The Command Decisions Series

• VOLUME 1 •
Aviation Weather

The Command Decisions Series • Volume 1

Aviation Weather
Forces to be Reckoned With

Richard L. Taylor

Belvoir Publications, Inc.
Greenwich, Connecticut

Also by Richard L. Taylor

IFR for VFR Pilots: An Exercise in Survival
Understanding Flying
Instrument Flying
Fair-Weather Flying
Recreational Flying
Positive Flying (with William Guinther)
The First Flight
Pilot's Audio Update (Editor)

ISBN: 1-879620-02-2

Printed and bound in the United States of America by Arcata Press (Fairfield, Pennsylvania).

Contents

Preface

On Monday, December 14, 1903, Wilbur Wright was able to get the *Flyer* into the air for a short hop of 105 feet, but the brothers didn't consider that a success. With the knowledge that the elevator control was much too sensitive, they spent Tuesday making repairs and adjustments and looked forward with great anticipation to the following day, when they fully expected to accomplish the world's first flight.

By Wednesday, repairs were complete and the *Flyer* was ready to go, but the weather didn't cooperate...a near-calm prevailed at Kitty Hawk, and the Wright airplane needed wind to fly. The brothers went to bed, hoping for more favorable winds the next day.

"When they awoke Thursday, they couldn't believe their ears. A subdued roar came to them, a rumble that rose and fell in the distance. They looked toward the ocean and saw the surf boiling before a bitter, howling wind of nearly 30 miles an hour.

"They went outside and stared. Finally, there was nothing to do but return to their shed to be out of the numbing wind. They sat about, depressed, listening to the wind shrieking through loose boards, blowing jets of sand around them.

"They shared the same thoughts. They were already two months behind schedule, and this wind could easily become a screaming gale or hurricane." (From *Kill Devil Hill*, Harry Combs, Houghton Mifflin Company, Boston, 1979.)

As we know, they screwed up their courage and accomplished the world's first flight on the 17th of December in 1903, despite winds that would keep most lightplane pilots on the ground today. And when they came back to Ohio and tried to fly the next spring, the warmer temperature and higher elevation created a density altitude that simply would not support the *Flyer*.

In other words, the world's first successful pilots were plagued by weather, and the situation has changed little in the almost-90 years since. Aviators continue to operate largely at the mercy of the elements. Strong winds, clouds, precipitation and violent manifestations of the energy in our atmosphere are the most frequent reasons for pilots altering their plans—or getting into serious trouble.

This volume in *The Command Decisions Series* is a compilation of educational articles and weather-related accident reports, creating a handy reference file for pilots who recognize the value of learning from the experiences and knowledge of others. As with other volumes in *The Command Decisions Series, Aviation Weather: Forces to be Reckoned With* draws heavily from accident reports researched by *Aviation Safety,* America's number one air-safety journal. Since its inception in 1981, *Aviation Safety* has provided reports on aircraft mishaps caused by weather, and has also attempted to educate its readers in ways to understand and cope with meteorological hazards. *Aviation Weather* is organized into chapters focusing on commonly encountered weather phenomena, and accidents that were caused by a pilot's failure to deal with changing meteorological conditions are presented and analyzed. It's hoped that this format of supplying critical weather information and supporting that information with actual case studies from NTSB files will help you form the necessary judgments when you're pilot in command.

There are precious few aircraft mishaps which can be attributed to just one proximate cause, and so you'll find a number of situations in this volume that smack of several problem areas. But we have limited our discussions to accidents and incidents in which weather played a major role; thunderstorms, low visibility, wind, turbulence, structural icing, and the all-time champ, attempts to continue a VFR flight into IFR conditions.

In virtually every case recounted here, there were options which, if exercised, would have prevented the mishap...perhaps the greatest lesson we can learn is to know the limitations of ourselves and our equipment, and have the good sense and fortitude to turn aside or turn back when we encounter a weather situation that is more than we can handle.

I hope as you turn the following pages you'll be able to learn from the mistakes of others and develop a decision-making process that will enhance the safety and enjoyment of your own flying. Above all, keep your eyes and your options open, and happy flying!

Richard Taylor
Dublin, Ohio
July 15, 1990

Wind and Turbulence

We wouldn't have to be concerned about the wind, if we could get the sun to shut down for a while and thereby stop the uneven heating of the earth. That would eliminate problems with crosswinds during takeoffs and landings, interminably long westbound trips when the prevailing winds are at work, and worries about wind shear and all the other unhappinesses that are generated by the movement of air. Of course, we'd also have to give up the benefits of tailwinds, and most people would become very bored by the never-changing weather that would result. It looks like we'll have to live with the winds. Just like sailors, we aviators must learn to cope with the negative aspects of wind, and make the most of the positive effects.

The bulk of this chapter is devoted to specific weather-related wind and turbulence phenomena and how they have affected your fellow pilots, often for the worst. But it's appropriate to review some important basics here. Wind is the end result when large-scale air masses are expanded or cooled. Pressure gradient forces move air from areas of high pressure to areas of low pressure—in a clockwise flow around the high and a counterclockwise flow around the low. (Our friends in the southern hemisphere, of course, encounter the opposite due to the Coriolis Force).

Surface friction will interfere with the orderly flow of air around large aggregate pressure systems, and localized forces will also dramatically change wind patterns. For instance, terrain or tree growth can influence wind patterns at a local field. Airports located near large bodies of water will experience sea and land breezes at certain times of the day due to heating differentials between the water and adjacent land masses. Valley winds are encountered when cool air over a valley sinks and begins to flow back upslope. Cool mountain winds—or katabatic winds—can flow downslope and displace valley winds. Mountain waves formed by prevailing winds skimming the high peaks will sometimes cause lenticular clouds, which we'll discuss shortly.

While fronts caused by the movement of pressure systems form the basic wind picture—which in turn affects local conditions—no frontal or terrain-induced wind pattern can quite compare to the winds produced by thunderstorms or other intense convective activities. Turbulence, murderous downdrafts, wind shear and microbursts—plane killers all—are the villainous by-products of thunderstorms large and small.

The complex, interrelated family of winds can also include turbulence induced by a multiplicity of factors—cold-frontal passage, clear-air turbulence at jet stream altitudes caused by wide frontal displacements, and man-made turbulence kicked up by heavily laden air transports poised to upset the kind of general aviation aircraft that you and I fly.

You can obtain a much more detailed understanding of the various types and characteristics of winds from any good aviation text. But the purpose of this book is to add depth to your understanding—and to illustrate how pilots have reacted when faced with the kind of tough weather choices you may be faced with the next time you fly.

Reading the Signs

Any discussion of a complex process—like weather—should build on the basics. Accordingly, one of the most fundamental pieces of knowledge about wind is its direction and velocity, especially important when a pilot is preparing to land or take off. Just about all airports worthy of the name have some sort of wind indicator, usually a wind sock, but sometimes a wind "tee," a name which comes from the shape of the device—a tetrahedron. A wind tee is mounted on a swivel base which allows it to rotate freely with the wind, and pilots know that they should land and take off in the same general direction as the pointy end of the tee. But as always in this business of flying, every single piece of information needs to be checked against something else. Here's a situation in which an experienced pilot should have looked a little deeper before making a commitment.

> An instructor taught his student pilot—the hard way—not to rely on just one indication when deciding which runway to use when the two pilots performed a landing overshoot at

Pilots often take a wind tee's indications for granted. But because many have to be positioned manually, always make sure the tee agrees with the windsock.

Whiteman Airpark, Pacoima, California. The accident left the aircraft, a Cessna 172P Skyhawk, with substantial damage but neither the commercially rated instructor nor his student were injured.

The student pilot, age 38, had 19 total hours. The instructor was also 38 and had 900 total hours, with 200 hours in Skyhawks.

They departed Burbank Airport around 9:20 a.m. on an instructional flight to Whiteman Airport to practice landings, and arrived at their destination about 20 minutes later. At 2,500 feet over Whiteman (elevation 1,004 MSL), the instructor and student checked the airport's wind tee. It indicated runway 12 was preferred. The instructor prepared to demonstrate the first landing. Another plane was at runway 12 preparing to take off, according to the student's statement after the accident.

The approach was normal, according to both pilots. The Skyhawk was flared out over the first third of the runway. But the airplane did not settle or lose speed as normal, the

A runway advisory from Unicom should be considered as just that. The pilot in command has to make his own judgments based on the windsock and wind tee indications.

pilots later told investigators. It touched down in the second third of the 3,725-foot runway. The instructor applied maximum braking, but the plane ran off the end of the runway, into a fence and some trees. Damage to the aircraft included minor damage to the nose and prop and severe damage to the wings. The pilots emerged to find that the wind was out of the north at 15 knots and they had made a downwind landing.

An hour later, an FAA inspector arrived at the scene. He found that the wind tee was indicating the wrong direction. The wind tee didn't swing in the wind—it had to be changed by hand, by airport personnel. The inspector also reported that, as he remained at the scene for the next hour, he observed several aircraft making go-arounds due to excessive floating and that both the wind and the runway in use changed from 12 to 30 several times.

When asked for ways the accident could have been prevented, the instructor wrote: "The airport should have manually had the wind tee pointing in the right direction. Also, the wind sock was faded and difficult to discriminate."

(However, it was also notable that neither the instructor nor the student mentioned having looked for—or at—the wind sock while checking the airport before landing. In addition, there was no mention of using other physical clues to detect the wind direction.)

The NTSB, in assessing the probable cause of the crash, said the primary flaw was the instructor's failure to go around when he realized the plane was floating excessively. A factor, however, was the airport operator's failure to position the wind tee correctly.

One of the most important words in FAR 91.3 is "final"—the pilot is the final authority as to the operation of his aircraft. If you get a surface wind report from a tower controller, you are entitled to rely on the accuracy of the numbers; but if it should turn out that a mistake was made, you are responsible to take appropriate action to keep from becoming a statistic. On the other hand, wind information on a Unicom frequency is not always the "right stuff," and the pilot is still responsible for figuring out that something is wrong. Consider another wind-related mishap at an uncontrolled field.

When a pilot is inbound to an uncontrolled airport and he asks on Unicom for the "active" runway, often a local pilot may supply an answer. There may be a moral obligation for him to answer accurately, but there is no legal one, nor is there any assurance that he might not make a mistake.

Such a lesson was placed before the pilot of a Cessna 414 which ran off the end of the runway at Coronado Airport, Albuquerque, New Mexico. There were no injuries in the incident, but the plane suffered substantial damage when it rolled into a culvert.

The pilot and his five passengers were completing a business flight from Abilene, Texas, when the mishap occurred at about 7:30 a.m. The flight, on an IFR flight plan, was conducted without incident until the plane descended for the airport, in good visual conditions.

The pilot told investigators that when he called on Unicom to learn the active runway, there was no response from the airport operator, but a pilot in a single-engine Cessna told him runway 35 was the active. The runway is 4,200 feet long and the field elevation is 5,270 feet.

The twin pilot therefore made an approach to runway 35. However, as the plane passed the threshold at an indicated airspeed of 95 knots, the pilot noticed that his ground speed was "a little fast." He now looked over at the windsock and for the first time noticed that it indicated a tailwind. He chose to attempt to stop the airplane using all available means—even managing to shut down the engines when an overrun appeared inevitable.

Winds at a nearby reporting station were listed as 180 degrees at 13 knots around the time of the accident.

Seems you just can't trust anybody...except yourself. There's an old rule that shows up in most pilot training programs that says if you're not able to land in the first third of the runway, go around. This decision must be tempered with good judgment, of course; if you're landing on a 10,000-foot runway, the "first third" rule would leave you another 6600 feet of concrete. But in any case, the secret is to plan your approach so that you touch down precisely where you want to...and if the plan doesn't work out, and there's any doubt that you have enough runway left to come to a safe stop, go around. The go-around is the ultimate escape valve, the universal remedy for almost all of a pilot's landing ills. The hard part is having the determination and discipline to use it.

Not Enough Energy

One of the best reasons for repeated landing practice in the traffic pattern is to develop in the student's mind a solid picture of a good approach. By doing the same thing over and over, the visual clues become easily recognizable, and if nothing else, a pilot can begin to see when an approach is going badly, and take the appropriate corrective action. During the learning process, a good approach can become a very mechanical procedure; set up on downwind at the same altitude, the same airspeed, the same power setting, and time after time, you'll wind up at the right place on the runway if the turns are made at the same places—and if the wind doesn't change.

Although pilots think in terms of their position relative to the ground, and can therefore see the effect of wind, the airplane responds only to "air miles"—the distance it's traveling through the air, and if there's a shortfall between required ground distance and air distance, the airplane is not going to make it to the runway without the addition of power. Other options include turning onto the base leg sooner, or using less wing flaps, or not powering down quite so much—all of which compensate for the wind, and serve to make up for the increased air distance you'll need to fly.

The integration of all these factors is a big bite for a beginner, especially one who winds up in a totally unexpected situation.

The student pilot, with approximately 18 total hours, suffered serious injuries when the plane apparently stalled on approach to her home base in a gusty crosswind after a bizarre series of events had left her on an unanticipated solo cross-country.

Investigators said the pilot and her instructor had set out on a dual cross-country from The Dalles earlier in the day, arriving without incident at Madras, Oregon. While having coffee, the instructor was stricken with an attack of kidney stones and asked to be taken to a hospital. After consultation, a flight instructor at Madras—who was the FAA-designated pilot examiner for the field—volunteered to sign off the student for a solo return to The Dalles.

When the student noticed some oil coming from the airplane and expressed concern, the Madras instructor, who also was a licensed mechanic, tightened some items on the engine and then released the airplane for takeoff, investigators said.

Although a round-robin flight plan had been filed by the original instructor, there was no evidence to show that a new flight plan for the return trip was filed, nor any check of weather made by the student or new instructor, NTSB's investigator said.

As the student arrived in the area of The Dalles, winds from 290 degrees had risen to 15 knots, gusting to 25, and there was considerable turbulence. The student entered the pattern for runway 25. Because her radio's comm and nav sides allowed reception only on one portion or the other, the student was unable to hear responses on Unicom, even though the local FSS and others heard and replied to her transmissions.

On final, the aircraft was observed to turn left and the nose pitched down, striking the ground at a steep angle. Wreckage evidence was consistent with a low power setting at impact.

Once again, a timely go-around would have saved the day. The matter of recognizing and coping with changing conditions is something that isn't developed overnight, and until that ability is well established, a pilot needs a lot of supervision and guidance.

Sometimes, Even a Go-Around Can Go Wrong

An actual short-field landing can be pretty spooky for most pilots, and gets even spookier when that short field is unpaved...most of us have grown accustomed to and comfortable with asphalt and concrete as the medium of choice for airports. Here's a situation in which the pilot did most of the things right, including a good decision to go around when he realized he was running out of runway, but a crosswind got the best of him as he tried to fly away from trouble.

> The pilot, who had logged about 100 hours in the Cessna 182P, was flying from Tamiami Airport to Tavernaero Park Airport—a private strip. The runway at Tavernier consists of a mixture of coral, sand, and grass. It is 1,800 feet long and oriented east-west.
>
> About three weeks before the accident, the pilot had flown into Tavernaero with an instructor. On that flight, they landed to the west.
>
> On the day of the accident, the pilot and his passenger departed Tamiami at about 2:40 p.m. They arrived at Tavernaero at about 3:10. The pilot chose to attempt his landing to the east this time. The winds were reported as from the southeast at around 15 knots.
>
> He later stated that he flew his approach with 20 degrees of flaps until clearing a house near the approach end of the runway. He characterized his approach as being a little high and a little fast.
>
> After passing over the house, he lowered the flaps all the way and touched down about one-third of the way down the runway. He applied the brakes, but realized that the Cessna would not stop before running out of runway. He then attempted to go around. The crosswind caused the airplane to drift off the runway to the left. It collided with trees and came to rest in a creek.

Here are two more examples of what can happen when a pilot, even a pilot with relatively high time in type, relaxes his vigilance with regard to wind direction and velocity.

The pilot apparently wasn't up to the task of landing a Cessna P-210N in a strong and gusty crosswind—and refreshingly, he conceded as much to investigators after a no-injury accident at DuPage Airport, West Chicago, Illinois.

The pilot, age 32, held a commercial license and instrument rating, with some 2,079 total hours and 300 in make and model. He was completing a flight from Crystal Lake, Illinois, when the accident occurred.

He was alone in the 1983 Pressurized Centurion during the landing attempt at about 2:55 p.m. The official wind observation, taken about eight minutes later, recorded wind from 040 degrees at 22 knots, gusting to 32 knots.

The pilot elected to land on runway 10, a 4,000-foot runway that is 75 feet wide. During his approach, he was given a wind report which he recalled for investigators as 040 degrees at 35 knots. He continued the approach and was on the rollout when he realized "the crosswind was too great and the aircraft weathervaned into the wind." The plane veered off into the mud and suffered a collapsed nosegear, propeller damage and a bent wingtip. The pilot was uninjured.

In his report to investigators, the pilot himself stated that he believed the accident was due to poor judgment, in that he had been "overconfident in (my) own ability to handle this strong a crosswind."...Actually, Cessna's P-210 handbook contains a statement that possibly might lead a pilot to believe even stronger crosswinds are manageable. Assuming a runway heading of 010 degrees and wind as the pilot reported it (040 at 35 knots), the crosswind component in the accident case was about 17-1/2 knots. In the P-210 manual, there is a note: "Maximum demonstrated crosswind velocity is 21 knots (not a limitation)."

An unauthorized student flight ended in death for a passenger and serious injury for the pilot when a Grumman American Cheetah attempted a takeoff in a 30-knot tailwind at Pryor, Oklahoma.

The NTSB investigator said the student had been endorsed for solo flight by an instructor who coincidentally sold him the Cheetah about a month before the crash. The instructor had informed the student that, because of other duties, he could no longer give him flight lessons. The passenger in the crash was reportedly half-owner and silent partner in the newly purchased aircraft, which was based at Harrison, Arkansas.

According to reports, the passenger called the pilot from a location near Pryor and asked to be picked up in the plane. When the pilot discovered that the pickup point would be an unimproved landing strip, he refused. The two then agreed that the passenger would go to Pryor for the pickup.

Witnesses at Pryor said the airplane landed and the engine was not shut down while the passenger was boarded. The plane then taxied the length of the 4,000-foot runway upwind, turned around and attempted a takeoff. Wind was 10 degrees shy of a direct tailwind, at 30 knots gusting to 45, during the attempt.

A witness watched the plane rolling down the runway at a high groundspeed, but clearly not achieving enough airspeed for safe flight. The plane was pulled off the ground at the departure end, but never left ground effect and bobbled on the verge of a stall for seven-tenths of a mile before the left wing dropped and the plane impacted a commercial building.

The pilot was thrown from the wreckage onto a nearby highway, where a passing highway patrolman who witnessed the impending crash had stopped. The patrolman helped the pilot to safety. There was a fire after impact, and the passenger did not survive.

Most airplane handbooks contain charts or tables from which a pilot can calculate range and endurance. But like all performance charts, the miles and/or hours it provides must be tempered by the stated conditions; in the case of range and endurance, the basic condition is no wind. Pilots who disregard the effect of wind during a cross-country flight are destined for problems, as this Cessna 210 driver found out.

The 52-year-old commercially licensed pilot-owner of a Cessna T-210 told investigators he had made the trip between Tyler, Texas, and Cortez, New Mexico, many times in the Mooney 231 he had owned previously, and fuel range had always been sufficient. It was therefore a surprise when he found himself running out of gas near Farmington, New Mexico. An ensuing forced landing on a highway left the pilot and his wife uninjured, but killed the driver of a pickup truck and seriously injured a youth in the truck when the plane's wing struck it.

The pilot, who had single- and multi-engine ratings, as well as a jet aircraft type rating and an instrument rating, had logged some 5,800 hours. He told investigators he had owned a Mooney 231 for some years, then acquired the Cessna T-210, which he had flown for virtually all of its 71 hours since new. While he had often flown the Tyler-Cortez trip in the Mooney, this was the first time he had attempted it in the Cessna.

The flight encountered headwinds up to 40 knots, according to preliminary information. The pilot told investigators he did not notice a problem until he was over Santa Fe and saw that the fuel gauges read about one-third on each side, then 20 minutes later were nearly zero. The pilot elected to divert to Farmington and called the tower there seeking an expedited clearance due to the low fuel state.

However, the airplane apparently ran dry about five miles short of the airport, and the pilot set up for an emergency landing, intending to touch down in the median strip of a four-lane highway. Upon nearing the ground, however, he noticed a tractor-trailer coming in the opposite direction. He repositioned the plane to land on the eastbound portion of the highway in order to avoid the semi, and the right wing impacted the pickup truck parked on the right shoulder of the road. The wing crushed the area of the cab, killing the driver with a blow to the head. The youth next to the driver had bent down to pick up something, and thus escaped death, according to one report.

The distance between Tyler and Farmington is about 690 nautical miles, the NTSB investigator said.

Low-energy accidents are no doubt the best kind to have, if you've just got to have one. In those situations where the airplane is moving at a high rate of speed and comes to a very quick stop, the chances of injury are much enhanced; but when the only energy involved is that of the wind, the damage is often confined to bent metal and a bruised ego. Such was the case with this professional pilot whose Cessna became a kite on a gusty day.

The pilot, holding a commercial license and an estimated 600 to 700 hours, was about to make a positioning flight to Manhattan, Kansas, for an air taxi operation when the accident occurred. A VFR flight plan was on file, investigators said.

Weather at the time of the 6:04 p.m. mishap included high scattered clouds and winds from 190 degrees at 22 knots, gusting to 40 knots.

Having completed his preparations, the pilot was waiting next to runway 19 when the tower cleared him to taxi into position on the runway and hold for the takeoff clearance. The pilot said as the aircraft turned to the runway heading, the left wing rose, lifting the nosegear and left main landing gear off the runway and allowing the aircraft to rotate 180 degrees. Although the pilot attempted to counteract the effects using control inputs and braking, it was not possible, since only the right main gear was grounded.

When the wind had spun the airplane 180 degrees around, another gust of wind came along and lifted the tail, flipping the plane onto its back.

Wind and Thunderstorms

Unless you've had the good fortune to have never experienced a thunderstorm close by, even on the ground, you are familiar with the tremendous rush of wind that usually accompanies the approach of one of these meteorological monsters. When you consider the physics of the situation, it's completely understandable; the air that has been lifted during the formation and development of the storm must return to earth sooner or later, and when it does, it's just like pouring water from a pitcher onto the kitchen floor...not only is there a very strong vertical component as the air descends, it moves out horizontally in all directions as it hits the surface. If your airplane happens to be in the immediate area when this occurs, you can count on a lot of things happening, none of them good.

This has been happening ever since there have been thunderstorms, but in recent years, the scientific community has figured out exactly what's going on, and has tagged the phenomenon with a very practical name—the "downburst." One of the acknowledged experts in this specific field of meteorology is Dr. John McCarthy, who is now Director of Research Applications Programs for the National Center for Atmospheric Research (NCAR) at Boulder, Colo.

"Wind shear has been known as a problem in aviation since the Wright brothers," McCarthy explains, "but it really didn't get identified as a catastrophic problem.

"Specifically, a microburst is an intense downdraft and outflow associated with a thunderstorm, although one can occur in less intense storms, particularly in dry climates. A microburst produces powerful, sudden headwind-to-tailwind changes below 1,000 feet AGL. An aircraft encountering this kind of wind shear may abruptly lose 80 knots of airspeed, which at low levels can be catastrophic."

While still at Oklahoma, McCarthy began to experiment with Doppler radar to measure wind shear. Doppler radar, basically the same type that police use in clocking speeders, was developed as a wind-measuring device in the 1960s at the U.S. Air Force geophysics laboratory.

"In the late '60s and early '70s, it became obvious that Doppler radar was a good tornado detector," McCarthy explains. "But it wasn't a wind shear detector, because nobody thought wind shear was a really big-time problem, so it became a severe-storm study tool." The advantage of Doppler radar over current systems that are being replaced—those which McCarthy would call "low-resolution" observation systems—is that it can pinpoint and measure wind shifts accurately and instantaneously and, most importantly, predict wind shear on a short-term basis.

For years, weather has been measured vertically by balloon-borne instruments launched 250 nautical miles apart. This doesn't provide much of a weather picture, considering that the majority of airplane flights, as McCarthy points out, are less than two hours, while wind shear forms intensify to hazard levels and dissipate within 5-15 minutes, sometimes in the path of an approach or takeoff.

In 1979, McCarthy moved over to NCAR. "One thing led to another," he recalls, "and in 1980, at a radar conference in Florida, Ted Fujita, Jim Wilson from NCAR and myself sat down over a glass of wine and put together the Joint Airport Weather Studies (JAWS) project to try and get a handle on the microburst."

In 1982, they set up a study at Stapleton Airport in Denver. In addition to Doppler radar, they also had an existing detection system called the Low-Level Wind Shear Alert System (LLWAS), consisting of wind sensors placed around the airport and a central data

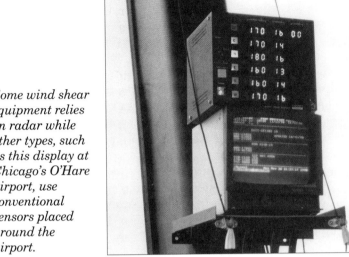

Some wind shear equipment relies on radar while other types, such as this display at Chicago's O'Hare airport, use conventional sensors placed around the airport.

processor. "The FAA just wasn't interested then, much to our chagrin at the time," McCarthy recalls, "but the National Science Foundation, NASA and the National Oceanic and Atmospheric Administration funded it. We pulled off this fairly small program on a shoestring." In more than one way, the project turned out bigger than they expected. They had anticipated that they would see 10 or 20 microbursts over the three-month period. Actually, they identified 150.

Then, on July 9, 1982, a tragedy occurred, which suddenly spotlighted their work and gave it a new urgency.

Pan Am 759 crashed at New Orleans, killing 153 people. "It was clearly a microburst," McCarthy says, "and it was the most catastrophic wind shear accident that had ever occurred." The accident prompted a wind shear inquiry by the U.S. Congress and the National Academy of Sciences, and the subject took on a national priority. Suddenly, FAA funding became available.

By the summer of 1984, NCAR had another project going at Stapleton. It had an even fancier acronym: CLAWS—Classify, Locate and Avoid Wind Shear. On May 31, a United jet encountered a microburst on takeoff and clipped off the localizer antennas at the departure end of the runway. The collision punctured the fuselage, and the aircraft could not be pressurized, so the pilot landed again. "It was a very close call," says McCarthy, "and the FAA called me and said, 'Look, could you protect Stapleton for the rest of the summer?' We weren't really in the operations business—we're a research organization—but we said, 'Yeah, we'll do that.'"

They put a meteorologist in the control tower, and when the researchers spotted a microburst, the meteorologist would inform the controller, who could pass it along to pilots. Over a six-week period, they identified 40 microbursts, and one pilot, at least, claimed that the alert and his decision to go around saved the airplane. On the basis of their success that summer, the FAA decided to adopt a national Doppler radar system for airport wind shear detection.

From 1985 on, NCAR worked with MIT's Lincoln Laboratory in perfecting a system.

As an outgrowth of their work, the National Weather Service, the FAA and the Department of Defense are working to install 150 of the radar systems throughout the U.S. Also, special-use Doppler radar, called Terminal Doppler Weather Radar (TDWR), will be installed to detect microbursts at 50 airports in midwestern, tornado belt states.

McCarthy's group, in fact, is working on a number of projects in addition to testing advanced radar products, including improved icing forecasts, winter storm forecasting, predicting the formation of thunderstorms and vortex detection and tracking. "The amount of weather training that pilots get is still woefully insufficient," McCarthy says. "You can take every written exam the FAA offers, flunk all the weather questions and still pass the exams. That doesn't make any sense, and we're pushing that hard. You've got to keep pinging on the system."

The Bigger They Are...

The catastrophic nature of a downburst or wind shear encounter by an airliner has led to sensational coverage in the media whenever one of those accidents takes place, and we have no doubt developed a mindset that excludes small aircraft from these problems. But, *au contraire!*...big jets seem to be more affected, but it's only because of their tremendous weight and resultant momentum. When several hundred thousand pounds of airplane starts downhill at a rapid rate, it takes time and a lot of power to arrest that descent; now and then, a downburst is encountered so close to the ground that there's no chance to recover.

On the other hand, a lighter airplane—and especially one driven by a propeller—will be able to pull out of the descent more rapidly. (A turbine engine requires some little time to "spool up" from idle to full power, but a reciprocating engine/prop combination provides near-instant thrust.)

Wind shear (a relatively rapid change in wind direction and/or velocity in a short vertical distance) will affect all flying machines, and if it isn't recognized and corrected promptly, you can wind up short of the intended touchdown point. There's no exemption from the effects of wind, not even for very light airplanes...the secret is in the timing.

FULL POWER, CAPTAIN...NOW!

The 23-year-old instructor and his 44-year-old student escaped unharmed when the Tomahawk crashed during an instructional flight. The 368-hour instructor, who had logged only 24 hours in the Tomahawk, was conducting a simulated engine failure while in the pattern. The 12.1-hour student had logged about half his time in the Tomahawk.

The instructor told investigators that when he simulated the engine failure, the student reacted properly, turning towards the runway and establishing the aircraft at its best-glide speed. He said everything seemed normal until the aircraft encountered what he called a "wind shear" on final approach. This caused a loss of airspeed and an increase in sink rate, and it became apparent that the Tomahawk would not reach the runway.

The instructor took control. He added power, but the Tomahawk contacted the ground at about the same time. Simultaneously, a gust of wind hit the aircraft, turning it to the right. The Tomahawk bounced and headed for a ditch. The instructor then cut the power, but the left wing hit the bank of the ditch.

Wind shear is a confounding sort of phenomenon. We normally think of the aerodynamics of an airplane wing in terms of its independence from outside influences. After all, weren't you taught in ground school that airplanes are not affected by movement of the air through which it's flying?

That's true enough, but all of that theory considered a steady-state environment, one in which the air was moving at a constant speed and direction, or not moving at all. When wind velocity or direction changes remarkably and suddenly, there are clear and significant changes in the aerodynamic behavior of your airplane.

Consider an airplane cruising at 100 knots, in perfectly calm air; the airspeed indicator would show 100 knots, groundspeed would be 100 knots, and the wing would be producing the same amount of lift it always produces in level flight at that speed. Now, crank up the wind so that you're flying into a direct headwind of exactly 100 knots; groundspeed would obviously be zero, but airspeed would still be the same, and the wing would continue to generate 100 knot's worth of lift. As long as the change in the wind took place gradually, there would be no changes except groundspeed.

Now, let's cause the wind to increase from zero to say, 20 knots...but this time, the change occurs suddenly, such as it might when you encounter a wind shear condition on final approach. At the onset of the increased headwind, the airspeed indicator would jump 20 knots or so, and here's the important part of the process; for the several seconds which might be required for the airplane to decelerate because of the sudden headwind, the wing thinks it's going faster, will produce more lift, and the airplane will pitch up momentarily until things come back to equilibrium. In order to keep things the way you want them, i.e., the airplane continuing on its glide path toward the runway, you'd need to pitch the nose down, and probably reduce power a bit to keep the airspeed on the mark.

When the opposite situation shows up—a sudden decrease in wind speed—things will happen the other way around; the nose will pitch down, airspeed will increase for a moment, and the airplane will begin a descent. In order to recover, you must add power and pitch up.

So far, not all bad as long as you have sufficient altitude in which to effect the recovery...and in most situations, the light weight and rapid power response give you the tools you need to stay out of the bushes. But when you encounter a wind shear condition that changes rapidly from headwind to tailwind or vice versa, that's the situation that causes big-time trouble. Imagine yourself having encountered a headwind shear (airspeed increases, nose pitches up, airplane starts climbing) and then just as suddenly the headwind shears to a tailwind; you are in a nose-high, low-power configuration, and now with a tailwind, the nose comes down of its own accord, the airplane starts to descend (sometimes very rapidly!), and you must crowd on the power right now, or pay the piper.

You should expect wind shear close to the ground whenever the winds are strong—perhaps 15 knots or more on the surface. The only safe procedure in this situation is to carry a bit more airspeed on final, and be sure to make your approach under power—even a little bit

Many pilots who have tangled with mountain wave conditions have learned by bitter experience that light airplanes simply don't have the climb rate to overcome severe downdrafts.

more than usual will make the difference—and don't hesitate to add power as required to keep the airplane on the glide path you want.

And of course, if it just doesn't look or feel right, even down at the bottom when you're ready to put the plane on the ground, go around and come back for another, more educated and more prepared try.

Why Mountain Flying Is Different

Whenever the air is moving rapidly anywhere, pilots must anticipate wind shear; but when the winds are blowing strongly over mountain peaks and ranges, the effect is increased remarkably. Every convolution on the surface disturbs the airflow, and even though most ridges and ranges are not all that smooth, they do the same thing that the curved upper surface of an airplane's wing does; they cause the airflow to accelerate. The end result, then, is that you must always expect stronger winds over and around the mountains. Frequently, this increase will produce downdrafts that will exceed the climb rate of a light airplane...and since flying down in the nap of the earth (as you well might be when trying to claw your way over a mountain ridge) means box canyons and dead-end valleys, the only alternative may be to "put it into the trees," a most unhappy ending to any flight.

Consider, for example, two flights that went wrong in mountainous conditions. The vagaries of wind played significant roles in each.

Three persons escaped injury and a fourth suffered burns when their Hawk XP crashed into trees in rising terrain about eight miles northeast of Aspen after encountering what the pilot said was a downdraft.

In command was a 32-year-old private pilot with 221 total hours, including 44 in the Hawk XP, 28 of which were hours as pilot in command. In the right front seat was a private pilot, age 43, with 75 total hours.

The command pilot supplied only a terse description of the accident and refused to be interviewed by investigators on advice from her lawyer. She stated, "We were flying northeast at 11,000 feet when a downdraft caused us to hit the trees." The other front-seat pilot gave a slightly more detailed description, and the passengers later gave their accounts in local newspapers.

The investigator said the four took off from Aspen at about 3:52 p.m. on what was intended as a one-hour local sightseeing flight. About eight minutes into the flight, in the area of Yekel Peak as the Hawk XP was negotiating a canyon topped by an 11,700-foot peak, the plane's rate of climb dropped from about 500 feet per minute upward, to some 300 fpm downward, the right-seat pilot recalled. He credited the pilot for not panicking and stalling the aircraft when it was clear that the plane could not outclimb the terrain.

The NTSB investigator said in the general area of the crash site, the terrain climbs 3,000 feet in three miles. He said handbook figures indicate the expected rate of climb for the plane at the weight estimated for the accident flight would be about 257 fpm, in the absence of downdrafts or turbulence.

This is bad enough when you can see where you're going; how about a similar experience on instruments?

The 936-hour pilot departed Torrance, California, for San Luis Obispo on an instrument flight plan about 8:45 a.m. The flight was uneventful until reaching the vicinity of Santa Ynez. He told investigators that, while cruising at 8,000 feet, the Cessna suddenly began descending at about 2,000 feet per minute. He was unable to climb out of this downdraft, and he pulled back on the yoke until the Cessna stalled.

He recovered from the stall and regained his airspeed. The Cessna was still descending, so he pulled back on the yoke again until the airplane stalled again. He recovered from this stall and, after regaining his airspeed, tried yet a third time. On this attempt, the Cessna broke into a spin.

The pilot was able to recover from the spin at about 2,500 feet MSL. He was able to see the ground at this point, so he made a forced landing.

Warning Signs in the Sky

"Surf's up!" is the rallying cry for those who love to ride the rollers in Hawaii, Australia, and a host of other seaside locations where surfing is the thing to do. And there's a similar call to action in the mountains, a call that raises the adrenaline level of certain aviators—"Wave's up!" will get the attention of every soaring pilot within earshot, because it means that the mountain wave is working, offering the prospect of super-long flights and perhaps new altitude records.

But most of these powerless pilots will have noticed what's going on, because they will have seen the "lennies" high overhead. Short for "lenticular," the term lennie refers to a unique cloud formation, created by high winds flowing over mountain ranges. As the air is forced upward by the rapidly rising terrain, it is cooled by expansion, and a cloud may form; the cloud thickens as the air continues to expand, but on the down side, compressive heating takes place and the cloud begins to dissipate. The result is a cloud that paints the standing wave; the cloud assumes the shape of a curved lens—in scientific language, "lenticular"—and thus the nickname "lennie."

For pilots who prefer to aviate behind a powerplant, the presence of lennies is a clear warning sign of high winds over the mountains, and in almost every case, the sight of lennies along the route of flight should give rise to serious thoughts of diversion. If the airplane in question has the capability of climbing well above these lens-shaped clouds, that is another option.

Here's a disturbingly graphic account of a pilot who found himself in a jungle of lennies. If this doesn't keep you from ever challenging this mountain-weather phenomenon, nothing will.

Of the many dangers that might be found in the clouds, it's rare that an IFR pilot thinks of a lenticular cloud—with its extremely deadly wind velocities and vectors—as a special danger. Lenticular clouds are generally thought of as isolated, but they can be embedded in other cloud formations.

Just such a surprise lay in store for a 59-year-old commercial pilot and his five passengers while on a personal flight in their rented Beech A36-TC Bonanza. As of the April 21, 1985 flight, the pilot had logged 2,685 hours with 46 in type, and had flown 359 hours in the last 90 days. The pilot's wife sustained minor injuries and the other five escaped unharmed when the Bonanza was literally ousted from the sky.

The pilot filed an IFR flight plan in person for the flight from Douglas, Arizona, to Albuquerque, New Mexico. Icing and turbulence prevailed along the route. The flight departed Bisbee Airport near Douglas at about 12:30 p.m. and the pilot climbed to his cruise altitude of 15,000 feet.

It was a little over an hour into the flight when the pilot noted the Bonanza was taking on rime ice at his assigned altitude. Being chronologically-minded and of a good memory, the pilot relates his experience:

1) IFR, in clouds, on oxygen, headset on, 15,000 feet altitude. Light rime icing—began to increase.

2) Obtained clearance to climb to 17,000 feet. Set climb setting—on auto pilot.

3) Glimpsed what could have been lenticular cloud through cloud break just before entry. Looked at map to check navigation radial and radio frequency.

4) Sudden hard jolt—like hitting a wall. Pitched downward. Wife was slammed back against seat so hard she incurred bruised back and compressed vertebrae.

5) Second hard jolt—less intense—but was aware of constant loud roar—like sound of tornado when shown on TV.

6) Sudden left bank—aircraft attitude indicator showed more than 80 degree bank. I applied right rudder and aileron but the aircraft continued to roll to the left causing temporary vertigo and disorientation.

7) Closed throttle—applied moderate back pressure on the wheel . Felt G forces pressing us into seats. Eased off of back pressure. I think we did a "split S" and I realized the gyros had tumbled.

Rugged mountains, such as the Wind River chain in Wyoming, are no place for an underpowered, normally-aspirated single.

8) Shifted to needle, ball, and airspeed only—for orientation. Airspeed never exceeded the green but was above the 152-knot triangle for extending gear and flaps. Therefore—left them retracted.

9) Returned to level flight and the door popped open at about the same time. Had descended from 15,000 to slightly below 10,000 feet. Still in clouds. Flying needle, ball, and airspeed with compass headings in moderate turbulence.

Flying on partial panel in the clouds, the pilot steered the Bonanza with the aid of controllers' vectors to the most convenient airport en route, Silver City, New Mexico. He descended the airplane to the minimum altitude advised by ATC and broke out of the clouds about five miles from the airport. The Bonanza landed without further incident. The pilot lauded the "great job" performed by ATC but did not think to report the occurrence for several days as he did not consider it to be an accident.

Actually, the damage was very serious. Shortly after the accident, an FAA inspector and a Beech representative inspected the airplane. Visual damage consisted of wrinkled and buckled wings. The wing bolts were removed and inspected; no stretching of the bolts was visible and they appeared to be in an airworthy condition. However, permanently deformed metal was discovered in the right lower section of the fuselage and wing root area. It was determined that the right wing butt rib and several stringers and ribs in the wings would need repair or replacement. These findings show the pilot had come perilously close to losing the wing.

Storm-Cell Turbulence

When you are flying comfortably above the clouds at an altitude limited by either airplane performance or the oxygen rules, one of Murphy's laws says that the clouds will rise to meet you. And when that happens, other unpleasantries often appear, as was the case with this pilot who encountered some Texas-size turbulence.

Neither the 46-year-old, 2,050-hour owner/pilot or his single passenger were injured during an encounter with severe turbulence near Midland, Texas, while cruising at an altitude of 13,000 feet.

The commercial pilot departed El Paso, Texas on an IFR flight plan, bound for Love Field in Dallas, Texas. The pilot cruised above the clouds for some time, but eventually the tops began to rise above his altitude. He flew in and out of the clouds, and eventually penetrated the upper 200 to 300 feet of a convective cumulus cloud. As the cloud was entered, the airplane encountered sudden, extreme turbulence and lost 1,500 to 2,000 feet of altitude before the pilot was able to resume level flight. After recovering, the pilot climbed to 15,000 feet. He then noticed that the gear-up light was no longer illuminated and the airspeed indicator was inoperative. In addition, he could see wrinkles in the wing skins as well as some areas where rivets had come out of the skin.

The airplane appeared to be operating normally, so the pilot elected to continue to Dallas. On arrival at Love Field, he found that the landing gear would not extend either electrically or manually. He decided to divert to Redbird Airport, a smaller field a few miles south of Love, and made an uneventful gear-up landing there.

On inspection, the wings and fuselage were found to be deformed as a result of the turbulence encounter, and in addition to the popped rivets noted by the pilot, there were skin tears near one wingtip. The personnel who removed the aircraft from the runway at Redbird noted that the landing gear motor release handle, which must be pushed forward in order to unstow the manual gear extension lever, was jammed. Once it had been freed, the manual landing gear extension system worked normally.

Penetrating Turbulence at Maneuvering Speed

When an airplane suffers that kind of deformation, it's a pretty good sign that the operating limitations have been exceeded—at least with regard to Va, or maneuvering speed. In very general terms, Va is the airspeed at which the airplane will stall before it suffers structural damage when it encounters a sudden increase in acceleration (G-loading). This could come as the result of a pilot pulling on the yoke hard, or flying into one of those brick walls of turbulence we've been talking about. In either event, the angle of attack is suddenly and remarkably increased, the effective weight of the airplane is also increased, and if airspeed is at or below maneuvering speed, a stall will occur, unloading the airframe and permitting a return to "normal" flight. You may have to launder your flying suit, but at least the wings won't come off!

The Va value listed for light airplanes is the maneuvering speed for a fully loaded airplane. There is some rather complicated aerodynamic reasoning involved, but suffice it to say that as aircraft weight decreases, maneuvering speed also decreases. (Larger airplanes are provided with a range of "turbulence penetration speeds," which take into account the wide range of weights at which these airplanes operate, and the rather large changes in weight that can occur during a flight because of fuel burn.)

The "light-weight" maneuvering speed for a small plane will not be much less than that quoted for maximum gross weight, so it's proper and safe to use that figure when you encounter really rough air. More important than the number is the approximate power setting and pitch attitude that will produce that speed, because once you're in the thick of things, the airspeed needle will probably be bouncing wildly, and trying to nail it down will prove difficult.

Turbulence Plus Icing Equals Disaster

Add icing to the difficulties pilots have faced in high wind conditions and you have the makings of a scenario that would tax the skill of even the most experienced aviator. This deadly duo joined forces and produced tragic results for the pilot/co-owner of a Piper Arrow and his lone passenger when their aircraft suffered a mid-flight breakup.

The pilot, a 48-year-old instrument-rated flight instructor, was en route from Bouquet Airpark near Pittsburgh, Pennsylvania, to Jacksonville, Pennsylvania, on an IFR flight plan. Earlier that day, the pilot had received a weather briefing lasting some 38 minutes from Altoona Flight Service Station. During the briefing he was advised of instrument conditions, moderate to heavy icing, and severe to extreme turbulence, particularly near the beginning of the flight.

The flight proceeded normally for the first few minutes, but investigators said that shortly after departure the pilot requested clearance to a higher altitude due to severe turbulence. This was granted, but he reported encountering icing, and was cleared back down to a lower altitude. It was during this descent that the airplane broke up.

Fly It or Watch It Fall

There are some circumstances so extraordinary as to leave a pilot to choose the lesser of two evils, thereby guaranteeing that he or she will make a bad decision.

One pilot who got caught between the proverbial rock and hard place (actually, a cliff and the wind) managed to get out of the situation with only minor injuries. His airplane was destroyed, but it's a fair bet that it would have been lost anyway, given the circumstances.

The airplane was a Piper Pacer. The pilot and three companions had gone on a late-summer caribou hunt to a ridge about 40 miles west of Delta Junction, Alaska. There was no airstrip there, but the ridge was clear and large enough to land on. The party set up camp near the north end of the ridge, which was bordered on the north and west by a sheer cliff between 1,000 and 1,500 feet high.

At about 3 o'clock one morning, the party was awakened

Stout tiedown ropes and chocks are the best defense against wind damage on the ground.

by the wind, which was beginning to blow very hard from the south. The pilot's estimate was between 60 and 80 miles per hour. He was helping his companions try to keep their tents from blowing away when he spotted the airplane trying to fly away on its own. The Pacer was bouncing up and down, with the tail off the ground in full flight.

The airplane was being restrained by only one tie-down—a "pigtail" type that screws into the ground, leaving a ring at ground level for attaching the rope. The four men ran to the airplane and tried to re-secure the other two tie-downs. Three of them held on to the bucking Pacer as the other tried to sink one of the loosened tie-downs back into the rocky soil. He no sooner secured the tie-down when it pulled out again. And now the wind was beginning to push the airplane backward towards the cliff.

The pilot recalled, "At that time I felt I had two options:

The gust front associated with a severe thunderstorm is more than enough to rip an airplane free of an inadequate tiedown with frayed or weathered rope.

watch my plane go over the side, 1,500 feet down; or fly it away. I opted to fly it away. I got in and they let it go. It took off in less than ten feet." The wind was blowing the aircraft toward rising terrain. The pilot tried to turn around but hadn't gained enough altitude, and the airplane hit the ground about 50 feet from where it started.

Two days later, the Pacer's ELT signal was detected, and the hunters were picked up by the Air Force. It is ironic that the rescue crew also picked up another pilot some distance away who had faced the same loser's choice and elected to leave his airplane to the mercy of the wind, rather than try to fly it to safety.

Bottom-Line Considerations

Wind, and the turbulence associated with rapid movement of the air through the atmosphere, are part and parcel of flying. The air is our medium, and we must learn to live with it when it's bearable, cope with it when it becomes troublesome, and respect it all the time.

The lighter the airplane, the more effect wind will have on flight operations, simply because a strong wind can move a lighter weight about more easily. With this in mind, there are definitely going to be days when the wind is just too strong for safe operations in a light airplane; it's important for each pilot to "side-step" his way to his personal wind/turbulence limits, as well as finding out gradually just how much atmospheric disturbance his airplane can handle safely.

Very much like a sensible sailor who stays on the dock because he knows that today's seas are just too much for his little boat, a smart pilot will take a look at a threatening sky or a forecast of lousy weather, and decide that "he who looks at the warning signs and turns away, will live to fly another day."

Structural Icing

Structural icing ranks with thunderstorms as one of the pilot's worst environmental enemies. Where an encounter with a thunderstorm is likely to be violent and noisy, icing is sinister and stealthy. Usually, a pilot will see its first traces on small things, like an OAT probe or sharp edges of the windshield seam.

What's happening is that very cold and unstable ("supercooled") water droplets are striking the aircraft and getting the jolt they need to freeze. Ice usually shows up first on small, thin objects because of what researchers call "collection efficiencies." It has to do with how much air a moving surface is displacing. An OAT probe, for instance, doesn't push much air ahead of it; and the supercooled droplets easily get through. Larger objects—such as the leading edges of the wing and stabilizers—push much larger "pressure waves," which tend to deflect some of the droplets.

Once ice starts building, though, it can be relentless. It can render unheated probes and antennas useless, or cause them to vibrate so much that they snap. As it coats the airframe, ice adds weight and, more importantly, changes airflow patterns. It can block the induction system and choke the engine. It can set up some very unsettling vibrations of the propeller and lead to blade failure. (In twins, ice being sloughed off the prop blades can create a terrific din when it hits the fuselage. In one case, a piece of ice thrown off a blade on a Dornier commuter plane went through a passenger window. Fortunately, no one was hurt, and the manufacturer took corrective action.)

The ability of an aircraft to climb or maintain level flight can be destroyed. In extreme cases, structural ice can render an aircraft completely uncontrollable.

Unlike thunderstorms, which can be detected by radar, areas ripe to cause airframe icing can be undetectable. Akin to catching a gnat with a net, conditions conducive for icing cannot be defined any more accurately than where there is visible moisture and temperatures at and below freezing. Like a broken record, the NWS issues forecasts for icing conditions all winter long. And even though an aircraft is as likely as not to come through an area of icing conditions with a clean airframe, forecast icing is the same as known icing in the eyes of some FAA enforcement types.

This all conspires to put a pilot in quite a bind. A prudent airman, however, will take an icing forecast for what it's meant to be: a warning. Pilots are required to report unforecasted airframe ice when they encounter it, and PIREPs are a good indication that the hazard is (or was), indeed, out there. SIGMETs and AIRMETs generally are based on PIREPs of known icing. But, just because there are no icing PIREPs doesn't mean you're home free—it could just mean no one else has been out there to make reports.

If there is an icing report, it's a good idea to find out who made it, keeping in mind the notion of collection efficiencies. What appears as "trace" or "light" to the first officer of a Boeing 737 may turn out as "moderate" or "severe" to the pilot of an Aerostar or Mooney.

Icing Myths

Almost any instrument pilot who regularly flies in cold weather will eventually have an encounter with airframe ice. How the pilot handles himself in that encounter—assuming he's successful on the first exposure—may determine his future attitude about flying into icing conditions.

Doubtless, icing encounters are responsible for lots of "there I was" stories in hangar flying sessions, and probably are the raw material for myths like "that Speedbird 250 will haul ice all day long." This kind of talk has the effect of whittling the specter of airframe ice down to size, while inflating the status of the pilot and airplane, until the contest can be viewed as a fairly equal battle between the aviator and the elements.

Unfortunately, all the facts conspire to prove this notion totally false. The preliminary rounds are only feinting and sparring, and when it comes to the real fight, the ice will always win. Unless the pilot withdraws from the ring while he's still able, the ice will eventually land a killer punch.

We introduce the issue of pilot attitudes because, although there can be no scientific proof offered, it appears to us to be the one factor which can explain general aviation's dismal record of accidents involving in-flight encounters with ice. With regularity (approximately 30 times a year), an iced-up airplane will slam into (or more usually, onto) the ground in another demonstration that there is always some icing condition that can beat any pilot, in any airplane. Since this is not some mysterious secret, but a well-publicized fact, we can only conclude that the pilot population has erected the myth of the intrepid, indestructible aviator, mounted on his trusty airborne stallion, to rationalize away the real danger the Ice Monster poses.

An in-depth study of in-flight icing encounters leading to accidents reveals these major points:

-Icing accidents usually involve experienced, well-qualified pilots.

-Icing accidents mainly involve pilots who got weather briefings, yet flew into the forecast icing conditions anyway.

-Despite the veteran pilot and his prior knowledge, in the majority of icing accidents the aircraft has little or no ice-fighting gear.

-Frequently—almost typically—the aforementioned pilot manages to keep the iced-up airplane flying, all the way to his destination airport in most cases, and have his accident on final approach.

-Icing accidents are more than twice as likely to involve fatalities as other general aviation accidents.

Studying the Problem

Although ice is mentioned in many dozens of NTSB accident reports yearly, a large number of these do not apply to the problem of in-flight icing encounters. A computer run of the NTSB reports will turn up many cases of carburetor icing in small aircraft, for instance. These are worth examining for their own lessons, but they are almost never related to airframe icing. Likewise, in about a dozen cases yearly, a crash results from attempted takeoff with ice and snow clinging to the airplane. These may be good examples of pilot misjudgment during preflight, but bear little relation to the in-flight icing encounter. Both these categories of ice-related accidents have been disregarded here.

NTSB investigators are often aware of icing conditions in the area

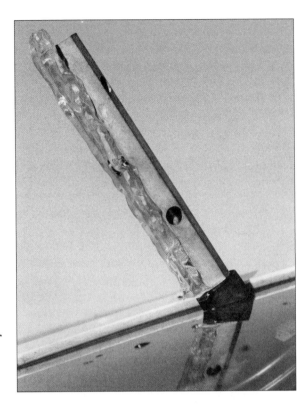

When icing is suspected, look for it first on sharp-edged objects, like the OAT probe.

of a crash that were probably encountered, but the wreckage (found perhaps days later) yields no proof of airframe ice. There are about two dozen accidents a year where ice is strongly suspected, but cannot be included as a causal factor.

Research conducted by *Aviation Safety* magazine revealed some 130 accidents during a statistical period selected between 1977 and 1980 where airframe (and windshield) ice, encountered sometime after takeoff, figured as a causal factor in a crash. This group of classic ice-encounter accidents is less than one percent of the general aviation accident tally for the four-year period, but amply demonstrates the deadliness of the icing encounter.

Typically, about 17 percent of all general aviation accidents result in a fatality. In stark contrast, icing encounter accidents result in fatalities about 38 percent of the time—or well over twice as often. Among the 130 accidents studied, 50 produced fatalities. In all, 118 people were killed, 55 seriously injured, and 175 left with minor or no injuries among the total group of accidents.

Pilots: Cream of the Crop

If it were imagined that the airmen destined to have ice-encounter accidents formed a social club, then it would be a very elite group indeed. Eligibility would be confined to the top five percent of all pilots nationwide.

Among the pilots in our study, only one misfit was a student, and all others had at least a private license. Indeed, well more than half had commercial licenses, and there were 18 of airline transport rank (though only a small number of the accidents studied involved for-hire flying, and none for scheduled airlines).

Moreover, 76 percent of the pilots held instrument ratings. The icing-accident pilots thus distinguish themselves from the general pilot population, where only about one-third have instrument ratings, and less than one-third have commercial or ATP licenses. Even further, those involved in icing accidents generally have a great deal of flying experience. Among the pilots studied, the average total flying time was 2,813 hours, and time in the type of aircraft averaged 496 hours. To stress the point, 63 percent of the icing-accident pilots had at least 1,000 total hours, and 70 percent had at least 100 hours in type. They were very experienced pilots.

Disturbing to report, we did also detect six pilots who filed and flew IFR even though they had no ratings.

The Airplanes

With all this collective aeronautical lore, one might think the pilots would venture into icing conditions in aircraft at least armed with the minimum of de-ice and anti-ice equipment. Not so. As far as the data go, it appears they mainly went in airplanes with no de-ice equipment at all. For instance, of 70 single-engine aircraft that crashed due to ice, 67 definitely were not equipped for icing flight, two others probably weren't, and the final one (a Cessna Centurion) had the equipment, but its wing boots leaked.

The list of single-engine aircraft downed by ice includes every conceivable type: Beech Bonanzas, Cessna Skyhawks and Skylanes, Piper Cherokees and Comanches, Mooneys, Rockwell singles, Maules, Bellancas, and even a Pitts, a Varga and a Globe Swift. At most, a few of these airplanes might have had a heated prop and heated pitot; but in the main, they had nothing at all to combat ice.

The story on the 60 twins involved is not as easily reckoned, since NTSB data don't make it clear how well equipped each airplane was. Many twins can have hot props, boots and heated windshields, yet

Pneumatic boots provide some protection against structural icing, provided they're kept in good operating condition. There's a limit to how many times a boot can be patched, however.

still not be FAA-approved for flight in ice. We tallied 36 twins in this category, where it couldn't be said for certain how fully equipped they were. Typical of this group were Beech Model 55 Barons and Cessna 310s. But of 24 twins where equipment level could be reckoned, the breakdown was 14 without de-ice, 10 with. Among the 14 were Piper Senecas, Beech Travel Airs (and one Duchess), and some Aero Commander Shrikes. Of the 10 twins that had equipment, seven had various portions of their de-ice kits inoperative.

In summary, pilots are getting themselves into icing conditions in airplanes that aren't at all ready for the challenge.

By the way, contradicting our previous study, the presence of the 60 twins (46 percent of the icing accidents) is well above the proportion of twins in the national fleet (about 13 percent). Even accounting for the greater exposure (a given twin flies more hours yearly than a single), this would seem to indicate a greater rate of icing accidents for twins than singles, although definitive data is not available.

Planning

Since a seasoned pilot in a no-de-ice airplane would be expected to know his limitations, it might be imagined that the icing accident results from a lack of forethought—the pilot never intended to get into ice (maybe not even into clouds), but was surprised by conditions after he got airborne. This is generally not the case. The data build a strong image of pilots who knew full well the risk they were taking.

First, whether they intended to fly VFR or IFR, the pilots definitely got weather briefings. In 110 cases where the presence or absence of a briefing was cited by NTSB, 96 of the pilots got briefings.

Second, of 118 cases where NTSB reported the presence or absence of a flight plan, only 23 pilots went without flight plans. Eleven were on VFR flight plans. And the vast majority—84 pilots— filed IFR flight plans.

Well, if the pilots were experienced, knew their airplanes weren't equipped, but flew into clouds anyway and got ice, were the weather briefers at fault? Did the FSS staffers give out misleading weather information to make the pilots think there wouldn't be any ice around? Not at all, it turns out. Where NTSB judged the accuracy of the weather briefing in relation to the actual weather at the accident site, it found the briefer's forecast "substantially correct" in 81 out of 88 cases. In the seven odd cases, weather was pronounced "slightly worse" than forecast. (Notice that in no case was it judged any better than the briefer had predicted.)

Awful Weather

In fairness, NTSB records assess the weather in the area of the accident site, not in the clouds above. Therefore, there could at times be substantial differences between what the pilot saw during most of the flight, and what he saw in the last few minutes. However, this distinction may seem trivial, in view of the absolutely horrible weather NTSB describes for typical icing accident cases.

Some precipitation was falling at the accident site 83 percent of the time. In a striking 30 percent of the accidents, the precip was freezing rain or drizzle—of all icing conditions, the most fearsome. Even assuming an airplane encounters no ice *en route*, but descends into freezing rain, the accretion of ice can be so quick and heavy as to prevent further flight within a few minutes. Depending on the frontal system, snow, rain and sleet are indicators of icing somewhere above ground level.

In 67 percent of the cases, there was some obstruction to vision

Electric prop de-ice is quite effective in keeping propellers from developing an out-of-balance condition due to icing.

underneath the ceiling. Usually, it was fog, but in 17 percent of the cases, it was blowing snow.

The congregation of accident site temperatures around 25 to 35 degrees is no surprise, but the temperatures well outside this range are a reminder that icing conditions do not always fall in line with the thermometer on the ground.

In 39 percent of known cases, it was nighttime when the airplane went down. It would not normally be worth mentioning that the icing accident season appears to run from November through late spring; this is obvious. But noticeably, the majority of icing accidents occur in January through March. This seems significant to us because in all likelihood, the pilots are not making their first sally of the winter. Could it be that the pilot who was nailed by ice in January had an icing encounter and "got away with it" the previous November? This would certainly fit the picture the other data paints.

In-Flight Decisions

While it is true that ice can bring down an airplane before it can get to an airport (this was the case in 45 percent of the accidents studied), it seems remarkable that a majority of the pilots do get near or on a runway before having their icing accident. What is more striking is that they usually get all the way to their destination.

Of 72 icing accidents on or near an airport, only five occurred during a return to the departure field, and 14 during a diversion en route. The remaining 53 occurred at the destination the pilot originally had in mind.

Of 58 icing accidents outside the vicinity of an airport, only four show signs of precautionary diversions from the planned flight.

In short, the record shows a predominant desire by pilots to "keep on trucking" in the face of icing conditions.

Arrivals

The off-airport accidents, as might be expected, involved the greatest number of uncontrolled descents into the ground. An iced-up airplane literally can "fall out of the sky," and there were 19 such accidents. Eleven airplanes hit terrain under cruise conditions. There were 17 successful off-airport forced landings, one hard landing, and eight stall-spins.

The on-airport group shows in great detail the operational aspects of ice on an airplane. There were 26 crunchingly hard landings, 19 stall-spins (usually on final), seven undershoots and two overshoots. There were 13 collisions with snowbanks or groundloops along the runway.

De-Ice Equipment Defeated

Even though one might expect pilots to gird themselves in de-ice-equipped airplanes for the battle against ice, they largely go unarmed. Rather than retreating from the ice, they resolutely press on to their destination, carrying the scars of battle all over their wings and tail, and have the actual icing accident there.

We must, of course, stress that equipped airplanes also have icing accidents, and no amount of de-ice equipment can stand up to the worst icing conditions. If the de-ice-equipped airplane stays in the conditions long enough, or the icing cloud is moist and cold enough, it can be overcome by ice even though the equipment is functioning properly. If the pilot fails to use the equipment correctly (for instance, inflating the boots too early) he can render the problem worse than before. Furthermore, ice can still stick to a plane even after the boots have worked.

The bottom line is that de-icing-equipped airplanes are not immune from the same icing problems as non-equipped ones. Whatever the airplane, the pilot's first thought must be to remove himself from the icing conditions (or not get into them in the first place).

Specific Examples

Some actual case histories will add life (and death) to the statistics.

A 3,375-hour private pilot departed Des Moines, Iowa, shortly after 8 a.m. in a Beech 58P Baron. The Baron was equipped for flight into known icing, and all systems were operational. The pilot had 1,418 hours in this make and model airplane. He held an instrument rating (830 hours actual) and had been flying regularly (85 hours in the past three months).

He was headed for Lockport, Illinois, a Chicago-area airport. He told investigators he left without getting a weather briefing, and without a flight plan, since it was his intent to return to Des Moines (which had clear weather) if he deemed conditions en route unacceptable.

About 17 minutes into the flight, the pilot checked with Des Moines Flight Watch for destination area weather. He was given Chicago's DuPage Airport as indefinite 200 sky obscured, visibility one-half to three-quarters of a mile, temperature 28 degrees, dewpoint 23. And for Midway Airport, indefinite 400 sky obscured, visibility one in fog, temperature 29, dewpoint 28. Flight Watch also noted that in the past hour, a Sabreliner climbing through 2,400 feet out of Midway had reported moderate clear ice.

About three minutes later, the Baron pilot air-filed to continue his flight IFR, destination DuPage. He stayed out of the clouds, on top at 15,000 feet, for most of the remaining flight. He checked the ATIS (ceiling now 500 feet sky obscured, pilot reports of bases at 200 feet, tops at 2,600, a PIREP of moderate rime ice on the approach) and got vectors for his initial approach.

He was still at 3,000 feet when cleared for a straight-in runway 10 ILS approach at DuPage. Investigators said prior to entering the clouds on the descent, the pilot activated his heated windshield and pitot systems, and the prop de-icers. It is interesting to note that from this point to impact was a period of just 10 minutes, meaning the airplane was in icing clouds only perhaps seven or eight minutes.

The pilot told investigators he noticed ice building up on

the unheated portion of the windshield, but did not "detect sufficient ice on wing surfaces to activate the deicing boots," as NTSB expressed it. Investigators also said, "Approximately halfway down the approach (the pilot) encountered a buffet at 120 knots which he attributed to turbulence."

The Baron arrived at the missed approach point and the pilot added power. However, the plane began to "mush" and lose altitude. As the pilot described it, he recovered from the half-stall (extremely low, according to eyewitness) and at the same time saw the runway off to his left. He banked toward it and the plane struck the ground (70 feet short of the threshold) with its left wingtip, slammed to the ground and slid down the runway for about 750 feet. It erupted in fire after coming to rest, but the pilot escaped the wreckage with minor injuries.

The fire prevented a complete inventory of the ice aboard the Baron, but about three feet of the left wing had broken off and lay 300 feet away. Investigators found its leading edge covered with one-half to three-quarters of an inch of rime ice.

CARGO FLIGHT

An ATP-certified pilot planned a cargo flight from Ohio to Michigan in a Cessna 402A. He would set out from Columbus for a short hop to New Lexington, Ohio, to pick up the cargo, then on to Lansing, Michigan.

The pilot had 3,056 total hours, 129 in make and model. He held an instrument rating and had logged 600 hours actual IFR. He had flown some 220 hours in the past three months. The aircraft had complete de-icing equipment, although, as it turned out, some of it wasn't working.

At about 2:30 p.m., the pilot called the Columbus FSS for a weather briefing, especially for the second leg of the flight. He said he would be leaving New Lexington around 4:30 p.m. and arriving in Lansing about an hour later.

The briefer gave him Toledo and Lansing weather. At Lansing, the ceiling was 2,100 feet, predicted to stay at 2,000, but with a chance of 1,000 and light snow showers. It was forecast to go to a 500-foot ceiling around 7 p.m. The briefer said there were no SIGMETs, but a pilot had reported light rime ice in the clouds around Dayton. A few hours later, the briefer received a SIGMET for occasional severe rime and mixed icing in clouds below 7,000 feet over lower Michigan.

The 402 pilot made his short hop and set out from New Lexington as intended, activating his IFR flight plan. He told investigators that, while en route, "all de-ice equipment was checked O.K." He was at 5,000 feet for a portion of the flight, but over Toledo, noticed light snow and obtained a descent to 4,000 feet, where he said he had "good ground contact." He told investigators he was about 30 miles from destination and had descended to 3,000 feet when he began to pick up "moderate rime ice." He said about 10 miles later, he contacted Lansing Approach and was sequenced second in line for the ILS 27L. At this point, he said, he found the wing de-ice boots were not operating, and the windshield alcohol system was not able to clear the windshield.

The pilot said neither the approach controllers nor the ATIS warned of "severe icing" on the approach. He said he got over the outer marker, dropped approach flaps at 160 mph, lowered the gear and continued the approach. He said he flew down to decision height, but found he could not see out the windshield. At this point, he added power and raised the gear. "Immediately thereafter the aircraft failed to accelerate, and settled to the runway," he said.

As luck had it, the plane descended onto the runway and slid to a stop. No one was injured. Controllers with binoculars said from the tower they noticed three or four people around the airplane moments after it came to rest, but the pilot was the only one around when crash trucks arrived. Thus, investigators considered the pilot the "only confirmed occupant" of the twin Cessna.

Investigators found evidence to dispute parts of the pilot's story. For one thing, "Although the Lansing Approach controller did not identify his transmissions as SIGMETs, he issued several icing advisories to inbound aircraft, including (the 402)," investigators said. "Shortly before the accident occurrence an aircraft that was inbound to Lansing cancelled his flight plan and advised he was doing a 'one-eighty' to avoid the icing conditions.

Controllers also said that shortly after Lansing acquired the 402, they asked the pilot whether he was picking up any ice. He replied, "Yes, moderate rime." A little later, the controller asked him what his speed was, and the pilot replied 140 knots. They asked if he could increase speed, and the pilot said, "No, not unless I lose some altitude." Investigators infer that the 402, which can cruise at 180 knots, was suffering performance penalties due to the ice accretion.

Investigators found ice all over the leading edges of the wings and tail, and tip tanks, of the 402. They also found that, despite the pilot's claim of having checked the boots, for reasons that are unclear, the pneumatic line that supplies pressure to the boots had been disconnected sometime prior to the flight; the boots could not have been operational. Moreover, they found the windshield anti-ice system working properly, but simply not able to clear the build-up on the windshield. (To be effective, an alcohol system must be used before appreciable ice collects.)

IFR WITHOUT A RATING

A 2,444-hour private pilot was planning a business flight with one associate from Salina to Kansas City, Kansas, (Fairfax Airport). The airplane in question, a Bellanca Turbo Super Viking, had no de-icing equipment.

Investigators did confirm that the pilot got a weather briefing at 10 a.m., but the FSS had routinely discarded the records, so authorities did not dispute the pilot when he said he was given no report of icing conditions.

In any event, it was 11 p.m.—fully 13 hours after the briefing—that the pilot departed Salina. He activated and flew under an IFR flight plan; he had no instrument rating, nor did he claim any instrument experience on his NTSB accident form.

History also does not record the circumstances of the flight itself, since it was unremarkable from an ATC point of view. The Bellanca flew from Salina to Kansas City, shot an approach, and landed.

Had the pilot obtained later weather, he would have found the current forecast called for low ceilings and low visibility at Kansas City, with light rain or drizzle on the ground, and moderate icing in the clouds.

At the time of the 12:30 a.m. arrival, local weather was reported as measured ceiling 900 feet overcast, variable between 800 and 1,000, visibility six miles, fog and icing conditions, temperature 34, dewpoint 29.

According to the pilot's description, he merely landed on runway 35 and after the maingear were down and the nosegear touched the runway, the nosewheel tire blew out and the Bellanca skidded off into a ditch. There were no injuries. But the pilot did concede to investigators that he had encountered icing conditions during the flight, and had knocked "some ice" off the leading edges of the wings after the landing. Investigators, who arrived at the plane about 10:30 a.m., found strips of clear ice next to the wing and tail leading edges. It cannot be estimated how much they might have melted since the touchdown time, but the strips were still 5/8 of an inch thick.

The NTSB ascribed the accident to a hard landing due to the accumulation of ice.

In yet another instance of structural ice fouling up the smooth airflow over the wings and causing the airplane to do things the pilot doesn't expect, an Aerostar pilot discovered a new stall speed; fortunately, it happened very close to the ground.

Moderate rime ice, accreting to the extent of one-eighth of an inch on a Piper PA-602P Aerostar, was enough to cause the airplane to stall out of the landing flare at 100 knots indicated, according to preliminary information in a crash at Bellaire, Michigan.

The pilot, a 39-year-old airman with 773 total hours, including 233 in make and model, was completing a trip from Grosse Ille, Michigan, with four members of his family when the accident occurred.

The instrument-rated pilot told investigators the flight departed Grosse Ille, entered the clouds at 2,500 feet and broke out on top at 6,000, then climbed to 14,000 in the clear, with light rime ice adhering to the Aerostar. After cruising, the plane descended for the approach at Bellaire's Antrim County Airport. It entered clouds at 6,000 feet again, and also broke out underneath at 2,500 feet, the pilot reported.

The pilot reported that he activated all the plane's de-icing equipment except for the pneumatic boots (no explanation was given for this choice, NTSB's investigator said), and flew the approach visually to runway 20. Gear and flaps were at normal positions.

However, just as he was entering the flare, at 100 KIAS, the airplane stalled, the pilot told investigators. It slammed down hard, hitting the ground about 100 feet short of the runway and shearing one main landing gear while driving the other up into the wing. However, none of the five persons aboard had any reported injuries.

The NTSB investigator said one-eighth inch of rime ice was seen on all the airfoils after impact.

Fatal Outcome

So far, we have cited only case histories where the pilot lived to tell about his adventure. In another case, a private pilot and his wife were not so fortunate.

The pilot held a private license and an instrument rating. FAA records show he had flown at least 400 hours, but NTSB did not recover a logbook to show how much IFR time he had logged. He intended an hour-and-ten-minute flight from Bloomington to Elkhart, Indiana, in a 1976 Piper Arrow. Other than pitot heat, the airplane had no de-ice equipment

The pilot called his local FSS at about 9:15 a.m. and outlined the flight, which would commence about an hour later. The briefer gave him a complete and accurate picture. Elkhart was currently reporting a partially obscured sky, ceiling estimated 400 feet overcast, visibility 1-1/2 miles in light snow, light drizzle and fog. A SIGMET was in effect for frequent moderate, occasional severe, rime or mixed icing in clouds in the area. Further, the briefer said there were "numerous" pilot reports of light to moderate rime icing during climbs and descents through the clouds. Tops of the clouds varied from 6,000 to 8,000 feet. The transcript of the briefing shows the pilot accepting this news without concern, then filing his IFR flight plan for a cruise of 7,000 feet.

The pilot left Bloomington on schedule, climbed to 7,000 and flew without incident out of Indianapolis Center airspace into Chicago Center's control. He was about 50 minutes into the flight when he radioed the controller, "I'd like to request higher, sir, I'm starting to build ice here." Within a minute, the controller approved a climb to 9,000 feet. The pilot immediately replied, "Roger. What's the possibility of going lower?" The controller was quizzical ("I thought you wanted higher.") but approved a descent to 5,000 feet.

Three minutes later, the controller suggested, "You can go down to lower if you need to." The pilot said, "Ah, (it) seems to be melting off a little bit. I'll stay here." A few minutes later, the flight was handed off to South Bend Approach, which is the control facility for approaches to Elkhart. The Arrow pilot was given a descent to 4,000 and was told Elkhart was reporting sky partially obscured, estimated ceiling 500 overcast, visibility one mile in light snow and fog. He was also told an airplane in the area had reported the freezing level as 4,700 feet. When reporting level at 4,000 the pilot mentioned, "I believe the freezing level here is around 4,300 to 4,400."

The flight received vectors to get ready for the Elkhart runway 9 SDF back course approach, and was descended to 3,000 feet. An Aero Commander twin arrived in the same airspace and the controller asked the pilots their speeds (to help decide which could be given the approach first). The Commander reported 220 knots in a descent. The Arrow pilot reported 150, then said, "make that 130 knots." The Commander was sequenced first, shot the approach, and landed.

The Arrow was now cleared for the approach. Meanwhile, a Piper Saratoga showed up, also bound for Elkhart. As the Saratoga was being given initial vectors, the Arrow declared a missed approach. "Did you have any ground contact on the approach?" asked the controller. "Yes, sir, I had the runway in sight. I was just a little high," said the Arrow pilot.

"Ah, say your intentions," said the controller. "I'd like to shoot it again, sir," said the pilot. He was issued vectors around for another approach. Along the way, the controller now asked the Saratoga and Arrow their speeds, again needing to make a sequencing decision. The Saratoga reported 160 knots, the Arrow 110 knots. The controller asked the Saratoga to slow to 120 knots, to let the Arrow get in first.

To help the spacing, he also asked the Arrow pilot, "If feasible, ah, increase your airspeed." Said the pilot, "Ah, that's all I can get out of her, sir." (An Arrow of this vintage can cruise at around 140 knots—without ice on it.) A few minutes later, the controller asked the Saratoga pilot whether he could slow to 100 knots. That pilot responded, "Ah, we can slow to about 110, sir, but a hundred...we're carrying quite a bit of ice, too." (The Saratoga later landed without incident. A Saratoga has no de-ice equipment.)

The Arrow pilot flew the approach, broke out and attempted the landing. Controllers in the tower saw nothing out of the ordinary, but the plane apparently stalled in the flare and slammed down on the runway, since it bounced back into the air immediately. Investigators later determined that the plane had hit so hard that the main gear struts were protruding through the top wing skins.

"Elkhart Tower, will you check my gear? I touched down a little hard there," said the pilot. "Understand you're going around?" queried the controller. "That's affirmative. I'm going to circle around. Would you check my gear for me?" The controller observed that the gear had not retracted, and the left main gear was cocked inward. He told the pilot. There was no answer, nor would there be.

Witnesses saw the Arrow climb to a few dozen feet, somewhat sluggishly even though the engine sounded as though it was at full power, then begin a slow left turn. As it got into the turn, it appeared to stall and drop off out of control. It hit the ground with the right wing down steeply. This sheared off the wing and slung the nose into the ground. The occupants were killed by the impact.

An investigator who arrived at the accident scene within moments of the crash found the leading edge of the horizontal tail covered with an ice formation 3/4 of an inch thick.

Leave Well Enough Alone

An iced-up wing is a true deceiver; the pilot is really never sure just how it will react to any changes in airplane configuration, such as major additions of power or flap extension. This pilot found out the hard way about the unpredictability of an plane carrying a load of ice.

The pilot escaped injury, one passenger suffered minor injuries and another was seriously injured when the Cessna 210 landed short of the runway and then struck a road embankment during an attempted go-around.

The pilot was completing an IFR flight from Buffalo, Minnesota to West Fargo Utility Airport when the accident occurred. The 63-year-old private pilot reported a total of 2,263 hours, including 468 in the Cessna 210, and some 403 hours of actual instrument time. He had recently passed a Biennial Flight Review.

The flight had made an approach and broken out under a

The Cessna 210 was damaged when it struck a road embankment short of the runway. A passenger reported seeing ice on the 210's wings during the approach. (File photo)

1,500-foot overcast when it was observed by a flight instructor at the field. The instructor said the Cessna entered a base leg for runway 17 at a somewhat low altitude, then turned final. On the approach, the instructor noticed the plane in a slow, nose-high configuration and remarked that it might stall if the pilot did not get the nose down. As the plane neared the ground, it apparently did stall and slammed to the ground. The instructor then heard the sound of full power being added, and the Cessna "seemed to hang just inches off the ground in a large sweeping arc until it hit a road embankment," witnesses told investigators.

One of the passengers later told investigators in a written statement, "I knew we seemed to be coming in too low before initial ground contact (I am not a pilot, but I have flown in small planes before)." Reportedly, the passenger in the back seat, who also was a pilot, had been telling the pilot in command to lower the nose, but this was not done.

The passenger also recalled seeing ice on the wings and on the outside air temperature gauge as the plane approached the airport. After the accident, numerous pieces of curve-shaped ice were found where the plane came to rest.

In his report, the pilot told investigators that during the vectoring for the approach, he did notice ice on the windshield. But, he said, use of windshield defrost removed it and he saw "no visible ice on the wing leading edge at one time that I looked."

The pilot also told investigators that final approach was "normal." He said he lowered 20 degrees of flaps and maintained 75 to 80 knots airspeed. "About a half-mile out I added power to extend glide because touchdown would be short of the runway. Because it seemed that the glide was not extending, I added more power. The wheels hit the grass. I added full power."

In the portion of the accident report where a pilot is invited to recommend ways the mishap could have been avoided, the pilot wrote, "I should have accepted landing on the grass short of the runway."

Now You See It, Now You Don't

There's little in aviation that can tax a pilot's discipline and resourcefulness more than coping with the hazard of structural icing. We know so little about the phenomenon. The best indication that an aircraft might start icing up in a certain area or along a certain route is reports from pilots who've been there recently and picked up a load.

Even when icing is "known" to have happened, there's no guarantee that other pilots will get ice in the same place. A NASA pilot once told us of how he eagerly launched several times into especially promising areas in a well-equipped and instrumented ice-research craft, only to return disappointed with a clean airframe and no data to show for the effort.

That's not to say he didn't eventually find ice—he did. The fact is that any pilot who flies regularly in winter—or high enough in spring and fall—has a good chance of someday being confronted with airframe ice. And when it happens, there are no hard and fast rules for escaping or handling the ice. Every encounter is unique.

A rather bizarre example of the vagaries of icing encounters involved two nearly identical aircraft operating within five minutes of each other near the same airport. The aircraft were Beech King Air 200s. Both had full de-ice equipment and were being flown by very experienced pilots. Both flew through moderate-to-severe icing conditions. One crashed. One didn't.

The critical difference in this case was that one of the aircraft was inbound for landing and encountered the icing conditions at a relatively high airspeed and low angle of attack. The de-ice equipment on this King Air was able to shed most of the ice that had built up. The other King Air was outbound and climbed through the supercooled water droplets at a relatively low airspeed and high angle of attack. As a result, ice rapidly built up on the bottom surfaces of the wings, behind the boots. It didn't take long until the aircraft became incapable of either climbing or maintaining level flight. It crashed while being vectored to the closest airport.

Running the Tapes

Seeking a clearer perception of how structural ice can affect light aircraft, we studied a printout provided by NTSB of accident reports involving icing conditions as a cause or factor. One of the first discoveries revealed by the files is that the nightmarish, fall-from-the-sky types of accident were relatively rare and usually involved other problems besides airframe ice.

In one case, the pilot of an A36TC Bonanza lost control while flying at 17,000 feet in an area of ice and moderate turbulence shortly after reporting that he had "lost the autopilot." The left wing separated in the uncontrolled descent.

A few of the loss-of-control mishaps had better outcomes. One involved another Bonanza, a naturally aspirated A36 model, that went out of control at 14,000 feet. In this case, the pilot was able to recover at 6,500 feet and make it to a safe harbor. After landing, though, the aircraft was found to have been severely damaged in the plummet.

Though one might expect ice to be primarily an instrument pilot's headache, the reports included several kamikazes who threw themselves into it during VFR flights. One pilot was lucky. His Cessna 210 iced up and was battered by moderate turbulence when he flew into clouds. He attempted to climb, but the aircraft soon became incapable of either climbing or holding altitude. The pilot and his passenger survived the forced landing, but the 210 was a write-off.

Of course, you don't have to be inside clouds to get ice. Another form of "visible moisture" is rain. Along a front, water droplets falling from warm air into much colder air can become supercooled. These droplets tend to be pretty big, and they can deposit a startling load of clear ice on an airframe in the wink of an eye, as illustrated by the following example:

A pilot had just purchased a Cessna 140 and set out to fly his prize back to his home field. The distance between the two airstrips was a paltry three miles. The ceiling was low—500 feet—but visibility was a good five miles in freezing rain. Only three miles—but the pilot didn't make it. He was forced to set the aircraft down short of his home field when the windshield iced up. The pilot escaped injury, but the 140 was substantially damaged.

In our opinion, a forecast of freezing rain is good cause for canceling any flight. (Even aircraft certified for flight in icing conditions are not required to prove that they can handle the stuff.) Launching into or pressing on in areas of known freezing rain (ZR), freezing drizzle (ZL) or ice pellets (IP), indicating that there's freezing precipitation somewhere aloft) is asking for trouble. One non-instrument-rated pilot in our sample did just that. He took off in freezing rain and killed both himself and his wife.

An old saw would have a pilot climb into the warmer air to escape freezing rain. However, ice accumulation from freezing precipitation almost always is severe, and, as the following example shows, there may be time only to choose a suitable field for landing. The accident occurred when a Cessna T210 ran into freezing rain while flying over mountainous terrain at 11,000 feet. Seeking to try for the warm air above, the pilot obtained clearance to a higher altitude—13,000 feet. The aircraft climbed only 300 feet before descending out of control, killing all six people aboard. It's interesting to note that at about the same time, another pilot, also at 11,000 feet, decided to start down when his Navajo began picking up ice. He had only to go down 1,000 feet before he found air warm enough to continue safely to his destination.

Warning Signs

Among other lessons provided by the accident reports is that, even though pilots may well be skeptical of forecast icing conditions, we should not ignore them. As illustrated by the following case, the forecasts sometimes are on the money: The pilot tried a route that was forecast to have not only icing conditions, but severe turbulence, as well. His Comanche 250 crashed out of control only about a minute after he reported encountering exactly what had been forecast.

Another pilot flew his Cessna 340 into an area in which he knew a SIGMET for severe icing was in effect. The ice that began accumulating on the twin proved to be only one of the pilot's problems. While descending to try to escape the icing conditions, he had to shut down the right engine. (He didn't say why, but extensive cylinder and magneto damage later was found.) The 340 eventually stalled and spun in while the pilot was attempting an emergency landing.

Don't Take an Icing Problem into the Air

Ice, in general, is where you find it, and one of the places it's easiest to find—and get rid of—is on the ground. A pilot who takes off in an airplane that is obviously ice-contaminated is really asking for trouble. Here's a situation that didn't have a high probability of a successful conclusion.

"It'll blow off on the roll," said the pilot of the ill-fated Air Florida flight. The snow on the wings that he was referring to did not blow off and the airliner crashed in the Potomac River. The lesson of the Air Florida crash is one that apparently must be retaught periodically.

In illustration of this was the January 19, 1986 crash of a Beech A-36TC Bonanza. The 43-year-old private pilot and his passenger were unhurt when the Bonanza ran off the end of the runway at Bowman Field, Louisville, Kentucky, but the airplane was substantially damaged.

According to investigators, the pilot and his passenger were observed loading baggage into the Bonanza in preparation for the flight. One witness—a retired corporate pilot—watched as the pilot "checked the oil and drained the sumps. He kicked the chock out" from under the wheel, but did not clean off any of the half- to three-quarter-inch layer of snow that had accumulated on the wings and tail.

The Bonanza pilot started the engine and began taxiing for the runway. The witness heard the engine being run up and the prop being exercised as the Bonanza rolled along. In his statement to investigators, the witness wrote, "At that point, I remarked to another pilot close by, 'I can't believe that he did not clean the snow off the aircraft. We are going to see an accident.'"

The Bonanza pilot later told FAA inspectors that since the snow on the windshield had blown off during runup, he thought the snow on the wings would blow off during takeoff. With this in mind, he started his takeoff roll on runway 32.

Witnesses saw the Bonanza accelerate down the runway. By the time it had reached the runway midpoint, it had reached an estimated 65 or 70 knots. They watched as it continued down the runway, still accelerating but with no attempt at rotation. Finally, with only a few hundred feet of runway left, the pilot decided to abort the takeoff.

He pulled the power off and got on the brakes. The runway was covered with the same wet snow, and the plane did not slow down. It careened off the end of the runway, sliding through the boundary fence. It came to rest with the nose-gear collapsed, the prop bent, and the right wing damaged.

Asked for ways in which the accident might have been prevented, the pilot showed he had learned a lesson. "De-ice or better snow removal from wings," he wrote in the space on the accident report.

Picking up ice in-flight is one thing. But taking off, knowing it's already on the airframe, is another thing entirely. Launching in an ice- or snow-covered aircraft defies all logic. Yet, each year, a few pilots do just that. The files include one report of a pilot and three passengers who set to work with credit cards and paper towels to try to scrape ice and frost off their Mooney while it was being refueled—an admirable but, apparently, futile effort. Witnesses said even more frost and ice were forming on the aircraft while this was taking place. This shouldn't have escaped the pilot's attention, but he elected to take off anyway. After a very long takeoff roll, the Mooney was in a steep climbing turn when it stalled and crashed into trees. There were no survivors.

Snow on an airplane does blow off sometimes, but only under rather special circumstances, and even then, there may be enough of it adhering to the wings and tail to cause real aerodynamic problems.

When an airplane has been sitting outside long enough to become completely cold-soaked—including fuel in the wing tanks—and dry snow falls on it, there's a pretty good chance that the snow will not stick. (We make special mention of the fuel, because a tank full of gasoline with a temperature just a few degrees warmer than the rest of the airframe will melt a thin layer of snow, which acts like super glue for whatever snow falls on top of it). And if the snow comes off so easily, why take the chance of blowing it off during the takeoff roll? Why not brush it off and fly away with a clean airplane?

There's another rather unique circumstance that can bring an "it'll blow off during the roll" operation to a screeching halt: Remember that the wing of an airplane creates lift primarily by reducing the pressure of the air flowing across the curved upper surface, said reduction accompanied by a lowering of the temperature. If there's a layer of wet snow on the wing, and the temperature drop is just enough to hit the freezing point, the wet snow can turn to ice—rough, lift-destroying ice—in the blink of an eye. And there you are, halfway down the runway, at the controls of a machine that won't fly, with perhaps not enough room to get stopped.

The smart winter-time pilot is a fervent believer in the "clean airplane" concept. Never, but *never,* attempt a takeoff if there is any ice, frost, or snow adhering to the airplane.

Safe Harbors

The first sign of ice accumulation is sure to raise a pilot's stress level and trigger the good old fight-or-flee response. A prudent pilot will flee, even if his mount is armed with boots and a heated windshield. The decision to climb, descend or turn around will be based on the pilot's knowledge of the weather.

If icing conditions can't be escaped, it's time to head to the nearest safe harbor—pronto. The situation can become grim, indeed, if flight is prolonged, as illustrated by a case that involved a Beech Queen Air on a scheduled commuter flight with two experienced pilots aboard.

> Moderate icing in light freezing rain had been reported by several pilots, and an AIRMET was in effect. The crew made it to the destination and shot an NDB approach. But below-minimums weather conditions forced a missed approach. After being instructed to climb in order to set up for another NDB approach, one of the pilots informed ATC that the Queen Air was carrying a heavy load of ice and was incapable of climbing.
>
> The crew then was given a revised clearance and vectors to the inbound course for the VOR approach to the same airport. At about this time, one of the pilots talked with an airline weather observer, who warned that conditions were below minimums and advised the crew to "get the hell out of there." Apparently, they did not heed the advice; the Queen Air later hit trees while circling to land. All nine people aboard perished.
>
> The crew had passed up a very promising "out." The VOR used for the second approach they made to the scheduled

destination was also an initial fix for a precision approach to
a nearby airport. Weather conditions at that airport were
above minimums at the time.

ATC is ready and able to provide guidance to a safe harbor, but it's
up to the pilot to ask for help. One report on a Beech A36 Bonanza that
crashed out of control noted that although the pilot had informed
controllers that ice was building up on his aircraft, he hadn't
requested assistance in locating a suitable place to land.

Easy Does It

One lesson that showed clearly in the accident reports is that an ice-
bearing aircraft requires a very gentle touch. Fully a quarter of the
accidents involved pilots who got very close to safe landing areas, only
to lose it at the last moment.

Some of the pilots just couldn't see out of their windshields and
either landed hard or hit something on the ground. Ice is more than
a match for most windshield defoggers, but with some experimenta-
tion, it is possible to use charts or books to rig up makeshift ducting
to concentrate the flow of warm air onto a small portion of the
windshield. Some resourceful pilots also carry scraping devices that
fit through the storm hatch on the side window.

The majority, though, involved stalls. Several occurred when
aircraft were being maneuvered to land or just after the gear or flaps
were lowered. One pilot felt his aircraft becoming sluggish during a
straight-in ILS approach; he added power, and the plane immediately stalled.

The aerodynamic properties of an iced-up aircraft are unknown.
The best bet is to leave an aircraft that's still flying alone as much as
possible. Any changes should be made cautiously, if at all. Keep the
power on and the turns shallow. Leave the flaps alone, and save the
gear for the last possible moment. If there's a lot of ice on the aircraft,
it might be better to slide it onto the runway gear-up at an airspeed
much higher than normal than to risk stalling out on short final while
reducing power or lowering the gear or flaps.

Doesn't Help At All

Whenever flight conditions include freezing temperatures and visible moisture, a pilot has got to expect icing...sometimes it happens,
sometimes not. But when the white crystals begin to form, you can
count on the accumulation being worse if the clouds are moving up

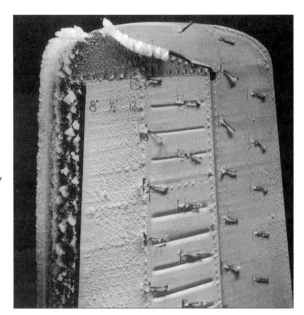

Even though the leading edges may appear lightly coated, the underside of the wings could be heavily iced, increasing drag and raising the stall speed.

and down (as in convection), or when you are flying near the tops of a cloud layer. In the case of vertical action in the clouds, the supercooled water droplets collide and grow, providing more water to turn into ice when you run into it.

Flying near the top of a cloud layer increases the potential of structural icing because the water drops have been lifted as far as they're going to go (otherwise, they wouldn't be "tops"), and again the more water in the air, the greater will be the ice that winds up on your airplane. Cloud tops and turbulence are to be avoided like the plague when temperatures are below freezing.

In the next example, a Lance pilot encountered both of these bad conditions, and got in deeper and deeper as the flight progressed, until there were no options left.

> The 33-year-old ATP had some 3,720 total hours, including about 200 in the Lance, which he owned. He left Memphis, Tennessee in VFR conditions and received a weather update at Little Rock, Arkansas, upon passing there about an hour and a quarter into the flight. Upon reaching Fort Smith, Arkansas, he activated an IFR flight plan and continued. The pilot said the air temperature at his VFR cruise altitude of 4,500 feet had been 45 degrees, and as he entered clouds and

flew at 4,000 feet it remained 45 degrees. The pilot stated he asked for pilot reports of any icing, and was given just one report about light icing at 16,000 feet.

The pilot's written accident report next states that he tuned in the ATIS for Wiley Post and got weather as a 500-foot ceiling, visibility three-quarters of a mile. While maneuvering for the approach, he heard the ATIS updated to include drizzle and fog. He said he asked for the surface temperature and was told it was 28 degrees. Although winds were from the north at 18 knots, gusting to 25, the approach in use was the runway 17L ILS. The pilot was vectored to the final approach course. As he descended below 3,000 feet, he noticed the plane was picking up light ice and the temperature had fallen below 32 degrees. He later said he did not consider the ice a problem.

Controllers stated to the pilot that the runway visibility was currently about 6,000 feet, allowing for a VOR approach to runway 36R if he wished, but the pilot elected to continue with the ILS approach.

The pilot said as he descended through 800 feet on the approach, the plane entered strong downdrafts, requiring large power and pitch inputs to correct. At 450 feet, he acquired the runway visually. However, he said he was in strong turbulence that required full power and full elevator to control. He said as he crossed the threshold, the plane instantly gained 30 knots of airspeed and nosed over. While recovering from this, the aircraft "ballooned" above the runway, then began to sink uncontrollably. Although he tried to recover with power and elevator, the nosewheel struck the runway. The pilot said the wind was blowing so hard that, when he opened the cabin door after coming to a stop, it was blown off its hinges.

Investigators noted that the Lance had about three-eighths of an inch of ice on the leading edges of the wings and tail surfaces.

Trial by Ice

When it rains—especially on a beginner—it really pours. Flying in icing conditions is a tricky business at best, and winning the battle usually requires a deep reservoir of experience, a lot of knowledge (gained through a series of innocuous encounters, building up to the "big one"), an airplane equipped with all the ice-control goodies, and a lot of good luck. This pilot had none of those working for him.

The education of a newly instrument-rated private pilot in icing conditions began as he flight-planned a trip from Denver, Colorado, to Casper, Wyoming. He planned the takeoff from Arapahoe County Airport in the early morning of the following day.

The trip was to be in his own Piper Arrow, which had not one piece of de-icing equipment. The pilot, age 30, had obtained his instrument rating six months earlier, now holding a total of 371 hours, with 60 hours simulated IFR and 14.7 hours actual.

He was a prudent flight-planner, calling the FSS at 4:30 p.m. to get a complete briefing, which included talk of a weather system moving through with ice and turbulence; but also had a forecast of colder temperatures and a change to snow. At 10 p.m., he watched the television weather forecast, and at 11 p.m., he called the FSS for an updated briefing. The briefer now gave a dour forecast of clouds, turbulence, precipitation, fog and ice, but noted the frontal weather was roughly overhead at the time. The airman asked for any pilot reports of ice, and the briefer responded that he had no PIREPs at all. The pilot then filed his IFR flight plan and promised to check before takeoff for icing forecasts or reports.

He did, calling the FSS at 3 a.m. before he left for the airport. The briefer gave him current observations that included low ceilings at Denver, Casper, Cheyenne and Laramie, but all with "light snow" as the precipitation. Queried the pilot, "Any reports of icing?" Said the briefer, "No, we haven't any reports at all."

A light freezing drizzle was falling as he got his clearance at 4 a.m. through the FSS and Stapleton controllers (the Arapahoe tower was closed); they made no reference to bad weather. The pilot took off, contacting Denver Departure on the climbout.

Arapahoe's elevation is 5,872 MSL. After establishing radar contact and okaying a climb to 12,000 feet, the controller now told the pilot, "Tops of the clouds are about 10,500. You might get light to moderate rime ice until you're out of the clouds." The pilot acknowledged and continued to climb.

In the next three minutes, the controller asked whether the Arrow was picking up ice, and the pilot reported none as he went through 7,800 feet, then 8,800. The controller then asked him to change frequencies, and with contact re-established, radioed: "(Arrow) 139, there's a twin Cessna out there that's been holding above, trying to burn off a little bit of ice, and you might explain to him what the situation has been weather-wise since you took off from Arapahoe."

"We haven't picked up any ice on the wings whatsoever. It's a light, drizzly, freezing rain on the surface, but shouldn't give you too much problems. The ceilings are about 500 to 1,000, wind is calm," the Arrow pilot reported to the Cessna 421 above him.

He spoke too soon. Ten minutes later, he found himself telling the controller, "We're unable to climb much above 10,000 here....We've got a little rough vibration in the engine. I bet we got some (ice) on the prop. She's not turning well." Shortly, the controller suggested, "If you like you can just make an ILS into Denver if it gets any worse there." The pilot responded, "Why don't we go ahead and do that." Vectors for Denver Stapleton's runway 26L ILS began.

Meanwhile, the Cessna 421 executed a missed approach at Denver. The controller asked that pilot to relate his experience for the benefit of the Arrow pilot. Said the 421 driver, "I had ice on the windshield and I couldn't pick up the runway environment until it was just too late. Recommend you turn the strobes on for him."

The Arrow's engine now began to run smoother, but ceilings at Stapleton were not going to allow a landing. "I executed the approach to minimums [5,531 MSL, 200 AGL] and observed the glow of the strobes, but not the environment," the pilot later told NTSB. He executed a missed approach, and noticed another problem: his climb rate was about 200 feet per minute. He now could see ice on the leading edges of the wings.

The Arrow pilot managed to regain about 8,000 feet, and turned eastward, hoping to find warmer air and marking time while he discussed his predicament with the ground. It was not auspicious: Five or six airports within a few hundred miles were checked, and the best ceiling reported was 1,600 feet at Laramie, Wyoming, which was out of the question due to high intervening terrain. Most other ceilings were around 300 feet.

Things looked up when the Cessna 421 pilot came back on the frequency and announced he had checked with the FSS, found that Trinidad, Colorado, (to the south) was reporting a ceiling of 25,000 feet thin scattered, and said he would divert there. Unfortunately, the Arrow pilot didn't have this option, again because of high terrain. But, reasoning that conditions seemed to be better somewhat south as indicated by the Trinidad weather, he decided to ask for a clearance to Amarillo, Texas, to the southeast.

This had progressed a ways when the controller announced, "Did you check somewhere and find out that the Amarillo weather was good, because we just checked for you and found out that it's not....They got 300 overcast, visibility three-quarters of a mile." Some more options were chewed up and spit out: Omaha or Lincoln, Nebraska; Alamosa, Colorado; Garden City, Kansas. Meanwhile, the ice accumulation seemed to stop, the Arrow got up to 8,500 feet, and then some more ice began accreting.

It was now time to discuss an attempted ILS back at Stapleton, or even a ground-controlled approach (GCA) at Buckley Air National Guard Base, if need be. The pilot showed aplomb. "You ever make a GCA before?" asked the controller. "We had to practice a lot of 'em to get this license," the pilot radioed.

Vectors for the 35R approach began. It was now about 5:30 a.m. and dawn was breaking, bringing hopes of better visibility, since the Arrow's windshield was covered with ice. "We can see a little bit better now. We may be landed out the side window, but I think we can get it," the pilot said. He even reported getting a brief look at the ground.

The controller then did a marvelous thing with some creative vectoring: "The reason I put you on that 290 heading," he said, "is if you get good contact with the ground again there's Columbine Airport....Because the weather right here at Denver isn't all that good right now. It's still like 400 overcast and (visibility two miles), light freezing drizzle, light snow. And if you do get a good hole out there and see the ground...you just might see Columbine."

Sure enough, seconds later the Arrow pilot announced

ground contact and the controller called out, "Columbine, three miles dead ahead." And just seconds later, the pilot radioed, "We have Columbine. We'll land there." He was VFR in sight of an airport, but his adventure wasn't quite over.

Here's how the pilot described the next events to the NTSB: "I made a normal downwind, base and final approach to runway 32. Forward visibility was slightly impaired by a small buildup of rime ice on the windshield, but not sufficient to noticeably affect the approach. "The approach had been rather steep. I made a close-in entry to downwind at 7,200 feet and the field elevation was 5,680, but all flight controls and indications were satisfactory. Upon turning final, visual indications appeared that I might be landing long, but as the final progressed it appeared that I was to be slightly short. I added power and pulled the nose up slightly, which corrected the problem.

"As I approached the threshold, the airplane suddenly dropped. I added more power and flared for touchdown, dropping approximately 10 to 15 feet in a normal landing attitude and configuration. I touched down very hard on the mains, right on the numbers. Rollout was straight forward, however I could see that the left main had been pushed up through the wing, as the skin on top was split. The rollout was very slow...and approximately 300 feet down the runway the left main collapsed and I allowed the aircraft to slide off the runway to the left." The pilot was uninjured.

His own self-critique of the landing was particularly apt: "I did not allow for the increase in airspeed necessary to offset the accumulation of ice. The airplane stalled without warning on final due to ice accumulation." Indeed, investigators who arrived two hours later found the aircraft's wings and tail still covered with approximately 1-1/4 inches of ice. The pitot tube was covered with a globe of ice the size of a golf ball; the pilot had not had a reliable airspeed indicator for the approach.

The NTSB's probable cause report put the onus entirely on the pilot. It found he had initiated flight with known deficiencies in the airplane (lack of de-ice equipment), and had set out in adverse weather, since he did mention there had been light freezing rain upon takeoff.

However, the pilot did have some points in his defense: "I

submit that had the 3 a.m. FSS weather forecast contained any report of icing conditions, I would not have contemplated the flight further," he told NTSB. "In addition, although I did not request an updated briefing at 4 a.m. when I called for my clearance, I would expect FSS to forward any report such as moderate to heavy rime ice to any pilot contemplating a departure at that time. Even Stapleton Approach—who I was instructed to call by FSS for clearance and who I submit was then in contact with the Cessna 421 with icing problems—at that time would have reasonably been expected to forward such weather conditions to any pilot calling for clearance.

"When I contacted (Departure Control) at approximately 4:15, then and only then was I aware of the actual existence of icing. I contemplated an immediate return to Arapahoe County Airport due to the controller's report of a Cessna 421 trying to 'burn off some ice.' At that point, however, whether I should have returned to Arapahoe or not was a moot question."

Certainly, the pilot might have recognized that the freezing rain at Arapahoe was good reason to cancel the flight, and he might have turned right around the first time he heard the icing report. But on balance, despite NTSB's cause report, we feel that the pilot and controllers acquitted themselves well once the trouble began, and the acid test was that the pilot walked away.

Home Field Lures Pilot into Crash

It's that old "home field advantage." Some pilots apparently feel that once a flight has begun, there is no going back—they can't return to their departure point and wait for the weather to improve. These pilots sometimes find themselves trapped, and escape routes can vanish quickly. "Having started, the flight had to terminate somewhere," the pilot wrote after the accident. But perhaps not where he intended. The story of his flight contains many lessons.

The 59-year-old, 999-hour pilot of a Cessna 172 found himself trapped by icing and below-minimums ceilings as he attempted to shoot a "modified" ILS into Greater Rockford Airport, Rockford, Illinois. The Cessna was destroyed when it hit trees and a building near the approach end of the runway. Only by incredible luck, the pilot did not terminate where the flight did—he escaped with minor injuries.

The pilot was rated and current for the flight. He held a private certificate with instrument rating, and had logged some 105 hours of instrument flight, 68 of which were in actual instrument conditions.

He was about to embark on a flight that would illustrate the incredible lure of the home airport, and the many small indecisions and mistakes that can tally up to one all-or-nothing roll of the dice. Perhaps the biggest single lesson is that there is nothing inevitable about a trip that starts VFR and ends in an approach to below-minimums weather.

BEGINNINGS

The pilot had spent the preceding two days skiing with a church youth group near Ironwood, Michigan. The youth group was planning to stay at Ironwood through the weekend, but the pilot wanted to get home to Rockford by Saturday evening to attend a church meeting on Sunday morning.

The adventure started at about 3:45 on Saturday afternoon when the pilot radioed the FSS at Houghton, Michigan, from Ironwood, Michigan. He filed an IFR flight plan for a trip from Ironwood to Rockford, with a departure time "as soon as possible," according to the statement of the FSS specialist. He listed Madison, Wisconsin, as his alternate.

There is a dispute on the record concerning a weather briefing. The investigator, in the accident factual report, asserts that "the pilot stated that he received a preflight weather briefing from Houghton FSS via radio telephone. However, the FSS specialist at Houghton said a pilot weather briefing was not given.

But according to the pilot, he had received a briefing. He could not recall what the weather was for his route, but the weather at his departure point, according to the pilot's observation, was "gorgeous...a beautiful day." (Indeed, the observation taken at Houghton, Michigan, at 2:52 p.m. listed conditions as a clear sky with a visibility of 40 miles.)

But weather at points along his route was not so nice. The 2:52 observation at Madison, Wisconsin (the alternate): sky obscured, measured ceiling 500 overcast, visibility three-quarters of a mile, light snow and fog. (The lowest published approach for Madison, the VOR-B approach, had minimums of 700 feet and one mile.)

Rockford, his destination, at 3:12 p.m. recorded a special observation: measured ceiling 500 overcast, seven miles visibility. Cedar Rapids, Iowa, offered a hint of what was to come for the Rockford area, though. The 2:52 observation: 600-foot obscured ceiling, visibility varying around two miles in light snow and fog.

But even the most complete weather briefing could not have prepared him for what lay in wait. There was no icing forecast for the area. Moderate mixed icing did exist, however, and would figure in the final outcome.

Options: Get more weather information; wait for weather system to pass; embark on flight.

Starting Small

By 3:56, the Skyhawk was in the air and the flight plan was activated. The pilot later reported that he had departed in VFR conditions from Ironwood. Weather at the destination had deteriorated somewhat. Rockford reported at 3:51 that the ceiling had fallen to a measured 400-foot overcast with five miles visibility in fog. His alternate at Madison: Sky obscured, 400 feet scattered, measured 500 feet overcast, visibility one-half mile.

The flight progressed uneventfully for the first hour and a half until the Cessna was over Wassau, Wisconsin, and darkness began to close in. The C-172 now began to pick up some rime ice, according to the pilot's statement in his accident report. The pilot later wrote, "I turned on my landing light and realized I was flying through light snowfall. I looked at the corners of my windshield to see if any ice was forming. There was a slight accumulation. Taking my flashlight, I turned the beam on the leading edge of the wing. A light coat of ice was forming."

Decision Point 2: Options: Return to Ironwood; get more weather information; continue the flight and try to get clear of ice.

He requested a climb from 7,000 feet to 8,000 to try to get away from the ice. He did not mention the ice to ATC at this time. The controller told the pilot that 8,000 feet and a little north of Madison would put the flight between layers. The pilot found this was true, and "the ice which had formed quickly sublimated." After passing Madison, ATC called for the Cessna to descend to 7,000 feet and turned the flight over to Rockford Approach.

The approach controller gave the pilot the current Rockford weather. This was the first time since takeoff that the pilot had received any updated weather information, according to the accident report. The news was not good. Rockford had dropped to an indefinite ceiling of 100 feet obscured, visibility half a mile in fog and light drizzle. The destination was below minimums.

Decision Point 3: Options: Get more weather information and divert to a field with weather above minimums; press on, hoping conditions will somehow improve without requiring a decision.

About 12 minutes later, the controller informed the pilot that the RVR at Rockford had dropped to 2,400. "Its been on the downward trend here for the last 20 minutes or so," the controller said. The controller thought of a field about 30 miles north of Rockford. "Do you want me to check to see what Janesville's got for weather?" "Why don't you try that?" the pilot responded.

DECISIONS, DECISIONS

About a minute later, the controller came back with the Janesville weather: "Estimated 500 overcast, visibility one and a half with fog. Wind 060 at five. Janesville altimeter two nine eight six. Their glideslope is out of service, but if that ceiling is good estimated at 500 feet, that still gives you minimums for the approach." (The minimums for a localizer 4 approach at Janesville were indeed 500 and one-half.)

"Glideslope out you say?" the pilot asked. The controller confirmed that the glideslope was not working.

"Okay," the pilot asked, "what runway would we use?"

"Probably runway 4, straight in off the ILS with the wind 060 at five," the controller shot back.

Decision Point 4: Options: Seek more weather information and divert elsewhere; continue to Rockford; try the controller's suggestion—Janesville.

The pilot didn't ponder long. "Okay, let's go in up there."

Meanwhile, weather in the rest of the area was changing. Madison was now reporting a 400-foot overcast, but visibilities had improved to five miles in light snow and fog. Cedar

Rapids, Iowa—just west of Rockford—reported an obscured 800-foot ceiling, visibility varying from two miles to one and a quarter miles in drizzle and fog. Weather at Chicago, to the east, was 600 feet overcast, visibility seven miles in light snow. None of this information was relayed to the pilot, nor did he request it.

FIRST ATTEMPT

The controller issued a vector to the northwest, outbound from the Janesville VOR, and called for a descent to 2,700 feet. "Report leaving 4,000," the controller told him, "I'll start your turn back inbound at that time."

"Descending to 2,700 feet resulted in an immediate build-up of ice on the leading edge of the wing as the plane descended from a much colder altitude," the pilot later wrote. Transcripts show that he never mentioned this to the controller, however.

Decision Point 5: Options: Treat the icing conditions as an emergency; say nothing and continue.

The Cessna was vectored to the localizer and cleared for the approach six miles from the outer marker, but as he got closer, the pilot asked the controller to, "monitor this thing as I come over [the outer marker]. I'm not sure this localizer is working."

"All right," the controller responded, "I show you just about on it right now." The pilot reported that his needle hadn't moved. The controller told him that radar showed the Cessna right on the localizer. "Okay," the pilot said, "This localizer, I don't think this localizer is working. We may have to come to Rockford and use the NDB."

The controller's response: "Okay, well, fly a heading of 040 for now. Let me know if you get the localizer. If not, why, we'll vector you to Rockford. What frequency you got set for the localizer there?"

"I'm not picking up the localizer," the pilot called.

"You say you are now?" the controller asked.

"We're not," the pilot reiterated.

"What frequency do you have set on the localizer?" the controller tried to confirm his radio setting.

"One oh nine point one," the pilot responded.

"Okay, that's the right frequency," the controller told him.

Decision Point 6: Options: Get more information and

divert elsewhere; try Rockford no matter how low it is.

"We'll try Rockford no matter how low it is," the pilot said, breaking off the approach. The controller gave him a climb to 3,000 feet and a heading back towards Rockford, telling the pilot that the RVR at Rockford was now up to 2,000. "Beautiful," was the pilot's reply.

THINGS CHANGE

Two minutes later, the controller told the pilot that the RVR had now dropped to 1,800 feet. He asked the pilot how much fuel he had on board. "Probably got two hours, a little less than two hours," the pilot said.

The controller brought the Cessna around for an ILS approach to Rockford's runway 36. Weather at the time was reported as indefinite ceiling 100 feet obscured, visibility half a mile in fog. Winds were given as 080 at five.

Realizing his localizer receiver was out, the pilot asked the controller to "give us like a no-gyro approach. You can monitor it as I come on down."

"Well, we can do that," the controller replied, "I just checked with Janesville. They said their localizer, they checked it out, the maintenance man says it's working."

"I don't think it's their localizer," the pilot said, "I think it's this thing."

The pilot said later "by this time, ice was forming more heavily and the propeller was vibrating. An occasional thump was heard as ice apparently broke loose and hit the fuselage. I realized it was becoming most urgent that I get the plane on the ground, or assuredly it would do it on its own." He did not tell the controller about this, though.

Decision Point 7: Options: Declare an emergency due to icing, maintain altitude and exit from icing conditions; press on silently.

OLD COLLEGE TRY

The controller started hunting around for alternates for the pilot. The closest better weather was at Madison. Five minutes after their regular observation at 6:50, observers there issued a special observation: 400-foot overcast with one mile visibility in light snow and fog. But this was still too low for the approaches available, and the Madison weather would continue to get worse.

The controller relayed this information to the pilot, who replied, "Okay, let's see what we can do here."

"Okay," the controller told him, "the RVR is still 1,800 here at Rockford, and our visibility now, ah, prevailing visibility is a quarter mile in light drizzle and fog."

Decision Point 8: Options: Get more weather information ("What's Chicago got? How about Cedar Rapids? Could I make it to Oshkosh?") and divert; continue to Rockford for the "old college try."

"Okay, we'll give it the old college try," the pilot said.

Why didn't he divert? Why didn't he look for better weather? "Rockford's my home base," he later said. "I'd made that approach hundreds of times. I was familiar with the terrain and the approach, so I thought I'd try there."

Meanwhile, the weather over the rest of the region had deteriorated. Madison was below minimums. Chicago, which was reporting a variable 600-foot overcast with visibility seven miles in light snow, "was not even mentioned," the pilot said. This was the best weather in the local area, however.

Cedar Rapids, to the west, was slightly better with an 800-foot obscured ceiling and two miles visibility in light snow and fog. The controller didn't mention this, either, but of course, he hadn't been asked.

At this point, even turning around and going back to the north was becoming a questionable option. Houghton, Michigan, had fallen to a 500-foot broken overcast. Oshkosh, Wisconsin, now offered the best weather within reach, with an estimated 1,500-foot overcast and three miles visibility during the 6:47 p.m. observation. This was deteriorating, though, and by the time of the next observation, one hour later, the ceiling had fallen to a 700-foot obscured ceiling with one mile visibility.

A NEW APPROACH

"What are your intentions?" the controller queried, "What kind of approach do you want to make, sir?"

Decision Point 9: Options: Get more weather information and divert; create a home-brewed approach procedure and try it.

"I'd like the ILS and, I think the glideslope's still working on this thing, but the localizer is out and we'll use the NDB to help us down," the pilot opted.

"You want to fly an ILS without a localizer and you're going to fly the glideslope and the NDB, is that correct?" the controller asked.

"Yes, yes that's affirmative," the pilot replied.

The controller chose a more helpful option. He offered to provide headings down the approach using Airport Surveillance Radar. The pilot replied, "That'll be super."

Now came the final series of events, and it would have all the appearance of inevitability.

The controller told the pilot to turn to a heading of 200, and had him confirm his altitude as 3,000 feet. "Affirmative," the pilot replied, "Where we at now?"

"You are four miles northwest of the airport," the controller told him. "Okay," the pilot replied.

"Cessna five five eight, the runway 36 RVR is now 1,600," the controller passed along.

"It's a little better," the pilot said.

"No, it's a little worse. It was 1,800 before," the controller told him.

"Okay, (unintelligible) tonight. Where's five five eight now?" the pilot asked.

"Your position is about three miles west-southwest of the airport," the controller offered.

"Okay, we'd like to turn in as quickly as possible," the pilot stated. The controller called for descent to 2,500 feet and, after confirming what frequency the Cessna was using, turned him over to the ASR controller.

LAST ATTEMPT

The pilot switched frequencies and the approach started. "Okay, five five eight's with you," the pilot called.

"Cessna five five eight, radio check. How do you hear?" the ASR controller queried. "Real great, loud and clear," came the reply.

The ASR controller started right up. "Five five eight, roger, fly heading 180, maintain 2,300. By vectors, surveillance final approach course runway 36. The minimum descent altitude 1,160 feet, the missed approach point is the runway threshold. In the event of lost communications, climb and maintain 2,500 feet, proceed direct to GILMY outer compass locator and execute the full ILS or NDB, whichever you have the equipment for."

"Roger, five five eight," the pilot replied.

"And five five eight, verify you're on a 180 heading."

"Let me check this thing," the pilot said, "Hold it, I think we got to move this compass over. We reset our compass."

"Five five eight, roger," the ASR controller said, "Fly heading 180. I will be turning you on the final five miles from the runway to give you time to line up on the runway."

"Okay, good deal," came the response.

"I knew it was going to be a tight approach," the pilot later wrote, "and would take all the concentration I could muster. In preparation for the final approach, I cinched my lap and shoulder harness as tight as possible."

"Runway 36 visual range now 1,600," the controller told him, "and if no transmissions received for one minute on the vector or fifteen seconds on the final, execute the published missed approach procedure."

"Roger," the pilot said.

"Cessna five five eight, would you like recommended altitudes on the final?" the controller asked.

"Wouldn't mind."

"Okay," the controller said.

"Take all the help I can get tonight," the pilot told him.

"Cessna five five eight, the wind direction is estimated, the indicators at the tower are out of service at this time. Weather bureau last sequence gave us winds at 100 at six knots," the controller told him. "Roger," the pilot replied. The Cessna was now on a left downwind about four miles south-southwest of the airport.

"Cessna five five eight, say your altitude."

"We're at 2,200 right now," the pilot told him.

"Altitude should be 2,300," the controller reminded him. But the pilot replied, "I don't know if we can pull her up. We're picking up a little bit of ice." This was the first time the pilot mentioned the icing.

"Cessna five five eight, roger," the controller said, "Turn left heading 090 and attempt to maintain 2,300 and the altimeter is two niner eight six."

"Roger. What was that heading?"

"090. We're turning a left base leg now for the approach," the controller replied.

"Roger, 090," was all the pilot said.

WANDERING

The Cessna was now five miles south of the airport on the left base leg of the approach. The pilot radioed that he was maintaining the 2,300 foot altitude requested.

"Roger," the controller said, "verify you're on an east heading 090."

"We're a little bit to the left. We'll be right back there," the pilot said.

The controller told him the RVR was 1,600 again. "Okay, five five eight, we know," the pilot replied.

"Cessna five five eight, prepare to begin descent in one mile. Published minimum descent altitude 1,160 feet. Turn left heading 060."

"Left to 060 and we're at 2,300 feet," the pilot stated.

"Cessna five five eight you can begin descent to your minimum descent altitude and let me know if you're receiving the glideslope. You're four and one-half miles south of the airport." The controller was now into the final approach phase.

"Just passing GILMY [the outer marker] inbound," the pilot called as he pulled on the carburetor heat. This, as the pilot later realized, was probably a mistake that robbed him of some vital engine rpms.

"Five five eight, that's correct and heading should be 060. You're left of course and correcting nicely and you're descending to your minimum descent altitude, is that correct?"

"Ah, that's affirmative," the pilot replied.

The Cessna was again drifting to the left of course as it came down the approach. The controller steered him back to the centerline and gave him a heading of 020, but he started drifting off to the left again. The controller gave him a turn to 030. The Cessna remained "slightly left of course and correcting nicely."

LAST WORDS

"Turn left heading 020," the controller told him, "You're drifting right of course rapidly. You're very slightly right of course and correcting back to course."

"You're one-half mile from runway. You're very slightly left of course now. Turn right heading 030." The post-accident weather observation would reveal the RVR had now dropped to 800 feet.

The Cessna disappeared from the scope. The controller called, "Cessna five five eight, Rockford, how do you hear?" But there was no reply.

The pilot later reported that he was coming down the approach and having difficulty maintaining airspeed. "I think what happened," he later told a local reporter, "was the plane was loaded with ice. I was keeping the power up. The tower was talking me down. I didn't have the radios I normally have. I thought I was higher than I was and I pulled the throttle back a bit. The plane sank like crazy."

Perhaps slightly rattled by the controller's call of "You're drifting right of course rapidly," the pilot gave a harder twist on the yoke than he should have. The 172 veered to the west, making almost a right angle to the approach course. According to the accident factual report, the final resting place of the Cessna was a straight line about 90 degrees left of the approach course from where it disappeared from the radar.

The pilot was about to make visual contact. "I saw a flash that lit up the windshield, then I looked up and saw another flash, and the next thing I saw was the trees." In his accident report, the pilot stated that after hitting the tree "the plane cartwheeled to the left, and after hitting another tree, collided with an unoccupied building." The Cessna's wing rode up the roof of the building, rolling the plane inverted before it hit the wall. It stopped, and dropped to the ground upside-down in front of the building.

The controller knew the Cessna had crashed. He called out the equipment and requested a special weather observation. Within ten minutes the Cessna had been found. It had slammed into the side of Camp Elmwood Singing Society Lodge 1/4-mile west of the approach lights for runway 36.

The pilot kicked out one of the side windows and crawled out of the wreckage. Rescuers arrived to find him "walking around," according to a local newspaper account. He had survived with only bruises and a cut on his ear from his skis, which "came flying through the cabin at the moment of impact." One of the pilot's friends was quoted as saying, "He was smiling and didn't seem to be in shock or anything."

"Sometimes the good Lord is sitting on your shoulder," the pilot told reporters. "It just wasn't my time."

The Investigation

The post-accident investigation confirmed that the localizer converter aboard the Cessna was not working. The probable cause of the accident, however, was laid to the pilot's "inadequate" preflight planning and preparation, his supposed failure to get a weather briefing and his flight into known adverse weather.

His own analysis of the accident? "A case could be made that the flight should not have been initiated. But having started, it had to be terminated somewhere. In the opinion of the pilot, the accident would have been less likely to occur if the primary ILS receiver had been operating, if icing had not accumulated during descent, and if these problems not been complicated by marginal panel lighting.

"The pilot also recognizes that he utilized carburetor heat on the approach and just prior to crash had reduced rpm by 100 to 200. This was a lesson not to be forgotten; that under icing conditions, the pilot should maintain the highest power level right down to runway threshold."

"My mistake was that I thought I was real high at the middle marker and I pulled power at a high angle of attack. She quit flying and dropped real fast. An FAA man later told me that if I hadn't pulled the power, I'd have flown right onto the runway."

The Feds Step In

Indeed, the FAA had taken notice of this accident. "About a week later," the pilot wrote, "I received a letter from the FAA indicating that my recent accident had raised a question about my competency to fly IFR and requested that I make an appointment for a review of the flight and a re-examination of my flight maneuvers.

"On the appointed day, in a rented plane, I flew to the regional FAA office located at DuPage County Airport. I was introduced to the FAA flight examiner and we proceeded to a conference room. Here we reviewed all my logbooks. Then we reviewed the conditions of my flight. The flight examiner took considerable time and patience to explain the circumstances so that if I ever encountered this situation again I would be well prepared.

"There was a question concerning my flight briefing [prior to takeoff]. The NTSB had initially reported that the briefer stated that

When low-IFR combines with widespread reported icing, it may be wiser to remain on the ground.

I was not given a briefing because 'he was in a hurry to get going.' Fortunately, I had kept a copy of my briefing which was recovered from the plane and I was able to give a detailed report of the conversation with the briefer. Later, a more thorough check of the Houghton FSS records did list the briefing. However, the examiner suggested that should I ever get a briefing in a remote area by telephone or radio to request the initials of the briefer. This will serve to confirm that a briefing was conducted should a question ever be raised."

The FAA man had other lessons for the pilot. "Keep the throttle wide open right down to the runway threshold and then pull the power. Better a fast landing and the application of brakes to landing short. Brakes are less expensive to replace than an entire airplane.

"Finally", said the pilot, "I have a greater respect for the spread between temperature and dewpoint. Never again will I take off when the spread between temperature and dewpoint is less than five degrees at the arrival airport. The 600-foot reported ceiling and the actual conditions at the airport three hours later gave adequate proof of how fast conditions change when nightfall occurs."

Proper Restraint

One thing he felt fortunate for was his restraint system. "The plane hit the trees and did a flip," he later said. "It's a good thing I had my belts on. I was wearing both my seatbelt and shoulder harness. I'm sore all over. Every place where my safety belts cut into my hips and chest hurts. It feels like I've been in a football game." Cinching the belts down tight during the approach probably saved him from more severe injuries.

Forewarned Should Be Forearmed

Determining the probable cause of an ice-related accident may be as mysterious as the search for a murder weapon when the victim choked on an ice cube—the evidence is gone by the time investigators reach the scene. In the next case we'll review, it will never be known exactly why the airplane crashed, but icing was certainly a prime suspect.

Part 91 of the Federal Aviation Regulations makes it crystal clear that pilots may not operate their aircraft in violation of operating limitations, one of which is frequently "flight in known icing is prohibited." The reasons for such a limitation can be many: lack of enough ice-protection equipment, lack of the proper kind, or unsatisfactory flight characteristics when structural icing is encountered.

> The pilot of a Cessna 402A on an air taxi cargo flight died when the plane plowed into the roof of a warehouse in North Kansas City, Kansas, while on the second attempt at an ILS approach to Kansas City International Airport.
>
> Investigators said the pilot held an ATP license and at least 5,000 total hours and was a former FAA inspector. The plane, out of Springdale, Arkansas, with a load of electric motor parts, was within maximum gross and center of gravity limits.
>
> The pilot had been weather- briefed and was on an IFR flight plan. Widespread forecasts and reports of light to moderate icing were recorded at the time of the arrival in Kansas City. In addition, aircraft landing before and after the 402A reported encountering ice on the approach. Cloud tops were at 3,000 feet, and in five- to seven-minute expo-

sures in the clouds, these aircraft accumulated up to an inch of ice, NTSB's investigator said. Since the Cessna pilot made two attempts at the ILS, the plane would have been in the same conditions even longer than the others.

In the attempted ILS to the southbound runway, the pilot first overshot the localizer inbound course and the controller gave him a left turn to rejoin it. However, the plane then overshot the course to the left, whereupon the controller suggested a left turn and vectors that would circle the pilot for another try at the approach. This was done and the pilot eventually tracked the localizer course. However, the controller then noted a loss of altitude, down to 1,900 feet in an area where the minimum altitude is about 2,600 feet. The controller's minimum safe altitude warning system also sounded an alarm, and the pilot was advised to climb.

A ground witness at that point reported hearing the plane's engines at what he described as normal full power, and the radar showed it regaining altitude up to about 2,400 feet. It continued inbound, with an airspeed in the normal approach area of about 120 knots. However, within about a mile of the runway, the radar showed the plane making an unannounced left turn and increasing its speed.

The aircraft struck the warehouse in a nose-high, right-wing-down attitude, continued through the building's lip around the roof, struck a large air conditioning unit and carried that several yards farther before coming to rest. The post-crash fire started immediately and virtually covered the building's roof.

The investigator said even though the airplane had all the equipment for icing flight, he could find no document showing that the 402A is certified for flight into known ice, although the later 402B and 402C models are certified. (A Cessna spokesman confirmed that the 402A is not FAA-certified for known ice.)

Preflight information often includes the boilerplate "chance of icing in clouds above the freezing level," but it's up to the pilot to decide whether he wants to stick his nose into the weather and find out if ice is truly there. Sometimes not a bad idea, but it requires a solid-gold alternate in the form of a cloud-free area or a layer of warmer air. However, when PIREPs of severe icing in the local area show up, all pilots should sit up and take notice; especially pilots flying airplanes with no ice-control equipment.

Two pilots were killed when a 30-minute flight in a Beech B-36TC Bonanza left the plane apparently so loaded with airframe ice that it became uncontrollable on a landing approach at Joplin, Missouri, after a flight from Springfield.

In command on the business flight was a 42-year-old private pilot who held an instrument rating and some 570 total hours, including about 48 on instruments. He was accompanied by a private pilot who obtained his license in late 1982 and whose logbooks could not be located.

The NTSB investigator said the pilots did not obtain a weather briefing per se. The two did stand in the Springfield Flight Service Station while the specialist there conducted a briefing of another pilot on the telephone. The investigator said the other pilot being briefed was going in a different direction from the Bonanza's intended route. Without seeking a briefing, the pilot left the FSS and returned a few minutes later with an IFR flight plan filled out. He submitted this to the briefer, asked when it could be processed, and left without further questions.

A few minutes later, the Bonanza pilot tuned in the clearance delivery frequency. Before reading the clearance, the controller advised the pilot that an Aerostar pilot who had just shot the approach to Springfield reported "severe" clear icing in the clouds from 6,500 feet down to 1,200 feet. This having been said, the controller read the pilot his clearance: "Cleared to Joplin as filed, maintain 4,000 feet." Without objection, the pilot accepted the clearance.

Other than pitot heat, the airplane had no de-ice equipment of any kind. By definition, "severe" icing conditions are conditions which even fully de-ice-equipped aircraft cannot surmount.

The plane took off and the clearance was amended to allow a climb to 5,000 feet. The pilot did report reaching 5,000 feet, but immediately reported picking up ice and began to ask for lower. During the succeeding minutes, the pilot many times referred to ice, with comments like, "I'm really picking up a load of it."

Due to equipment constraints, the lowest radar vectoring

available in the area is 4,200 feet. When the pilot said he couldn't maintain 5,000 feet, he was cleared to 4,200, and when he later said he couldn't maintain that, controllers cleared him to 3,000 feet if he could perform his own navigation to the Joplin runway 31 outer marker. This was accomplished. The controllers' original aim was to give the pilot a back-course ILS approach to runway 31. Instead, the pilot was cleared for and made a front-course approach to runway 13, with a circle-to-land on runway 31.

Airport lights were turned up to full intensity for the 7:15 p.m. approach. The plane flew over the airport and was seen to enter a turn from a downwind to a base leg. It then apparently lost control and hit the ground at a high rate of speed. There was a fire after impact, obliterating evidence of how much ice might have been clinging to the airframe.

An iced-up airplane often does strange things, and a circling approach is certainly not the way to go. But here's a case of a pilot who really stacked the deck against himself; overweight, out of CG, no approach charts, a load of ice. And to top it all off, only one eye.

Coincidence resulted in NTSB's investigator being on the scene within about three minutes of a crash that took the lives of the pilot and his wife aboard a Cessna 414 which spun into a back yard in Aurora, Colorado, a Denver suburb.

The NTSB investigator, who would normally have been on call to investigate the accident anyway, happened to be in his home a few blocks from the crash site. He not only had heard the plane go overhead, but was listening to a news program that was interrupted by a bulletin about the accident. He was able to make his way on foot to the site where the Cessna was still burning when he arrived. Despite the heat of the fire, he was thus able to observe that ice was coating many surfaces of the airplane.

The investigator said the 62-year-old pilot had been in California for a month, taking training in a Cessna Citation, and was returning home to the Denver area when the accident occurred. It was two days before Thanksgiving, and the pilot's children had arrived in Denver in anticipation of a holiday reunion. In fact, they were waiting at the airport for the plane at the time of the crash, the investigator said.

The pilot held an ATP certificate and current medical, had some 4,400 total hours and 1,468 in make and model (he had owned the Cessna twin since it was new) and held an instrument rating. He was the president of a local oil company. The pilot's children mentioned to investigators that he "hated to go around and hated to fly instrument approaches." The pilot was returning from California with not only his luggage after a month's stay, but also a collection of furniture picked up en route, including such items as antique marble-topped tables. The pilot and his wife had left Maryville, California, and flown to Reno, Nevada, a day earlier, where they had stopped overnight due to weather.

The day of the accident, the pilot was briefed on the weather (including a forecast of icing conditions at Denver) and filed an IFR flight plan for Arapahoe County Airport.

The loading of the aircraft included some baggage in the nose, but most of it—about 500 pounds—was put into the plane's aft compartment. The pilot's wife sat in the aft-facing seat behind him. The rest of the cabin seats were empty. The NTSB investigator calculated that the plane was thus loaded some six inches aft of the rearmost c.g. limit.

Nonetheless, the flight left Reno and was uneventful (perhaps because the en route portion was in the clear) until the descent into the Denver area shortly after 5 p.m. Soon after reporting in the clouds, the pilot told controllers he was beginning to pick up ice. (The airplane was equipped only with propeller de-ice boots, and was not certified for flight into icing conditions. A Beech King Air that landed after the accident had a measured 1-1/2 inches of ice on its unprotected surfaces after shooting the approach.) The pilot asked for a descent to a lower altitude, but the controllers stated that this could not be authorized due to minimum terrain avoidance limits. The pilot then asked to climb. But controllers now offered to vector him directly onto a final approach for runway 34R at Arapahoe, which is served by an ILS. This was accepted and promptly was accomplished.

However, Denver Approach is a radar facility located at Denver's Stapleton Airport. At Arapahoe, tower controllers noticed the plane going overhead the field at about 500 feet, just inside the ceiling. They called Denver Approach by phone to report that the pilot apparently had missed the approach.

Controllers now issued the pilot the missed approach procedure, which called for a climb and a turn. However, the plane did not turn or climb, but proceeded on runway heading to a point about six miles north of the field. The pilot initially read back the missed approach procedures incorrectly, then did not follow them once the misreading was cleared up.

The plane was seen by witnesses to arrive over a well-lighted library in Aurora and circle it perhaps six times, staying just below the ceiling and remaining in control. It then rolled onto a straight heading, climbed into the clouds and soon after, descended out of them in a flat spin. Ironically, about 15 or 20 seconds before the crash, the pilot reported in a calm voice that the plane was iced up and was stalling. He reported his altitude.

The observed airframe ice, the calculated weight of it, and the c.g. problem might account for the flat spin, NTSB's investigator said. As for the loss of control, NTSB's investigator learned that for perhaps most of his life, the pilot had worn a glass eye in place of his left eye, even though he held no waiver or any limit on his license. The investigator pointed out that with a windshield covered by ice, the pilot might have had to use the side window for ground reference. Since his left eye was sightless, it would have required nearly a 90-degree turn of his head to look out the side window. Turning in this manner back and forth to the instruments and the window is extremely conducive to vertigo.

The investigator also noted that the pilot's approach plates were found in the back of the airplane, suggesting that he may have been attempting to conduct the approach into his home field from memory.

Sorry, There's Simply Not Enough Power

Sometimes, a forecast—that's a forecast, not a promise—of clear air above a layer of potential icing conditions can lead a pilot to challenge the elements, in hopes of being able to climb through the troublesome area. And sometimes, it doesn't work.

Airframe ice of between half an inch and one inch over various parts of a Cessna 182M was noted when the plane crashed at Dalton, Georgia, after being unable to continue an IFR flight. The pilot suffered serious injuries in the hard-landing crash. Another passenger suffered minor injuries, and three others escaped without injury.

The NTSB investigator said the pilot, age 63, held a private license and had about 1,930 total hours, including about 500 in type. The pilot had obtained an instrument rating in July of 1983 and in his accident report stated he had some 560 hours of actual instrument flying.

The flight, originating at Atlanta, Georgia, was intended for Chicago, Illinois, the pilot's home base. According to the pilot's statement to investigators, he obtained a weather briefing before the flight which indicated that the tops of the clouds would be 5,000 feet and that there would be a chance of light icing on the route of flight. He therefore requested and was assigned a cruise altitude of 6,000 feet. He said the reports indicated he would be clear of clouds after passing eastern Tennessee.

The pilot said he climbed to 6,000 feet but did not reach the tops; however, he cruised for half an hour in the clouds without any signs of ice or precipitation. At this point, light rain began, and shortly, he noted ice collecting on the wing strut of the Skylane. He now requested a climb to 8,000 feet and was cleared to do so; however, the ice accretion suddenly began to increase. The pilot said the plane wasn't able to climb above 7,300 feet, and still couldn't get clear of clouds. In addition, the ice began to "noticeably disturb the airflow," he said.

After consultation with controllers, a diversion to Chattanooga, Tennessee was begun. But after five minutes as the plane steadily lost altitude at about 300-400 feet per minute, the pilot told controllers he couldn't reach Chattanooga. The flight was cleared to divert to Dalton, and due to terrain, was advised to stay at 4,000 feet until on final approach.

The Skylane shot the approach at Dalton and the pilot estimated he broke out of the clouds at 1,200 feet MSL (or 500 AGL), with visibility of about a mile (these are minimums for the localizer approach). He said about 20 seconds after breaking out, he sighted the airport and headed for a landing maintaining 95 miles per hour on the approach.

Nonetheless, as the plane was over the runway about 50 feet up, control was lost. The pilot said the plane seemed to veer as though left rudder had been applied, even though the rudder pedals had not been moved. The Skylane slammed down heavily on the runway.

A witness who observed the plane after the crash said it had about three-quarters of an inch of ice on the leading edges of the wings and tail, about half an inch on the fuselage, and about an inch on the belly and underneath the wings.

Preflight Actions

One of the cornerstones of aviation survival (i.e. living to be an old pilot) is the ability to recognize the inherent limitations of your equipment, and knowing when to leave the bird in the barn.

Flight planning for IFR trips in cool or cold weather just naturally includes a consideration of the icing level. The freezing level (a common datum) is often stated as some fixed value—say, 5,000 feet—as though to fly at 4,999 feet would be safe, but 5,001 would not. Of course, experienced pilots know that no reckoning of freezing level is this precise, and considerable leeway must be allowed. It could be easily 1,000 feet or more off the level reported.

When a report states ice can be found from 3,000 to 7,000 feet, this does not mean that just because a pilot gets to 3,500 feet without finding any ice, he is home free. He simply may not have gotten into the clouds which contain the ice—yet.

Nor does it make the weatherman a liar to find no ice in the strata where he predicted it—it might be sheer chance that one pilot finds it and another does not. Keeping a wary distance from the icing level is the wiser course, as it defeats this element of chance.

Finally, to find ice and report it to the controller is not to trigger some alarm in the radar room. Ice is an emergency if the pilot says so. Some controllers may understand the icing predicament a lot better than others.

Such considerations applied in the planning and execution of a flight that ended in a crash near Wapakoneta, Ohio, seriously injuring the lone pilot aboard a homebuilt VariEze. While some may question the wisdom of taking a homebuilt into IFR conditions, the aircraft was equipped with the basic required gear and the pilot was properly certified. The type of aircraft was not found to be a factor.

The VariEze had a nav, a comm, and a transponder (though no encoding altimeter), as well as the primary panel instruments. The pilot, age 52, was the builder and had a total of 457 hours, 215 of them in the airplane. He also had an instrument rating and 13 hours of actual IFR, plus 44 hours simulated. The trip was intended from Toledo, Ohio, to Rolla, Missouri, and eventually to California to deliver the plane to a person who had agreed to buy it.

The pilot got a weather briefing the night before the flight, and called again shortly before 7 a.m. for another one. After some preliminaries to establish the destination, etc., the briefer told him:

"We are calling for—down across Michigan and southwestern Ohio, Indiana—for frequent moderate, occasionally severe rime or mixed icing in the clouds, and precip from 3,000 to 7,000. That runs from Saginaw to Detroit, down to Lafayette and back up to Duluth. And calling for occasional moderate turbulence below 10,000 across this area. Your surface chart shows a low up over Lake Huron and an occluded front running east and west to off the east coast.

"Your current weather at Toledo, 2,300 broken, 5,000 overcast, visibility 10, light rain showers, surface winds 280 at 20, they're gusting to 25. Here at Findlay we've got 2,300 overcast, visibility 10, light rainshowers. Indianapolis: 1,500 scattered, 3,400 overcast, visibility 15. And pilot reports: 15 east of Indianapolis, a Seneca, tops 8,000, he had light rime. And..." The pilot broke in: "Where was that one? That tops?" "Fifteen east of Indianapolis." The briefer and the pilot began a dialogue: "Fifteen east of Indy and rime in the clouds?" "Yeah." "I guess I'd better go underneath, huh?" "Uh-huh. Terre Haute's reporting 2,200 broken, 3,000 overcast, visibility 15. St. Louis: clear, visibility 10."

"Well, because of icing I might as well stay underneath. I'll be under the radar minimums in places." "Yeah." "But I don't want ice. It's a little experimental airplane; it doesn't need that junk."

The pilot obtained winds aloft forecasts. He asked for the temperature at 3,000 feet, but (as is standard) it was only reported at 6,000 feet (-1 degree F was the report) and higher. The pilot continued: "Okay, I've got to unfold a chart here and get me some minimum en route or I won't know what altitude to give you...ah, you're looking for ice in the clouds and uh, probably at 3,000. I'm going to miss the ice, aren't I?" Said the briefer: "Hmmm, should be getting pretty close...yeah, okay, freezing level for Ohio should be running, well, this time of the morning, about 3,000 to 5,000, and, uh, we call for that icing here in the Indiana area about between 3 and 7."

Pilot: "Three and seven. In other words, I probably can't file below three anyway. Okay, I guess I've got a flight plan for you." And the pilot proceeded to file—for a cruise altitude of 3,000 feet.

At about 7:58 a.m., the pilot was off and climbing. He contacted Toledo Approach and was given a transponder code and cleared to climb to 3,000 feet, via flight plan route (Victor 47 to Findlay VOR, Victor 14 to destination).

About 10 minutes after takeoff, the Toledo Approach controller asked, "Are you proceeding direct Findlay now, sir?" The pilot's response was, "Ah, copy. I'm correcting now." Controller: "Roger. I was wondering there. You was proceedin' ah, southeastbound there." Pilot: "Copy."

A minute later, the controller threw the monkey wrench into the equation. For reasons that were not entirely explained in the NTSB accident report (but had to do vaguely with traffic), the controller now told the pilot, "Four Eight Echo Zulu, climb and maintain 4,000, advise level at 4,000." The pilot did not take this casually. He said, "Do you have any ice reports at four?" The controller said, "Ah, no, sir, I have received no ice reports." The pilot now took what would be the fateful step: "Okay, out of 3,000 for 4,000." The pilot reported level at 4,000, and was told to advise when he passed the Findlay VOR. He acknowledged ("EZ copies").

Six minutes after the plane had reached 4,000 feet, the controller advised, "Radar contact is lost, eight miles north of Findlay VOR." The pilot acknowledged. About four minutes later, he reported over the VOR. The flight proceeded routinely for 10 minutes, into another handoff (to Indianapolis Center).

Within a minute after joining Center, the pilot said: "I'd like to descend lower, please." The controller replied: "All right, unable lower at the present time, ah, maintain 4,000." Pilot: "EZ copies. I'm just gettin' a little bit of ice." Controller: "And 48EZ, report the NADIR intersection. I won't have lower until NADIR due to thousand—three thousand traffic. And, ah, I will not—I do not have you on radar at this time." Pilot: "48 EZ."

Eight minutes passed. At 8:39 a.m., the controller asked, "And 48 EZ, you still picking up ice there at four?" "Say again for EZ?" "Ah, are you still picking up ice?" "Ah, that's affirmative, just a little bit." "All right, can you maintain 4,000?" "That's affirmative at this time."

The controllers were at this point doing a bit of horse-trading, so to speak. The Center controllers were trying to get airspace where he could descend to 3,000 feet, but ahead on Victor 14, at REDKE intersection, Muncie Approach had a Twin Beech holding at 3,000. The controllers were looking at other routings that would allow the VariEze down lower. "All right, ah, maintain four and if you have any trouble let me know." "EZ copies."

Another eight minutes went by, and at 8:48, the pilot now requested, "Four Eight EZ would like to descend down to three and get rid of this ice." "Four eight EZ, have you gone by NADIR intersection?" "Ah, I'm having trouble picking up Rosewood (VOR). I must be past it." "How about BOOKS intersection—and that's off of Fort Wayne?" "Ah, I've only got one nav and I'm havin' trouble switchin' back and forth and keepin' it all together." "Ah, 48EZ, I'm going to have to have you tune in either Dayton VOR or Fort Wayne, to give me a position report, 'fore I can get any altitudes."

"Ah, EZ copies. Stand by." The center controller now went back to Muncie with a more urgent-sounding request. "Now, listen to this real close," he told his Muncie colleague, and outlined the pilot's predicament and his uncertainty about his position. When this was laid out, the Muncie controller at first stated that 3,000 feet would be approved. However, the two controllers discussed it further, and noted that the icing was reported from 3,000 to 7,000. They began to consider whether the pilot might be able to climb above it, which might also allow them to receive his transponder signal.

The controllers were thus occupied when at 8:52 a.m., the pilot radioed, "EZ has just lost an engine and I'm descending." It was the last the controllers heard from the flight. Other flights in the area heard an ELT signal at 8:56 a.m.

The pilot descended out of the 1,600-foot ceiling and remembers heading for a cornfield, but when interviewed afterward couldn't recall details of the crash landing, which destroyed the plane and seriously injured the pilot.

Getting It on the Ground

That said, it appears the next problem needs extra attention: getting the iced-up airplane all the way to the runway without incident. There is no handbook around that offers complete advice on this subject.

A first point to consider is that landing an iced airplane is a dangerous proposition, as discussed below, and possibly the danger can be avoided if there's a way to get the ice off before landing. If a pilot has plenty of gas, he might consider going somewhere completely different—such as a place that's quite a bit warmer. Or, if he went through VFR conditions on the way to the ice, he might just turn around and go home. This is really no time to be shooting an instrument approach, because it won't be anything like a normal approach.

Once on an airplane, ice sticks tenaciously, and it isn't easy to get off. In general, heat works best, so if there's a place where 40-degree temperatures exist, it may pay to go there. However, it may also occur that the weather system is a winter warm front, where there is risk of more ice as one goes toward the warmer side. If it's necessary to go somewhere colder but get into VFR conditions, we'd opt for that.

Another way ice leaves the airframe is by a kind of sublimation, or simply evaporating away, even though the wing and air temperature is below freezing. This is much slower, but it may work, or at least dispense with some of the ice accretion. A pilot's first encounter with ice may be of the trace-ice kind, a frosty film which blows away within minutes of leaving the icing cloud (this may explain why a pilot becomes sanguine about icing conditions). Half an inch of ice won't blow away easily. But, with enough gas, and an hour or so of VFR conditions, the trip back home might just cure the icing problem.

The point is, there is hardly ever any overwhelming reason to continue to the destination, and sometimes it's the worst place to go (i.e., if there's freezing rain on a night IFR approach).

Icing's order of business starts with the smallest objects on the airplane. It builds first on the antennas, rendering them perhaps useless or breaking them off. Then it gloms onto the propeller blades. Then it builds on the leading edges of the tail surfaces, then on the leading edge of the wing, on the windshield, etc. It may even cover the induction air supply, and that's surely the end. Again, no pilot has to witness these events if he stays out of icing conditions, or at least gets out promptly.

Ice leaves in roughly the same sequence it came (assuming it has stopped forming). The antennas will likely vibrate and either break, or shed the ice. The propeller will probably throw off most or all of its ice load. Because this is rarely symmetrical, one blade often retains ice a little longer and the imbalance shakes the whole airplane violently. If this doesn't shake the engine out of its mounts, the problem goes away fairly quickly. Pumping the throttle or prop control sometimes helps to shed prop ice.

This still leaves the wings and tail with ice, and the major problems arise here. First, the tail ices faster than the wing by about a three-to- one ratio. If you see half an inch of ice on the wing, the tail may have 1-1/2 inches.

Ice's main threat is aerodynamic, and it's a big threat. The ice typically does not lie smoothly along the airfoil curve, but builds into a forward-projected ridge, or horn. This alone is an awesome source of drag. In the most detailed studies on ice effects we've seen, Cessna Aircraft presented graphs to show that a T-210 Centurion with an inch of ice on the wing leading edge (and corresponding amounts elsewhere) requires all its 285 horsepower to maintain a cruise at 120 miles an hour (normal full-power cruise is around 200 mph).

Also, to deal with the drag, the wing will be flown at a higher angle of attack—nearer to the stall angle. What is the margin above stall? In the T-210 case, Cessna didn't present stall speeds for an inch of ice; the data might be frightening. With just a quarter-inch of ice, the Turbo Centurion stalled gear and flaps up at about 102 mph, versus a normal 75 mph. With 20 degrees of flaps, stall came at 82 mph, versus a normal 70.

Thus, an iced-up airplane might require full power to maintain level flight at a speed which is only 10 to 15 mph above stall. The pilot will learn soon enough how much the ice has slowed his airplane; he may not recognize how much it has cut his stall margin. Likewise, the drag will mean an unbelievable amount of power will be needed just to fly down final—in the extreme, perhaps 80 percent of available power, depending on the ice. In our study data, 19 pilots stalled or spun in the pattern or on final. We'd guess many of these came after a power reduction to what seemed a more believable setting to the pilot at the time.

Because the stall margin is so low and drag so high, the airplane generally will not flare at all in the normal sense when power is reduced at the runway. A pilot coming over the fence at 110 mph might expect a long "float" before touchdown; actually, there may be no float, just a thud as the stall arrives at 105 mph. (This is no exaggeration; in the study data, an iced Bonanza stalled at 110 mph.) The study data revealed 26 hard landings at the destination airport. "Hard" means enough to damage the airplane substantially.

All this is predicated on the wing stalling, as a normal aircraft behaves. An iced-up aircraft isn't normal, and presents a rather frightening new problem: a tail stall.

Because the tail typically ices more than the wing, because of the high angle of attack required to keep a given altitude or rate of descent, because of a possible forward c.g., and especially because flap extension causes a change in downwash off the wing and a dramatic increase in nose-down pitching moment, the horizontal tail may arrive at a stall (negative) angle of attack before the wing does. This is an event that never happens on a conventional airplane, and no pilot can train himself for recovery, since relaxation of back pressure during the consequent nose drop will probably not do any good—the tail goes further into its stall as the nose drops. There may be no aerodynamic buffet to warn of the stall. Only lots of altitude and the ability to regain airspeed will allow for recovery.

The tail stall problem may explain some of the stalls on final (which could have come at flap extension), as well as the stall-hard landing at the runway, when the pilot attempts to flare.

The vast majority of flight manuals do not even allude to the tail stall possibility (most do not give any advice about landing with ice). Cessna—without doubt the leader in providing such information to its lightplane pilots—recommends that only about 10 or 20 degrees of flaps be used with an inch of ice or less. If there's more than an inch? "Approach with flaps retracted to ensure adequate elevator effectiveness."

What To Do?

In summary, then, there are some reasonable guidelines about landing an iced-up airplane that a pilot can and must keep in mind. These are based on the assumption that the airman has been prudent in getting out of ice and is not collecting more on the approach:

1) Find the longest runway possible (5,000 feet isn't asking too much) with the clearest approach, both with regard to terrain and weather. A long, stable final with tiny power changes is going to be necessary. You'll need to be VFR and clear of the hills to accomplish it.

2) Fly somewhere near the top of the airspeed indicator's white arc at all times. If you're going to use some flaps (only 10 or 20 degrees

at most), extend them while still at altitude. Extend the landing gear now, too.

3) Upon entering the pattern, do not expect "normal" power reductions. It may be that the power you've got is necessary just to maintain altitude. Make a wide pattern with shallow turns to avoid a stall.

4) On final, adjust power in minute increments to maintain a descent at the runway, at an airspeed no less than 20 percent above normal approach speed. Hold this speed all the way to the runway.

5) Go-arounds are dangerous with ice, but if you must contemplate one, make the decision at least 500 feet above the field elevation.

6) Above all, do not expect a normal flare and landing. Drive the airplane to within 10 feet of the runway, assume a level attitude, and drive onto the runway, then pull back the power. There will be no "float" and the stall will come abruptly.

7) Because of the high speed and power held until landing, touchdown will occur much faster than you've likely ever seen, and it will take an incredible amount of runway to come to a stop. Make sure the power is off, flaps are up and hit the brakes hard but evenly, relaxing pressure at any sign of locked wheels. In general, it will be better to accept running off the end at a slow speed, than to attempt a go-around now and hit trees because the airplane has a sickly rate of climb.

8) Remember that, until the airplane stops, you are in the midst of an emergency procedure. Ice on an airframe is an emergency, not an inconvenience.

Moral: Amend Attitudes

In summary, the icing accident is one of the few types which demonstrate almost without exception that the most important factor is the pilot, not the equipment. Somewhere in the country, there is always enough ice to bring down even a big, powerful twin with full de-ice equipment, working perfectly; in a lot less ice, a small single doesn't stand a chance. But in any ice, the pilot is responsible for getting into and out of his predicament.

The typical pattern: An experienced pilot with IFR skills—who perhaps has lost his fear of ice—gets a briefing, knows about the potential for ice, but goes anyway, even though his airplane is ill-equipped. He gets into ice and not only does not treat it as an emergency, but typically continues for his destination, often even though conditions are very poor there. Depending on his latent skill and the airplane, he crashes on the approach or in a stall on landing.

The pattern can be broken. Pilots can adopt new attitudes. First, pilots in winter can resolve never to go without timely and complete briefings—and continue to update weather throughout the flight. Pilots without de-ice systems can choose not to fly if there's a reasonable likelihood of icing conditions. Whether a pilot has de-ice equipment or not, he can treat it as an impending emergency when ice starts to form.

The key is to do something about it, not continue waiting for more ice to form. Our advice would be to immediately get the controller's help to find conditions where the ice will stop accreting. But one reasonable choice is always a 180-degree turn.

In any event, once ice is on the aircraft, it is hard to get off, and even though the plane continues to fly, the emergency is not over. If there's enough gas, we'd think about diverting to someplace substantially warmer, in hopes that the airplane can shed its ice before landing. If that's not possible, at least a diversion to the biggest airport around is not being overly cautious.

The big airport provides better navaids and assistance, but most importantly, it gives the pilot the longest runway he can get—and he'll need it to get down safely.

There's a children's game, "Scissors beat paper; paper beats stone; stone beats scissors." And just as surely, ice beats airplanes. The pilot who remembers it may not have the best story to tell when he gets back to the pilot's lounge, but at least he'll get there.

Thunderstorms

When Don Quixote sallied forth to do battle with windmills, he probably reasoned that even if the worst happened, he'd wind up with nothing more than a slap on the head from one of the blades, so the risk was justified. But when a pilot tangles with a thunderstorm—we're talking full-blown *thunderstorm* here, not just a cumulus cloud with a lot of ambition—the possibility of catastrophe looms very large indeed. Especially in light airplanes, the odds of coming out the other side in one piece are not encouraging. At the very least, you'll have the ride of your aeronautical life. You've been hearing that ever since you started in ground school, but believe, *believe*; there are forces at work inside a thunderstorm that simply cannot be successfully countered.

The more we find out about thunderstorms, the more we are convinced that the only safe procedure is complete avoidance. But given all this warning and all these predictions of the dire circumstances, pilots continue to get themselves into compromising positions with regard to thunderstorms. Most of the accidents seem to occur during a cross-country flight, when a pilot apparently is driven by a strong urge to get where he's going; and if a thunderstorm stands in the way, he is reluctant to detour far enough—if at all—to avoid the nasty weather.

Many pilots seem to rely on air traffic controllers, hoping that the ATC radar will steer them around the storms; but the primary purpose of traffic-control radar and the controller's duty priorities usually preclude any worthwhile guidance from that quarter.

Our objectives in this section of *Aviation Weather* are (1) to re-educate the reader in the principles of thunderstorm formation and development, (2) discuss ways of avoiding these meteorological monsters, and (3) point out the dangers of challenging thunderstorms through accident reports that illustrate various methods that should *not* be utilized.

What Makes a Thunderstorm?

A thunderstorm is a very complicated atmospheric engine. A well-developed storm may contain turbulence, icing, hail, rain, and snow at the same time, and may cover hundreds of square miles of the earth with its heavy clouds. It is not at all uncommon for the vertical currents to carry cloud tops well over 50,000 feet.

But in spite of its complications, thunderstorm formation depends on just two simple physical properties of the atmosphere; a quantity of unstable air, and some sort of lifting action. The *degree* of instability and the *amount* of lifting determine how big a thunderstorm will grow, but without these two, there will be no storm. It's important for pilots to be aware of the conditions that will set this meteorological machine in motion, and plan their flying activities accordingly.

Atmospheric instability is best understood by first getting a handle on the "normal" situation—a *stable* atmosphere. When a parcel of air is lifted (by whatever means) and cools at the same rate as surrounding air, there is no tendency for the lifted parcel to continue its vertical movement; it is quite satisfied to remain where it is. But if a lifted parcel contains a great deal of water vapor, which retards cooling, it will arrive at some higher altitude at a temperature warmer than that of the surrounding air. It will continue rising—at a rate commensurate with the difference in temperatures—because of its lower density. That's *instability*, and building cumulus clouds are the pilot's primary visual clue that conditions for thunderstorm formation are present.

Air that's dry and has a standard lapse rate (2 degrees Centigrade per 1,000 feet) generally is stable. Displace the air upward and it will cool and settle back down to where it was after whatever disturbed it in the first place goes away. Stable air resists vertical development and, therefore, is unsuitable for brewing thunderstorms.

But air displaced in a higher-than-standard lapse rate will tend to remain warmer than the air surrounding it and continue to rise in a convective current. The vertical development is helped along by heat released when water vapor condenses.

Mother Nature's thunderstorm recipe isn't complete without the second ingredient—a yeast, if you will—to start the moist, unstable

The forces inside some thunderstorms—such as this mountain-country supercell—simply can't be countered by any aircraft, regardless of size or type.

air moving upward. Textbooks refer to this ingredient as a *lifting mechanism*. Lifting action, can come from a number of sources; among them are orographic lifting (caused by air flowing over hills, mountains, ridges, or up-sloping terrain), thermal lifting (usually the result of the surface being heated unevenly by the sun, although cool air drifting over warm ground or water also counts), and frontal lifting (the result of air being bulldozed aloft in advance of a cold front, or rising somewhat less vigorously up the slope of a warm front). No matter the source, when unstable air is propelled upward, clouds will begin to develop when that air is cooled to its dew point; if there's enough lifting and enough moisture, a thunderstorm may happen.

Life Cycle

A thunderstorm usually comprises many separate cells. The individual cells may be in any one of three stages of development—cumulus, mature or dissipating.

As air rises and moisture condenses in a developing thunderstorm cell (the cumulus stage), water droplets grow and, at some point, become too heavy to be lofted further. Powerful downdrafts are created when the droplets fall, taking some air with them. Downdrafts and rain showers are the mark of the mature—and deadliest—stage of a storm's life.

Usually, downdrafts tend to choke off the flow of air into the storm and hasten its dissipation. But strong winds aloft can tilt a thunderstorm, so that the incoming flow isn't blunted by the downdrafts. Such a thunderstorm, usually with a characteristic anvil top, can last for hours.

Water droplets freeze if they are forced high enough, but the resulting ice balls eventually get too heavy to remain aloft. Before that happens, though, a hailstone can grow to the size of a pea or, if the lifting force is particularly powerful, a grapefruit. Though we usually picture hail as being round, it often develops in very weird and lethal-looking shapes.

Turn for the Worse

The worst weapon in a thunderstorm's arsenal is a vortex that can form when a rising column of air starts to spin. If the vortex pops out the bottom of the storm and hits the ground, it's called a tornado; if it hits water, it's a waterspout. Vortices are usually formed in storms that build above the tropopause (about 40,000 to 60,000 feet over the U.S. in summer).

The helter-skelter movement of air in and around a thunderstorm causes other hazards, such as severe turbulence and icing, wind shear and lightning. The latter is the thunderstorm's signature. Lightning occurs when a storm sheds an intense electrical field built during collisions of zillions of charged particles. Lightning gives off heat, which causes the air around it to expand rapidly and produce the sound of thunder.

Thunderstorm Advisories and Warnings

Perhaps the best advance warning of potential thunderstorm involvement in the weather conditions for an upcoming flight is your general knowledge of what's going on in the atmosphere. Hot, muggy weather and an approaching front are clear indicators, as are the same moist conditions in an area where the air is being lifted over rough terrain or up a slope.

Here's where the smart pilot begins to check further, and there's a series of weather information products available for the asking. When planning a flight, there are several sources of clues to the possibility of thunderstorms along the route. One is the area forecast, issued three times a day and providing a 12-hour regional forecast and a six-hour outlook.

Terminal forecasts, issued three times daily and good for 24 hours, focus on conditions expected within five miles of an airport, but they can also include advisories of potential thunderstorm activity in the "vicinity" of the airport—that is, within about 25 miles.

Another good source of clues is the convective outlook—the "AC note"—which plots areas where there are slight, moderate and high risks of *severe* thunderstorms, as well as areas where thunderstorms could approach severe limits, over a 24-hour period. The output from these sources usually take the form of SIGMETs and AIRMETs, in-flight advisories of significant meteorological conditions.

The National Severe Storms Forecast Center—which prepares AC notes, as well as weather warnings for commercial broadcasts—considers winds of 50 knots or more, hail three-quarters of an inch or larger in diameter, or tornados signposts of a severe thunderstorm.

At Large

The National Weather Service uses the same basic criteria for tagging a severe thunderstorm. In hourly surface reports, "T" indicates that, at the very least, thunder has been heard. But "T" indicates there's a severe thunderstorm lurking near the airport. If a funnel cloud is spotted, "tornado" is spelled out in the report.

Radar cannot "see" wind or hail, so radar reports attempt to correlate storm strength by the amount of precipitation that's being painted. The NWS uses six "VIP" (video integrator and processor) echo levels:

A precipitation echo of Level 1 intensity marks a "weak" storm in NWS's book. A Level 2 return is considered "moderate" and means that light to moderate turbulence and lightning may be found there. Level 3 is "strong"; severe turbulence is possible, lightning is likely. Level 4 is "very strong" and means severe turbulence is likely. Level 5 is "intense" and correlates with an area of severe turbulence, lightning, organized wind gusts and, probably, hail. Level 6 is "extreme" and marks large hail, severe turbulence, lightning and extensive gusts.

One item to look for during a preflight briefing is a convective SIGMET, which will warn of lines of thunderstorms, scattered severe thunderstorms and widespread storms of Level 3 or greater. The warnings are issued whenever one of these conditions is spotted, and they are updated at 55 minutes past each hour as long as necessary.

Ask for It

The importance of a thorough preflight weather briefing cannot be overemphasized. Ignoring this basic point has brought several pilots to grief. For example, one airman apparently became impatient with an FSS specialist who was having trouble calling up information on his computer. He declined to contact another FSS or call back later and, therefore, never learned of a convective SIGMET for embedded thunderstorms with tops above 45,000 feet. His Centurion crashed after losing its left wing.

It's a good idea to stay alert for anything that might be missed during a briefing. If you access DUAT via a home computer, make sure you check out all the hazardous weather menu items. On the phone, if a specialist doesn't specifically mention convective SIG-METs or weather warnings, it doesn't really mean there are none. Go ahead and ask, just in case the specialist might have overlooked something.

Keeping Tabs

Equally as important as getting a thorough preflight briefing is updating the information after you're on the way. NTSB's files of accidents involving thunderstorms are rife with cases in which important information did not get to pilots in time.

In one, a Bellanca Viking was taxiing out to take off on an IFR flight when a SIGMET was issued for storms topping 45,000 feet. A half hour later, the aircraft fell in pieces in an area of Level 4 thunderstorms.

It bears repeating that thunderstorms can develop very quickly. Controllers are supposed to read convective SIGMETs when they're issued, but the broadcasts can be missed. It's a good idea to check in frequently with Flight Service or Flight Watch and monitor ATIS broadcasts along the way. It certainly doesn't hurt to simply ask ATC about any current weather warnings. Meteorologists with color weather radar are on duty in all ATC centers and, in a pinch, a controller can summon information. But most of the time, you've got to ask for it.

Radar Traps

Radar is a great tool, but it's no panacea. Controllers often help pilots pick their way around areas of heavy precipitation, but pilots should realize that ATC radar is designed primarily to keep aircraft from bumping into each other. Its ability to paint weather is limited and often inhibited when traffic is heavy.

Navigational guidance is a secondary service, and controllers can turn down requests when they're too busy. If a controller tells you he's painting no heavy precip on his radar, it may mean just that. His scope may be configured to inhibit precipitation echoes.

Several years ago, a pilot departing from a major airport saw a large echo on his airborne radar and asked a controller what his radar was showing. The reply was "nothing." Meanwhile, an ATIS broadcast at another major airport nearby included an advisory of a Level 6 storm, 28 miles wide.

It's risky business to launch into IMC with embedded thunderstorms, counting on ATC to shepherd you through.

Hooks and Shadows

It makes sense not to fly in IMC with embedded thunderstorms unless you've got radar aboard the aircraft—and know how to use it.

Radar can get you into trouble if you don't really know what you're looking at. Several years ago, a pilot was climbing out in a P210 when a rather innocuous-looking cell floated onto the radar display. There appeared to be nothing behind it, so he simply zig-zagged around it— and promptly got onto a roller coaster that would have put Playland's to shame.

Only later, while attending a radar seminar, would that pilot learn about radar "shadows"—attenuation-induced blank areas that can hide some real monsters.

Pressing Ahead

The NTSB's files on thunderstorm-related accidents reveal several other common mistakes that prudent pilots should try to avoid. One error involved in many of the accidents was failure to heed warnings and advice.

For example, a pilot of a Cessna 182 departed into an area covered by a convective SIGMET and pressed ahead after being told there was a cell ahead of him. The Skylane crashed five minutes later.

An N35 Bonanza pilot set off IFR into an area of known Level 3 and 4 thunderstorms. The aircraft was last seen descending at a high rate of speed out of a 400-foot overcast.

During recent years, about a dozen pilots crashed after being advised that VFR flight was not recommended. One non-instrument-rated pilot pressed on at night, knowing there was a convective

If you know how to interpret it, airborne radar is an invaluable tool for use in avoiding thunderstorms.

SIGMET for active thunderstorms along his route. Another braved a night flight in an area covered by a tornado watch.

Proof Positive

It might sound silly to say that one of the easiest ways to avoid a thunderstorm is not to take off in one, but it has happened. In one case, a Comanche 260 pilot apparently was trying to depart before an IFR clearance-void time. But as he did so, the airport was in a heavy downpour of rain and was being pelted by small hailstones and buzzed by lightning. The Comanche crashed about a mile and a half from the runway.

The matter of taking off or landing when a thunderstorm is in the vicinity of the airport is an important one, for the huge quantities of air descending from the storm act very much like water when it is poured from a bucket onto the floor. The column of air, sometimes descending at thousands of feet per minute, rushes out in all directions, creating a 360-degree spread in wind directions, and wind gusts that can easily reach 60-70 knots. The moment of liftoff is no time to encounter a 60-knot tailwind. Witness this accident, which happened as the pilots hurried to beat a storm.

Two pilots in a Beech 19 Sport survived with burns in a crash while taking off downwind from College Park, Maryland, in conditions that included a thunderstorm "roll cloud" directly over the airport, as well as a tornado watch in effect, and while a local pilot was waving his arms attempting to warn about the severe conditions.

The pilot-owner, holder of an ATP license and 6,800 total hours, including some 400 in the Sport, was accompanied by a commercial pilot who was his student for a course on multi-engine training. Nevertheless, the flight was listed as personal in nature.

The ATP pilot told investigators he left St. Mary's, Maryland, around 3 p.m. and flew to College Park—in the Washington, D.C. area—where he picked up a desktop simulator. The subsequent flight was to be to Cambridge, Maryland.

The pilot told NTSB investigators he had noticed some weather formations west of Washington as he arrived in the area, and also stated that he was in a hurry to pick up the simulator and leave College Park, since it was beginning to rain. Neither pilot had obtained a weather briefing, the NTSB investigator said.

Shortly before 4:40 p.m., the plane was observed taxiing to the displaced threshold markings of runway 15. Witnesses reported that the windsock indicated wind from 330 degrees in excess of 20 knots and that a "roll cloud" was directly over the airport. A traffic reporter/pilot for a local radio station attempted to warn the pilot of the Sport by waving his arms. Nonetheless, the plane attempted a takeoff.

Witnesses said the airplane started to roll on runway 15 with about 2,200 feet of runway remaining, and became airborne with about one-eighth of the runway remaining. It stall-mushed and settled to the ground off the end of the runway. The plane struck some trees, went through a chain-link fence and onto a tennis court, then crashed through the opposite chain fence before coming to rest.

The pilots, who had been wearing seatbelts and shoulder harnesses, were able to extricate themselves, but a fire breaking out on the left side of the aircraft caused severe burns to the pilot and lesser burns to his companion, who helped him from the plane.

Paying Little Heed

The southwestern part of the United States is one of the prime areas for thunderstorm development. Huge quantities of moisture from the Gulf of Mexico frequently sweep northward in advance of a cold front, and the steep slope of the frontal surface provides a strong vertical boost. All the ingredients for monster thunderstorms are there, and he who decides to press on despite warnings of severe weather often gets more than he can handle, as this Cardinal pilot found out...the hard way.

The 34-year-old private pilot and his dog were killed when the Cessna descended out of a severe hail shower while the pilot was attempting to extricate himself from a storm.

Investigators said, according to information provided when the pilot obtained his last medical certificate, he had 2,200 total hours. He held an instrument rating, although it was not clear how much instrument time he had logged.

The pilot had departed Gallup, New Mexico, around 8 p.m. in VFR conditions and had air-filed an instrument flight plan around Albuquerque, with a destination of Addison, Texas. He arrived in the Dallas area after midnight. Controllers had guided him south of the area and informed him that a line of thunderstorms extended over DFW and Addison airports; they suggested a diversion to Dallas Love Field. However, the pilot mentioned that he had a friend waiting for him at Addison, and that he could see the ground, so he wished to continue to Addison.

Controllers gave the pilot vectors for Addison, but warned that it "might get very rough" and asked that he apprise them of conditions.

The Cardinal entered the vicinity of a thunderstorm, and in a short while, the pilot reported that it was raining very hard and he thought there was some hail. Soon thereafter, he reported that the hail was "extremely hard." A few seconds later, the pilot radioed "I just lost my windshield—I need to get out of here." Controllers issued a vector for a course reversal, to 180 degrees, but the plane was lost from contact.

The wreckage was discovered in a lane when fire department personnel were dispatched to deal with the damage to homes caused by the severe hailstorm, which dropped hailstones ranging in size from golf balls to tennis balls. In a house 150 feet from the crash site, the hail had been so loud that the occupants never heard the airplane hit.

The NTSB investigator said the plane's windshield had indeed broken, but in addition, the leading edges of the wings had been hit by hailstones, pounding them as flat as though the plane had hit a wall. He said Cessna engineers originally gave the opinion that a Cardinal with a broken-in windshield could not continue to fly, due to both the extreme drag and to the likely turbulence over the tail surfaces.

Yet another pilot made the fateful choice to fly in the face of a line of killer thunderstorms.

The pilot and four passengers were killed when a Beech A-36 Bonanza suffered an in-flight break-up near Zolfo Springs, Florida, during an apparent encounter with severe weather. The pilot, with 188 total hours, including 57 in the Bonanza, had no instrument rating. The airplane was seen to descend out of the clouds in pieces after dropping off radar scopes while receiving VFR flight following service from controllers. Thunderstorms were in the area at the time.

The plane, a 1982 Bonanza, had been rented from an FBO in Orlando, Florida, a day earlier for a round-trip flight to Key West, Florida. It departed Key West at about 4:24 p.m. on Sunday for the return flight.

During a preflight briefing at Key West, the pilot was advised that VFR flight was not recommended and that there was a SIGMET in effect for the route of flight calling for thunderstorms with tops to 45,000 feet. Nonetheless, the pilot departed VFR.

Investigators said the pilot filed a VFR flight plan, but failed to activate it after takeoff. However, he did contact controllers to request flight following, and was in contact with Miami Center until just before the 5:37 p.m. break-up occurred. The flight had been at 7,500 feet and a last radar return at 7,000 feet was observed before contact was lost.

Investigators said the pilot, age 29, had obtained his private license in late 1982. His medical certificate had expired at the time of the crash.

The NTSB investigator said the Bonanza's right wing failed about six inches inboard of its attach fittings, and the left wing separated, tearing away the remainder of the wing's carry-through structure beneath the cockpit. The wing failure was indicative of positive overload. The empennage also separated, but was held to the fuselage by the rudder and elevator cables.

Although the warnings of thunderstorms don't mean that you can't or shouldn't go flying, let them put you on notice that you must have an out, an alternate, a "Plan B" to implement if things go sour. Especially when you have been warned, there's no flight so important that it requires intentional penetration of a storm area...not even true love.

The 22-year-old commercial pilot was killed when the Bonanza crashed out of control during a night IFR flight. The 12:39 a.m. accident occurred in an area of thunderstorms.

The 357-hour pilot also held an A&P license. He had logged some 50 hours in the S35 Bonanza since being checked out, and reportedly had flown this aircraft exclusively for the last two months.

The pilot was attempting to fly from Sanford, Florida, to St. Louis, Missouri, to see his girlfriend. Originally, he intended to take a commercial airline flight. However, the owner of the Bonanza, for whom the pilot worked, learned of the pilot's plans and offered to let him use the aircraft for the trip. The pilot then cashed in his ticket and prepared for the flight.

He received a weather briefing from Orlando Flight Service and filed an IFR flight plan for the trip, departing Sanford at 9:26 p.m. The flight was routine until ATC notified the pilot of some weather activity along his route. ATC's initial warning came when the aircraft was still some 50 miles from the weather. The pilot chose to continue on his planned route and soon found himself in the weather.

He reported to ATC that he was encountering "heavy

lightning" and he requested vectors out of the storm. Controllers told him that the quickest way out was for him to continue straight ahead.

A few moments later, the pilot again asked for vectors out of the storm. Again, controllers told him that the fastest way out was straight ahead. However, they said that if he felt he had to turn, they suggested he turn right. One further, unintelligible transmission was received from the Bonanza before it dropped off the radar scopes.

The Bonanza crashed into trees, cutting a narrow swath. Investigators said the aircraft, which had been modified with the Beech V-tail beef-up kit, did not break up in flight. They noted that the tail section was the most intact portion of the wreckage. They also stated that there was no evidence of a lightning strike on the airframe.

Investigators are examining the possible impact of fatigue on the pilot's performance. The owner of the Bonanza told investigators he had approved the pilot's use of the airplane earlier in the day. However, he said that if he had realized that the pilot was going to depart so late, he would not have allowed the flight to commence.

Investigators are also examining the possibility of engine failure or malfunction. They reported that the fuel selector was found in the "OFF" position in the wreckage. It had not been determined if it was moved to that position by the pilot, or as a result of the crash, or if a rescue worker on the scene had moved it.

Tag, You Lose

The files also show that pilots often lose races with thunderstorms. In one case, an F33C Bonanza pilot saw a storm approaching from the west and tried taking off to the east. The wind was calm when he began to roll, but then a sudden gust hit the tail, sending the Bonanza off the runway into the woods.

In another case, two pilots attempted to squeeze in a short training flight in an ultralight aircraft with a thunderstorm about 20 miles away. The instructor recalled that the wind suddenly went from calm to gusting over 40 knots, blowing the ultralight into trees.

Several other accidents occurred when aircraft conducting takeoffs or go-arounds were unable either to climb or maintain altitude with full power and best indicated climb speed.

Using Airborne Radar for Thunderstorm Avoidance

The ubiquitous advice to "go around a thunderstorm, never *through* one" is well-founded; the risks of penetration are truly monumental compared to the benefits, which are *zero*. Cumulus clouds tend to stand out rather prominently in almost any skyscape, and give ample warning of the potential danger that lies within, making the eyeball the best thunderstorm detector in this situation.

But when thunder bumpers are obscured by other clouds or the dark of night, the ability to "see" them can be remarkably enhanced by airborne weather radar. Once available on only the twin-engine airplanes in the general aviation fleet (those old radar antennas were so large and cumbersome there was no room for them on a single), weather radar is today not an uncommon feature on one-motored flying machines.

Weather radar will normally reflect radio energy from liquid water (rain) in the atmosphere, and will display areas of precipitation on the cockpit scope. It's very important to understand that radar does *not* detect or display turbulence; the reason that we are taught to stay away from radar-detected areas of precip is that in general, heavy rainfall and turbulence within a cumulus cloud go together. (By way of contrast, the Stormscope works in an entirely different manner, displaying the location of electrical discharges that are associated with atmospheric turbulence.)

Radar technology has truly wrought some miracles; from yester-year's monochrome displays (on which one interpreted shades of green to figure out where the heaviest rainfall was located) to the current crop of multi-color radar sets, with green, yellow, red and sometimes purple to show various intensities of precipitation...and in the most advanced units, turbulence as well. There is even a new generation of radar which can display a vertical slice of the weather ahead; pilots flying with that kind of gear can really "take a storm apart" to see what's making it tick.

In any event, we don't intend to offer a lesson on how to use airborne weather radar; rather, we want to make the point that no matter how you figure out that there's a storm in your path of flight, the very best thing to do is *avoid* it. Some pilots, even when equipped with radar, fail to give a thunderstorms a wide enough berth...

> The pilot and his wife were killed when the Bonanza descended in pieces at around 1:20 p.m. as the couple were en route on an IFR flight and deviating around thunderstorms.

The NTSB investigator said although full logbook records were not available, the pilot was believed to be very experienced, and a logbook from the airplane showed he had been flying regularly. The couple had taken off from Oklahoma City and were bound for Houston, Texas, on an IFR flight plan when the accident occurred.

Investigators said the pilot was at his assigned altitude of 11,000 feet when he asked for and received permission to deviate around a thunderstorm cell. At about the same time, he was given a frequency change, but never checked in on the new frequency.

Witnesses at the scene first heard an explosion, then saw pieces of the plane descending. Witnesses said there was no rain at the time, but there was a large thunderstorm just north of the crash site.

Investigators found both wings had separated from a negative overload (tips bending downward and aft). In addition, they found the horizontal tail surfaces also failed in the same manner. The tail surfaces were among the earliest pieces in the wreckage swath.

The NTSB investigator noted that the plane had a color radar set, which presumably was being employed to circumnavigate the thunderstorm, and it had a flight director and autopilot, although whether the autopilot was engaged at the time of the breakup could not be determined.

Sometimes, it's not good enough to have a "near-miss" with a full-blown thunderstorm. In the case just mentioned, the pilot may have seen the storm on radar, and figured he was well clear of the bad stuff he saw on the cockpit display. Unfortunately, there's little or no useful correlation between the appearance of a thunderstorm on radar and the severity or amount of turbulence or hail in the vicinity of the storm. The radar image represents only the precipitation portion of a turbulent system whose updrafts and downdrafts often extend far beyond the visible storm cloud. Severe turbulence can be expected up to 20 miles from severe thunderstorms. This distance decreases to about 10 miles in less severe storms.

Having weather radar on board makes it very tempting to consider penetration of a precip area rather than to take the time to go all the way around. But remember that a well-developed thunderstorm may contain areas of turbulence, hail, and other assorted nastiness

The Stormscope, such as the 3M Series II model shown here, is a popular and effective storm-avoidance device.

that may be masked by the very intensity of the precipitation; after all, there is just so much radio energy available to the radar set, and when it's all soaked up by really heavy rain, there's nothing left to warn you of what else may be there.

Remember that ATC radars are set up to keep planes from running into each other, not to interpret weather returns. There are only two levels of precipitation displayed on today's ATC radar scopes; light, and heavy. You may not be bothered by that kind of "light" precip and the associated turbulence (if any), but you can bet that you won't like what you'd get into if you traverse the "heavy" stuff.

Here's an account of a pilot who not only ignored a thunderstorm warning from an air traffic controller, but who was operating at an altitude that introduced yet another hazard—heavy icing.

An experienced pilot and his two passengers died when their Cessna 421C broke up in flight near Fort Lupton, Colorado, after an apparent encounter with severe weather, the flight having continued even after a controller warned the pilot of a Level 6 thunderstorm directly ahead. There was evidence that a lightning strike may have preceded the break-up.

At the controls was a pilot who listed his profession as "cabinet maker," and who had been a business associate of the plane's owner for a long time, although he had only begun to work full-time for the owner's company in the past one to two years, investigators said. The company owner and his son were the passengers.

The NTSB investigator said while logbook records of the pilot have not been obtained, he had reported some 1,800 hours of military and 2,200 hours of civilian flying time when he obtained his most recent medical certificate. In the same application, the pilot reported no flying in the past six months. However, the NTSB investigator said records of the company's airplanes—a Cessna 310 and the Cessna 421 that crashed—showed the pilot had flown one or the other "almost daily" during the past year or more. The pilot was qualified and current for the IFR flight being conducted.

The flight had departed Amarillo, Texas and was bound for Helena, Montana when the accident occurred. It was at 22,000 feet under control of Denver Center, with the controller providing vectors around weather cells.

The controller advised the pilot that there was a "Level 6" thunderstorm (the highest level detectable on the radar scope at that time) directly ahead of the airplane. The pilot replied that he "didn't see anything." It was unclear whether the pilot was referring to not seeing anything on the color weather radar display in the airplane, or was in conditions that would permit him to identify thunderstorms visually. In any event, no course change was made.

A short while later, the controller again advised of the thunderstorm ahead, and the pilot now replied that he was "picking up something" and requested, "Maybe you'd better vector me around to the west." A vector to accomplish this was issued.

Within a few minutes, the pilot reported that the plane was "picking up heavy icing," and moments later, he transmitted, "We're going in," the plane's N-number, and, "We're going in." At about the same time, the plane's target, now down to 21,300 feet, dropped off the radar scope.

Witnesses who saw the airplane descend said they saw an in-flight flash of fire. Additionally, there was a post-impact fire. The Cessna's left wing and portions of the empennage separated prior to impact.

At the right wingtip were discovered holes which, upon

examination by Cessna, were determined to be the exit holes of a recent lightning strike, probably cloud-to-cloud in nature. The entry area of the strike could not be determined.

The investigator said that a Convair 580 in the vicinity of the accident site near the time of the crash had reported severe turbulence, and another pilot had called in an urgent pilot report after sighting a funnel cloud 20 minutes prior to the accident, moving in the direction of the accident site 14 miles away.

Into the Unknown

Assembling the bits and pieces of weather information that show if a route can be flown safely is one part artistry and two parts hard work. During thunderstorm season, conditions can change quickly, and pilots have to be relentless in their pursuit of information.

But in our natural drive to complete our missions, we have to guard against the impulse to embrace information that provides the green light while disregarding or failing to seek out that which suggests our best alternative is to stay on the ground.

A few years ago, several elements conspired to rob a professional flight crew of a true picture of violent weather that would take their lives, as well as those of their five passengers. The elements included an incomplete briefing, unfortunate timing of a weather warning and a malfunctioning radar system in the aircraft. As we shall see, however, in each case a better give and take of vital information could have provided the crew a glimpse of what lay ahead.

Up Before Dawn

The crew began duty very early on April 4, 1986. The Israeli 1124A Westwind was wheels-up out of New Jersey's Teterboro Airport at 8:30 a.m. and landed at Redbird Airport, south of Dallas, about three hours later with four executives of Singer's Kearfott Division aboard. (Another missed the flight and had to take an airliner to Dallas.)

The pilots were young but very experienced. The captain was a 35-year-old ATP with 7,353 hours of flight time, including 657 in the Westwinds. His copilot was 22 and had a commercial license with 2,745 hours, including 895 in type.

The return flight was scheduled for 2:30 that afternoon, but one of the execs called at 2 o'clock to say that their meeting had been delayed and to release the pilots to return to Teterboro without them. The captain then checked with his flight operations manager and was told to wait and take the passengers back if they could be airborne by 7 o'clock, Dallas time.

AFTERNOON BUILD-UPS

During an earlier briefing by the Dallas Flight Service Station for the anticipated 2 o'clock flight, the captain had been told to expect thunderstorms in northeast Texas and Arkansas. He learned that the storms were being generated by a stationary front and would build throughout the afternoon.

The captain called the Dallas FSS again at 5:14 p.m. At the time, both a SIGMET and an alert weather watch were in effect and calling for severe thunderstorms with tops to 55,000 feet, three-inch hail and wind gusts to 75 knots. The captain was informed that there was a line of cells running from the south to the northeast of Dallas, but he was not specifically told (and did not ask) about the SIGMET or alert weather watch. The alert had been posted at the FSS but the effective times had not been updated, leading the specialist to believe it had expired.

Furthermore, the specialist said the line was moving slowly and would probably affect only the initial portion of the flight out of the Dallas area. She did suggest, however, that the crew check again before takeoff "to see what this line is going to do." Scheduled departure time was an hour and a half later.

DARK NIGHT

Neither of the pilots checked back with the FSS, but they did use an automated commercial weather service at the FBO a half hour before takeoff. Evidence indicates, however, that they did not access information about severe weather.

When the passengers arrived, they were driven out to the Westwind, which departed Redbird's Runway 13 a scant four minutes before the 7 o'clock deadline. It was a dark, moonless night. The captain had flown down that morning, so it was the copilot's leg. The captain handled the radios.

The Westwind, N50SK, was flying a standard instrument departure that included ATC vectors to a jet route connecting the Dallas and Texarkana vortacs, when the following conversation between the captain and a Dallas/Fort Worth Departure controller took place:

"Departure, SK. We are passing nine point five. You painting anything out in front of us?"

"Well, ah, about your 11 o'clock, 10 miles, I'm showing an area. Everybody's been going to that, then turning northwest-bound."

"Sounds real good to us."

"Roger."

"Would like vectors around these build-ups. We would appreciate it. Our radar is not doing very well this evening."

"SK, turn 10 degrees to the right."

RADAR GLITCH

Note the captain's rather ambiguous remark about the Westwind's weather radar system. Though he asked for help in avoiding any areas of heavy precipitation that might be showing on the controller's radar screen, his comment that the on-board radar was "not doing very well" was open to interpretation.

Indeed, the departure controller did not interpret the captain's statement to mean that the on-board radar was unusable, and he did not mention the problem while coordinating the hand-off to a Fort Worth Center controller.

The Westwind was climbing through 13,000 feet when the captain switched to the center frequency and acknowledged clearance to Flight Level 230. He told the controller, "If you help us pick our way through here, we'd appreciate it." The captain did not mention any problem with the on-board radar. He accepted a vector from the controller but later asked, first, to fly a specific heading (075 degrees), then to fly direct to the Texarkana vortac—suggesting that the crew was capable of picking their own way through the weather.

IN THE CLEAR?

The Westwind was handed off to another center controller and cleared to climb to FL 370. Later, the controller asked for a pilot report:

"50SK, how's your ride through there?"

"Oh, some light bumps every now and then, but we've topped it."

"You remember what the tops were right along there?"

"Well, off the left, they're still building...topping out about 38, 39. But off to the right, where we were just passing through, they're topping about 36 to 37."

Remember that the weather briefing by the Dallas FSS had left the captain with the impression that the aircraft would be out of the heavy weather after leaving the Dallas area. In fact, the Westwind was heading directly into an area of severe storms around the Texarkana vortac. At the time, several other aircraft, which apparently were painting the weather on their on-board radar, were deviating around the area. The controller apparently believed—from the captain's report that he was on top of the clouds and from not being advised of the aircraft's radar malfunction—that the crew did not need to be advised of the weather.

TURBULENCE UPSET

The next transmission from the Westwind was by the copilot, indicating that the captain had assumed control of the aircraft. "Center, Westwind 50SK. We need to maintain the heading we're presently on and would like to request 390, if you can."

The controller acknowledged the request and said he'd check (i.e., coordinate via land-line with the next sector controller). About a minute later, the copilot advised, with stress evident in his voice, "Center, Westwind 50SK needs to get up."

"N50SK, climb and maintain Flight Level 390. Go ahead."

After repeating the clearance, the controller received a garbled transmission from the Westwind, which may have included the words "negative thrust."

The National Transportation Safety Board determined that the Westwind was thrown out of control by the turbulent outflow from a VIP Level 6 thunderstorm cell seven miles ahead. The upset occurred in clear air but the aircraft then entered and descended through the storm, which was building through 45,000 feet (4,000 feet above the service ceiling of the Westwind at the time). The Garrett TFE731 engines flamed out, and the attitude instruments may have been unreadable in the severe turbulence within the cell. It is likely the aircraft encountered severe icing during the descent, as well.

The Westwind emerged inverted from the clouds at a very high rate of speed at about 4,000 feet. The crew's attempts to regain control of the aircraft were unsuccessful, and N50SK struck the ground near Redwater, Texas.

Corollaries

The NTSB determined that the Westwind's radar malfunction, the severe thunderstorm and the "improper" weather briefing were the probable causes of the accident. Through the Board's efforts, the Airman's Information Manual was revised to recommend that pilots report weather radar malfunctions to ATC, and the Air Traffic Control Handbook was changed to require controllers to pass such information along during hand-offs.

It also was discovered that a convective SIGMET was issued just as the Westwind was lifting off the runway at Redbird Airport. As required, the SIGMET was broadcast by the center controller—but four minutes *before* the Westwind checked in on the frequency. It was another piece of vital weather information that never reached the crew of N50SK.

That indicates one more lesson to be derived from the accident: When severe weather is possible, it's a good idea to ask controllers along the way about any new SIGMETs or alert weather watches. A busy controller might only be able to provide the SIGMET or AWW number, but you can always ask to leave the ATC frequency momentarily to get the scoop from an FSS or Flight Watch. The information obtained could significantly change the picture of what lies ahead.

One important fact to remember is that when conditions are ripe, a thunderstorm can build extremely rapidly. The file on the crash of a Delta Airlines L-1011 on approach to the Dallas-Fort Worth airport a few years ago provides a good example. According to the ATIS broadcast, the weather was good VMC with calm winds; but as the L-1011 was being set up for an ILS approach, the pilots were told there was "a little rain shower" north of the airport.

By the time the aircraft was on final approach, the little shower had grown into a Level 4 thunderstorm, spitting lightning and downing the L-1011 with a microburst. The pilot of another aircraft approaching DFW at the time was painting the thunderstorm on his radar. He described the display of the storm's development as like "an atomic-bomb explosion filmed in slow motion."

Under or Over?

You've probably heard pilots talk about flying beneath storms to "wash the bugs off." Several pilots have found that it's also a great way to reduce an aircraft to scrap metal.

It's not a good idea to try flying over a developing storm, either. Without breathing heavily, a thunderstorm can build much more rapidly than most light aircraft can climb. And there can be some nasty turbulence above even harmless-looking cumulus clouds. One Mooney pilot found out the hard way while flying at 8,500 feet.

An encounter with an unforecast severe thunderstorm may have led to the crash that took the lives of the private pilot and his two passengers. The accident came during a flight from Kirbyville, Texas, to Saint Joseph, Missouri.

Investigators said the pilot did not have much IFR experience, and preliminary information indicates he had not flown any actual IFR in several months prior to the accident.

Weather conditions along the proposed route of flight were forecast to be good with scattered clouds. The only forecast rain was well north of course.

However, at about 2 p.m., the time of the accident, the local sheriff's department contacted the National Weather Service inquiring about a severe thunderstorm in the area. An NWS specialist replied that they had nothing on their weather radar. But when they depressed the antenna's scan, the storm showed up as a pinpoint. The sheriff later told investigators that the storm came up suddenly and dumped an estimated nine-tenths of an inch of rain on the area in three minutes. It then quickly dissipated.

A farmer heard the Mooney in its final seconds. He reported hearing the engine rev up to high speed, followed by the sound of impact. Subsequent examination of the engine found nothing amiss.

Examination of NWS weather radar data showed the storm was isolated and could have been easily circumnavigated. Investigators noted that it was apparently the pilot's habit to navigate directly between points using RNAV. Charts found in the wreckage indicate he was doing so on this flight. However, investigators have been unable to explain why he did not go around this storm.

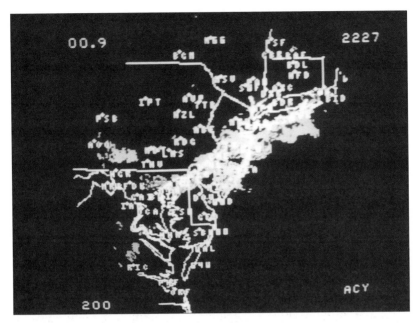

When ground-based weather radar paints a line of fast-moving severe storms, it makes more sense to wait them out. Often, they'll pass over in less than an hour.

The Experience Factor

A good instrument pilot, one who is competent, current and proficient would have his hands full in a thunderstorm; the forces exerted on an airplane are greater than you can imagine, and the noise alone is enough to curl your hair. But what would it be like for a non-IFR pilot? Here's a graphic example.

The go/no-go decision all pilots must make before a cross-country flight is seldom an easy one. The desire to get to the destination must be balanced against considerations of aircraft and pilot capability, and most particularly, weather. Often a pilot will get just enough information about what lies ahead to sway him one way or another, and make the choice based on an incomplete set of facts. Just such a decision proved fatal for a 299- hour private pilot and his passenger when he lost control of his Cessna 210L in an intense storm near Lake City, Florida.

The 31-year-old pilot had been visiting his parents in New Port Ritchey, Florida, and decided to leave for his home in Michigan on the morning of the accident, but his departure was delayed by fog at the airport.

A witness at the airport who spoke to the pilot said the ceiling had risen somewhat by 12:15 p.m., at which time the Cessna took off and disappeared into an overcast estimated at about 600 or 700 feet. (This observation is corroborated by NWS observations. For instance, St. Petersburg, approximately 15 miles to the south of New Port Ritchey, reported measured ceilings of 700 feet broken, 3 miles visibility in fog at 11:47 a.m.)

The non-instrument rated pilot was intending to fly to Michigan VFR; he did not file a flight plan, nor was there any record to show he obtained a weather briefing. His father stated that he did make a phone call from the airport to get weather information, however. Interestingly, a witness said the Cessna 210 pilot prior to departure had spoken to a pilot who had flown in from the north that morning and who said that the clouds were in a thin layer with tops about 1,500 feet.

The area forecast for northern Florida, issued at 3:40 a.m., called for isolated rain and thunderstorms with tops at 40,000 feet, becoming widely scattered by 1 p.m. local, with an outlook of IFR conditions. Though the pilot was not instrument-rated, the aircraft was very well equipped for IFR, having RNAV as well as an autopilot.

Radar contact was established with the Cessna by Jacksonville Center at 12:30 p.m., and the flight was provided with VFR flight following service. At 12:46 the pilot reported level at 11,500 feet. Eight minutes later, however, Center terminated his VFR radar service due to heavy IFR traffic.

Then, at 1:08, the pilot called in and stated that he was in clouds at 7,500 feet and descending. He requested information on the ceilings in the area; he was apparently attempting to fly out of the clouds to VFR conditions (by this time, he was in the immediate vicinity of a large storm cell).

Controller: Turn right to a heading of 180, a slow turn, sir, and advise me when you break into VFR conditions, please.

Pilot: Going to get it level first—I'm in a dive—I'm level, now I'm climbing.

Controller: Have you leveled off, sir?

Pilot: (Unintelligible) hold on for a second—All right, I'm heading 180.

Controller: Okay, sir, have you leveled the aircraft off?

Controller: Have you leveled the aircraft, sir?

Controller: How do you read now, sir?

Controller: If you read, ident, please, ident.

Pilot: I'm going down two thousand foot per minute.

Controller: Are you able to level off, sir, able to level off?

Pilot: How to (unintelligible) any clearing (unintelligible)

Controller: Yes, sir, just continue eastbound, you should be out of the weather in five miles; continue eastbound, sir.

Controller: Are you able to level off, sir?

Pilot: No, I'm still diving, I'm trying to but I can't figure out...

Controller: All right, sir, are you holding on to the yoke?

Controller: Let go of the yoke, sir, let go of the yoke momentarily.

Controller: Let go of the yoke, sir, let go of the yoke.

Pilot: (Unintelligible) I'm—I'm descending fast, I think I'm upside down—what should I do?

This was the last transmission from the Cessna. Radar contact was lost less than a minute later.

At the time of the crash, weather radar was showing Level 5 storm activity over the crash site (radar echoes are categorized by NWS on a scale of 1 to 6, with 5 being characterized as "intense"). Though witnesses on the ground did not observe thunder or lightning, they did report that it was raining very hard.

The wreckage was scattered in a line three-quarters of a mile long. Subsequent analysis showed that the right wing had been overloaded in flight, and had separated, taking part of the tail with it.

The pilot was clearly unqualified for the flight. He had a total of only 1.2 hours of simulated instrument flight time, the last 0.2 of which being on his private pilot checkride 18 months before the crash.

His decision to take off into instrument conditions is difficult to fathom. However, Florida weather tends to be localized and is often easily avoided (it's not uncommon to be able to fly VFR even with known thunderstorms in the area). But beyond the local conditions, it's a puzzle how the pilot could lack the judgment to obtain a live weather briefing for a flight of nearly 1,000 miles. While it's possible that he did get some form of automated weather briefing (such as PATWAS), winter weather seldom remains VFR over that much of the country, and a PATWAS recording will only deal with the local area.

There is no known reason that the flight could not have been delayed a day: Neither the pilot nor his passenger had to be back in Michigan until the following Monday. However, the passenger's sister said that an ice storm had been forecast for Michigan late that day, and it was her understanding that the pilot wanted to leave Florida early to be sure of beating the weather at his destination. (NWS records show that there was a weather advisory in effect for lower Michigan that afternoon and evening, calling for occasional snow and freezing drizzle, with temperatures near freezing.) The pilot's father said he did not know of this, and said that the pilot had not mentioned it, though he did say that he wanted to get to Michigan before dark.

So What Do You Do If You Get into One?

It's a pretty safe bet that every pilot has been admonished to never, but *never* get into a thunderstorm. And it's equally safe to say that the vast majority of the pilot population will never have that experience. Let's be clear that there is little or no excuse for anyone blundering into a thunderstorm he knows is there—there are too many warning signs for that to happen—but on occasion a storm is masked by either clouds or darkness, and an unsuspecting pilot gets too close. When that pilot is not well prepared for hard-core instrument flying, and especially the kind of instrument flying required to cope with the turbulence and wind shear and violent weather found in a thunderstorm, the results are more often than not catastrophic.

Nevertheless, if you fly on instruments long enough in those parts of the country which produce cumulonimbi, you can count on getting close enough to feel some of the effects, and if you like to live on the edge, you may indeed come face to face with one of these monsters some day—or night. In this circumstance, where you suspect that you might encounter a storm, you don't have to fly on totally unprepared. There are some things you can do to prepare for the turbulence that might show up. Once again, the FAA has some good advice in this regard: Tighten your safety belt, put on your shoulder harness, and secure all loose objects in the airplane.

–Plan and hold your course to take you through the storm area in a minimum of time.

–To avoid the most critical icing, establish a penetration altitude below the freezing level or above the level of 15 degrees Centigrade.

–Verify that pitot heat is on and turn on carburetor heat or jet engine anti-ice. Icing can be rapid at any altitude and can cause almost instantaneous power failure and/or loss of airspeed indication.

–Establish power settings for the turbulence penetration airspeed recommended in your aircraft manual.

–Turn up cockpit lights to the highest intensity to lessen temporary blindness from lightning.

–If the autopilot is being used, disengage the altitude hold and speed hold modes. The automatic altitude and speed controls will increase maneuvers of the aircraft, thus increasing structural stress.

–If using airborne radar, tilt the antenna up and down occasionally. This will permit you to detect other thunderstorm activity at altitudes other than the one being flown.

Spend some time reviewing the POH, especially the emergency procedures, and brush up on systems, including how the induction system works and what should be done in heavy precipitation or ice. Do you know what power and trim settings will set your aircraft up for maneuvering or turbulence penetration speed? A short test flight is all that's needed.

The information will come in handy if things get crazy. Most thunderstorm encounters are over in a few minutes, but they seem to take forever. It may be a roller-coaster ride in which you'll be doing well just to hold on to the controls, let alone see the flight instruments, which will be blurred by the turbulence. Rain may be hammering the

Thunderstorm Dos and Don'ts

We'd be remiss if we left this subject without reminding you that even if you do your best job of avoiding, and still tangle with a thunderstorm, there are some things you can do to better the odds of survival. At the top of the list is DON'T GIVE UP THE SHIP—keep flying the airplane, no matter what. The *Airman's Information Manual* takes it from there:

DON'T attempt to fly under a thunderstorm even if you can see through to the other side. Turbulence and wind shear under the storm could be disastrous.

DON'T fly without airborne radar into a cloud mass containing scattered embeded thunderstorms. Scattered thunderstorms not embedded usually can be visually circumnavigated.

DON'T trust the visual appearance to be a reliable indicator of the turbulence inside a thunderstorm.

DON'T change power settings; maintain settings for the recommended turbulence penetration airspeed.

DON'T turn back once you're in the thunderstorm. A straight course most likely will get you out of the hazards most quickly. In addition, turning maneuvers increase stress on the aircraft.

DO avoid by at least 20 miles any thunderstorm identified as severe or generating an intense radar echo. This is especially true under the anvil of a large cumulonimbus.

DO clear the top of a known or suspected severe thunderstorm by at least 1,000 feet of altitude for each 10 knots of wind speed at the top. This will probably be the altitude capability of most aircraft.

DO circumnavigate the entire area when there is more than 6/10 cloud coverage.

DO remember that vivid and frequent lightning indicates the probability of a severe thunderstorm.

DO regard as extremely hazardous any thunderstorm with tops 35,000 feet or higher whether the top is visually sighted or determined by radar.

DO keep your eyes on your instruments. Looking outside the cockpit can increase danger of temporary blindness from lightning.

DO maintain constant attitude; let the aircraft "ride the waves." Maneuvers in trying to maintain constant altitude increase stress on the aircraft.

fuselage—you'll think it's hail—and lightning may render you momentarily blind. When hail starts hitting the aircraft, you'll know it.

Don't Panic

Stay calm? Well, that may be impossible. But try not to panic. Concentrate on controlling the aircraft. Keep the wings level, gently. A wing-leveler or the autopilot roll mode can help, but disconnect altitude-hold and accept altitude changes. (Let ATC know they'll have to accept them, too.) Use small control inputs; don't manhandle the aircraft.

You've already set power and trim to reduce airspeed to the maneuvering value. You might want to lower the gear to help stabilize the aircraft. But leave the flaps up.

Most storms travel west to east. If you're westbound, the best bet is to keep going. If you're eastbound, a 180-degree turn might be the quickest way out, but be very careful making the turn so that you don't overstress or lose control of the aircraft.

Many pilots have encountered thunderstorms and survived with interesting stories to tell. But there are storms that can give a pilot a heart attack (it's happened), wrest an aircraft from his control, pull it apart with turbulence, batter it shapeless with hail, sear it with lightning and choke it with water and ice.

That's definitely something to think about.

One More Time

A comedian's goal is to "leave 'em laughing." Our goal in this part of the *The Command Decisions Series* is to "leave 'em remembering" that no matter how big your airplane, no matter how much fancy storm detection gear you've installed, no matter how wonderful an IFR pilot you may be, there's a thunderstorm out there that's bigger than you are.

If there was ever a situation that should bring out a pilot's humility and awe and respect for things meteorological, it's a thunderstorm. If we do nothing more than leave you with the indelible impression that the *only* way to handle thunderstorms is to avoid them, we'll consider our mission accomplished.

VFR in IFR Conditions

The National Transportation Safety Board has a wealth of categories available for assignment as the probable cause in airplane accidents, and "Pilot in Command—Continued VFR into Adverse Weather Conditions" is one of the most-used. These words have been the epitaph for literally thousands of pilots over the years. Most pilots feel, "Oh, that won't happen to me." After all, weather is such an easy thing to avoid.

One can get an instrument rating. That should take care of an unplanned encounter with weather, right? And, of course, flying the right equipment should also keep pilots out of weather trouble. They can get a nice big airplane with lots of instruments and avionics, and maybe an autopilot, too. All this should be able to handle most anything that nature can throw their way. With an instrument rating and a "wonderplane" like that, who's afraid of some clouds?

Yet, every year scores of pilots come to grief by pressing on into the weather. Whether scud running or going on instruments "for just a few minutes," the results can be fatal.

The Stats Speak

Pilots pressing the weather have been a problem from the earliest days, and the problem has stayed with us since then. NTSB has been trying to get a handle on the problem for a long time. But their data collection and analysis suffers from some limitations.

In one study, the Board examined some 13,571 crashes involving

33 different models of aircraft, and was able to conclude that weather was a cause or factor in 3,438 of the crashes, or 25.3 percent. More significantly, when the Board examined fatal accidents the numbers became more dramatic. Of the 2,172 fatal accidents they studied, 970—44.7 percent—involved weather as a cause or factor.

These numbers are a little misleading, though. The Board counted weather as a cause or factor in some accidents where it had a rather tenuous link (fuel exhaustion accidents, for example—unfavorable winds leading to extended flight beyond fuel available to reach the destination). But the Board was able to determine that low ceilings, fog and rain ranked second, third and fourth, respectively, as the most frequent weather conditions in all accidents. When the focus was on fatal accidents, these conditions eclipsed all others as leaders of the pack.

Years later, the Board's analysis techniques became a little more refined. In 1984, continuing VFR flight into instrument conditions accounted for 96 accidents. Although these 96 crashes accounted for only 3.5 percent of all accidents that year, they amounted to almost 15 percent of all fatal crashes.

Again, though, these numbers are not an honest assessment of the incidence of VFR into IFR. For various reasons, the Board's numbers do not count all instances of VFR into IFR. An example of this is illustrated by an accident involving a student pilot who flew a Piper Seneca into an area of intense thunderstorms over the Gulf of Mexico. Only one wing of the Seneca was recovered and so the accident was listed as "undetermined." The rest of us would no doubt agree that this VFR pilot continued flight into IFR conditions way over his head.

New Numbers

There are many questions the NTSB numbers raise, and they provide few answers. *Aviation Safety* has examined its own database of aircraft accidents amounting to some 5,944 accidents involving all types of light aircraft. Of these crashes, 1,035 were fatal.

In this collection of crashes there were 276 instances of pilots continuing VFR into IFR conditions. This amounted to 4.9 percent of the total. This is a rather higher number than NTSB's total.

When it comes to fatal crashes the numbers become almost shocking. Of the 276 VFR-into-IFR accidents, 230 were fatal (about 83 percent). In the overall context, these 230 fatal VFR-into-IFR crashes accounted for more than 22 percent of all fatal accidents in our database.

Myth Conceptions

The database provides more than just good numbers. It explodes some of the myths long held dear regarding VFR-into-IFR accidents. It also reinforces what should be some obvious points.

For example, one might imagine that most of the pilots involved in these crashes were not instrument rated. And that's true, to an extent. Some 188 of the pilots in our database *did not* have an instrument rating, although 87 of them did (31.4 percent).

The puzzling failure of an instrument-rated pilot to file IFR before hitting a cloud-covered mountain figures as a major issue in the investigation of a crash of a Beech A-36 Bonanza near Midland, Arkansas. The pilot and a woman passenger were undertaking a flight from Ft. Smith, Arkansas, to Abilene, Texas. The plane was owned by an Abilene company, and the pilot was the company president. Earlier, the pilot had flown IFR from Youngstown, Ohio, to Ft. Smith.

However, after obtaining a weather briefing including warnings of marginal conditions, the pilot nonetheless filed VFR out of Ft. Smith. Weather at the time was marginal VFR, with a measured ceiling 1,600 feet overcast, visibility seven miles.

At 8:32 a.m., the flight was cleared for takeoff. Soon thereafter, Ft. Smith Tower advised the pilot that a frequency change was approved. At 8:37 a.m., the tower again advised a frequency change was approved and told the pilot to squawk 1200 on his transponder. No further contact was made until 8:39 a.m., when the pilot requested a frequency to obtain a clearance to get on top of the clouds. He stated that he was running into low visibility. Ft. Smith Tower gave him the Approach Control frequency.

At 8:40 a.m., the pilot contacted Approach Control and was given a discrete transponder code. He acknowledged the code and stated he was 19 DME south of Ft. Smith. At that moment, the ATC tape contains the sound of a woman's voice in the background and the first sounds of impact.

The airplane was found on the northern slope of Sugar Loaf Mountain, where it had impacted in a slight climbing attitude on a 170-degree heading. The first rescue team said the accident site was in clouds when they arrived.

One might think that trying to outrun the weather is something low-time private and student pilots would do, but not those with higher tickets. Yet, some 28.3 percent of all the pilots in our survey held commercial tickets or better. And the low-time part of the myth doesn't hold much water, either. The average total time for pilots in these accidents came to 2,114 hours.

Equipment didn't make much of a difference. The accidents involved airplanes ranging from lowly Cubs and Cessna 150s up to big cabin class twins like the Piper Navajo and Cessna 421.

It's also apparent that winding up in the weather is generally not an unintentional maneuver. The accident reports made it clear that the pilots in most of these accidents knew what they were getting into, but continued anyway.

NEW PILOT

The crash of a Piper Warrior took the lives of four young people when the plane struck the ground in a left-wing-low descent at high speed shortly after a night takeoff from Kirksville, Missouri.

According to NTSB, the pilot, age 22, had flown into the area in the rented airplane from Illinois on the previous Friday, intending to return the night of the crash (a Sunday). He did some local flying on Saturday, but on the following day made several calls to the FSS and consistently got weather briefings that discouraged him from attempting the return trip. Eventually, he called the plane's owners and was assured that it would be acceptable to keep the Warrior another day.

Nevertheless, at a gathering late in the evening, the pilot apparently decided to offer some friends a ride in the airplane, according to NTSB's investigator. The youth called the local FSS at about 11:14 p.m. and obtained a briefing in which he was advised that VFR flight was not recommended. Conditions included a 12,000-foot overcast and ground fog on a moonless night.

Accompanied by another young man and two young women, the pilot went to the uncontrolled airport and took off in the Warrior. Judging from records and the airplane's Hobbs meter, it was in the air only about one-tenth of an hour. Although there were no witnesses, this and impact evidence is consistent with an attempted takeoff to the south followed by a descending 180-degree turn into the ground. The time was believed to have been 12:08 a.m.

Toxicology reports showed no evidence of any alcohol or other incapacitating substance in the body of the pilot. While it is not considered to be a primary factor, NTSB's investigator did estimate that the Warrior was 15 pounds over maximum gross weight and the center of gravity was probably near the aft limit.

The investigation concentrated on whether the pilot was likely to have been able to handle an essentially IFR condition that would have existed assuming he climbed above ground fog, which would have combined with the overcast to eliminate all visual references.

Unfortunately, the evidence suggests that such ability was unlikely. The pilot had only a private license and 66.5 total hours. During his flight training he logged only three-tenths of an hour of dual instrument instruction—one-tenth during regular training and two-tenths during his practice flight test.

The NTSB also noted that the emergency locator transmitter in the plane operated properly, but did not aid in locating the wreckage, which was spotted at 8:30 a.m. by a passing motorist. Authorities were not even aware that the plane might be missing until about 5:30 a.m., when a relative of one of the passengers called the police. The ELT signal was not detected until after the wreckage had already been located; then, tuning a radio to 121.5 MHz at the nearby airport easily brought in the signal. However, the NTSB investigator said the crash was definitely not survivable, and all aboard were killed at impact.

The decision to continue into the face of known danger is one that often proves fatal, as it did for one commercial pilot of a vintage Stinson 108-1 and his passenger late one night near Lewiston, Idaho.

Old Pilot

No logbooks were found for the 39-year-old pilot, though the Idaho State Bureau of Aeronautics determined that he had been an aerial application pilot, but he had not made his living in aviation for six years. The NTSB listed him as having flown 10,000 hours.

It was determined after the accident that the flight departed from an unnamed private agricultural strip near Pullman, Washington, at 10:20 p.m. It was apparently bound for Boise, Idaho some 200 miles to the south-southeast.

There was no record of a weather briefing before departure, nor was a flight plan filed. The first contact with the flight came a few minutes after departure, at 10:33, when the pilot called the Walla Walla Flight Service Station from over Lewiston, Idaho and requested a weather briefing for the route to Boise.

The briefer asked if the pilot was VFR, and the pilot said yes. The briefer told him that VFR flight was not recommended along the route, and that the ceilings would be likely to obscure the mountain tops. The terrain in that part of Idaho is rugged, and the minimum altitudes found on the sectional charts for the route range up to 9,200 feet MSL. The forecast was calling for scattered to broken clouds at 8,000 feet MSL with gusty winds and rain showers.

Ceilings along the route were in the vicinity of 3,000 feet, which would have obscured many of the mountain tops, but left the valleys clear. Visibility below the clouds was good, at 10 to 12 miles in light rain, according to the FSS. However, a local resident located about 15 miles south of the crash site told officials that the mountain tops were obscured, the visibility was "almost black," and there were high winds and rain. Campers further south told of thunderstorms in the area, though there was no mention of these in the weather briefing. An official with the Idaho Bureau of Aeronautics recalled that it was raining hard that night.

The next contact with the Stinson came about 25 minutes after the weather briefing, at 11:03, 2-1/2 minutes before contact was lost with the flight. A transcript of the radio conversation between the Stinson and Walla Walla Flight Service indicates the pilot was disoriented and distracted:

Pilot: Ah, we're, ah, about two-thirds lost and we've lost our compass. Do you have DF [direction finding] equipment?

FSS: Okay, stand by one...what is your type aircraft and last known position, sir?

Pilot: Ah, we were trying to get over towards Grangeville. [About 35 miles southeast of the Lewiston VOR—Ed.]

FSS: What was your last known position and what is your heading and altitude?

Pilot: (Unintelligible) over towards Grangeville.

FSS: Okay, what is your heading and altitude, sir?

[Ten seconds later]

FSS: Stinson...Walla Walla Radio.

Pilot: Ah, go ahead.

FSS: Roger, what is your present heading and altitude, over?

Pilot: Ah, (unintelligible) north and we're at 6,500 feet.

FSS: Okay, are you in VFR conditions now?

Pilot: Negative.

FSS: Roger, do you have transponder equipment on board?

Pilot: Say again?

FSS: Do you have a transponder aboard, over?

Pilot: Negative.

FSS: Okay...what type of navigational aids do you have?

Pilot: Ah, we've got a VOR but it's...we're not picking nothing up right now.

FSS: Okay, what are you tuned into, sir?

Pilot: What are you tuned in...what VOR are you tuned into?

There was no further contact with the Stinson.

An official who listened to the tape of the radio conversation said: "My impression was that his stress level was pretty high. He seemed pretty scared. His voice went up a couple of octaves."

Later reconstruction of radar data beginning eight minutes before the pilot called Flight Service for the weather briefing shows that the airplane flew south towards Lewiston until it was almost over Lewiston airport. The pilot turned southwest (away from the track to Grangeville), then made a 90 degree turn to a southeast heading. After about five miles he turned right, parallel to the Snake River and directly away from Lewiston VOR. After a further five miles he turned north and flew up the other side of the river,

Using DF steer equipment, a Flight Service Station can often locate a pilot disoriented in marginal weather.

directly toward the VOR. After flying north for five miles, he turned east, and radar and radio contact were soon lost.

The Stinson impacted steep, heavily wooded terrain at the 4,500 foot level. The airplane was heading east-northeast at the time of impact. The outer panel of one wing was lodged in a tree about 60 feet above the ground, and the rest of the wreckage was found in a small area. The pilot and passenger were apparently killed by the impact, and a post-crash fire destroyed the rest of the airplane. According to the NTSB, the ELT did not operate—it either was not set off, or was destroyed in the crash and fire.

Over the next five days, 121 search-and-rescue sorties were conducted over an area 40 miles wide from Pullman to the Boise Valley. The aircraft was then declared missing, but was still thought to be within the five-mile circle centered on the last radar contact.

More than one year and three months later, a U.S. Forest Service aircraft reported an unusual pattern in the trees at a location near the suspected accident site. A ground party was dispatched and located the wreckage.

A report prepared by an official of the Idaho Bureau of Aeronautics said that the pilot was "Reportedly, a very good stick-and-rudder pilot with considerable night cropduster experience...some of the information received on his exploits suggest heroic experiences had little or no effect on him and there were also reports of operations that many would say showed questionable judgment."

Of the plane, the report said it "had been a 'hangar queen' for a number of years....This aircraft reportedly had vintage radios which for the most part were not functional. The communications transmitter was reported to be very weak."

The reason a highly experienced pilot would choose to fly a poorly equipped airplane into marginal and worsening weather at night when he had just received an unfavorable forecast while practically on top of an airport remains unanswered. According to the Idaho official, "We never did figure that out."

A large number of VFR-into-IFR accidents fall right into the "standard" picture. A low-time private or student pilot finds himself in an unintended encounter with weather. Or, picking his way through thunderstorms and trying to stay VFR, he gets cornered. In way over his head, the pilot loses control and crashes.

An example of this was a 27-year-old, 184-hour student pilot in a Cessna 150 on a night solo cross-country flight over Washington state. During the flight, fog rolled in and covered the ground. The pilot became lost and started to run low on fuel. He was able to contact Seattle Center and the controllers vectored him to the airport at Forks. Despite the runway lights being turned up to full bright and state police vehicles using their emergency lights, the student couldn't see the field through the fog which had formed.

Finally, low on fuel, he initiated a descent into the fog, lost control and crashed. Miraculously, he escaped with only minor injuries.

Or consider the case of the 45-year-old, 99-hour private pilot in a Piper PA-28-160 Cherokee. He was trying to fly from Knightdale, North Carolina to Chattanooga, Tennesee. He departed under VFR conditions, but about 90 minutes into the flight the weather started to worsen, so he decided to turn around. But the weather at the departure airport had also gotten bad, so he decided to head for a third airport.

Weather there had also dropped. In desperation, he turned toward yet another airport, only to find the weather had closed in on that field as well. He turned toward a fifth airport, only to run out of gas before reaching it. He crashed in a wooded area, but he and his passengers escaped with serious injuries.

Low-Time Pilot, High-Performance Airplane

Thunderstorms, being fairly localized, can usually be circumnavigated. They also provide yet another avenue for VFR pilots to find themselves socked in. The temptation to try and pick a way around thunderstorms should be tempered by a good overall weather picture before the flight.

An example might be the crash of a Piper 601P Aerostar south of Wickenburg, Arizona. The 311-hour pilot, holding a private certificate with no instrument rating, had called for a weather briefing at about 10:00 that morning. He told the briefer that he wanted to fly from Torrance, California, to Florida with a planned overnight stop in Texas.

The briefer told the pilot of possible thunderstorm activity along his route. He went further and advised the pilot to get an updated briefing before he went and to use the inflight weather services to keep up to date on weather developments during his flight.

The pilot did neither. At about 10:45 that night, Phoenix TRACON got a call from the pilot in his Aerostar. He told the controller that he was in the clouds at 17,500 feet and that he wanted to land at Phoenix. Four minutes later, the Aerostar dropped off the radar screen. It was found with its wings ripped off 28 miles west-northwest of Luke Air Force Base.

But it's not always the low-time private or student pilot who finds his way into the weather and can't find his way out. Others with far more experience have found themselves behind just such an eightball.

Consider the case of the 4,609-hour private pilot in a Piper PA-34-200T Seneca. Like the Aerostar pilot, he too had called for weather before the flight. And, like the Aerostar pilot, he

The low-time private pilot with no instrument rating, flying an Aerostar, became disoriented in IMC. The aircraft was later found near Luke Air Force Base, minus its wings.

did not have an instrument rating. Unlike the Aerostar pilot, this aviator never established contact with anyone during the flight.

He had planned to fly from Kaiser, Missouri, to Olathe, Kansas. The weather briefer told him of severe weather along his route of flight, including a tornado watch in the Kansas City area. The pilot took off anyway. Controllers monitored the progress of the Seneca on radar, although the pilot did not contact them. At 10:33 p.m., the target dropped off the scopes. The aircraft was found three days later where it had crashed in a densely wooded area after a steep, high-speed descent.

"I'll Keep On Going"

Continued VFR flight into extremely poor weather was strongly suspected in the crash of a Mooney M20C near Shelby, Ohio, according to the investigator in charge.

The Mooney evidently broke up in flight in weather that included thunderstorms, high winds and heavy rain. The investigator said the pilot and his wife had left the EAA convention at Oshkosh, Wisconsin, intending to stop at Mansfield, Ohio on the way home to New Jersey, in the company of another couple flying a Piper Cherokee.

The NTSB said neither pilot obtained a weather briefing nor filed a flight plan, and neither contacted any FAA facility en route. NTSB's investigator said weather at Oshkosh at the time of departure was good, but a briefing would have revealed rain already reported at Mansfield, with a storm front expected to move through.

The Cherokee pilot told investigators the pilots were in radio contact and, when they got to Ohio, the Cherokee pilot saw the deteriorating weather and decided to turn back and land near Willard, Ohio. He said the Mooney pilot radioed, "I'll keep on going and meet you in Mansfield." The plane was about 15 miles short of destination when it descended in pieces. Mansfield weather at the time included a 200-foot ceiling, visibility one-quarter mile in heavy rain, with thunderstorms in the area. At the crash site, winds were strong enough to blow down standing corn.

NTSB said the pilot's total time had not been obtained, but he held only a private license, with no instrument rating.

I Dare Ya'

In some cases, it seems like the pilots simply thumbed their noses at nature and the regs. Knowing the weather and their limitations, they launched into it anyway, sometimes flaunting their unauthorized, unwise flights into the weather.

For example, there was the case of the 50-year-old, 350-hour private pilot in a Mooney M20C. He was not instrument rated, but this didn't stop him from filing an IFR flight plan. He took off from Indianapolis International, bound for Kirksville, Missouri.

The weather that afternoon was pretty bad. Low ceilings, turbulence, and thunderstorms were on his route of flight. He made it as far as Brocton, Illinois, before he finally lost control and crashed.

Or the case of the 90-hour private pilot in a Grumman AA-1. He called ground control at Westhampton Beach airport, New York and requested a VFR departure. Ground control told him the field was IFR, so he filed an IFR flight plan.

From the NTSB brief: "About 15 minutes later, he called for his clearance. He had trouble copying his clearance and read it back four or five times before getting it correct. The pilot was cleared to takeoff from runway 24, [with a] left turn direct to Hampton VOR. He was instructed to contact New York departure control after takeoff.

The pilot acknowledged the instructions and contacted departure control. Departure control answered by stating, 'Three seven Lima, if that is you, stand by a second.' That was the last reported contact with the aircraft." The little Grumman vanished and was never found. The pilot was presumed dead after the search was given up.

Another example involved a 170-hour, 28-year-old private pilot in a Piper PA-28R Arrow. With no instrument rating, he had departed Valkaria, Florida on an IFR flight plan, bound for Charlotte, North Carolina. He and his two passengers made it as far as Jacksonville, Florida, before he lost control. The Arrow broke up in flight, showering debris into the pine forests of Florida. The NTSB noted the probable cause as "Pilot in command—attempted operation beyond experience/ability level."

In a similar vein, the crash of a Beech V-35B Bonanza near Irvine, California shows how far these pilots can get.

Although the 58-year-old private pilot had accumulated 1,768 hours, he had not gotten an instrument rating. Nevertheless, he filed and flew an IFR flight plan from Visalia, California to Irvine.

The weather at Irvine was very poor. An observation taken at the time of the crash showed an indefinite ceiling of zero with an obscured sky. Visibility was one-half mile in fog. The pilot attempted an ILS approach, but missed, telling the controller he "had a localizer problem." He tried the ILS again. During this attempt, controllers twice issued low altitude alerts. Finally, controllers told him to break off the approach and climb to 3,000 feet. The Bonanza dropped off the radar screen and crashed in a parking lot about a half-mile from the airport.

A "One-Eighty" Isn't the Only Solution

The situations we've discussed so far have almost always resulted in accidents in which the airplane crashed completely out of control, or cruised into obstacles in its path. But once in a while, a pilot who finds himself in intolerable weather conditions makes the uncomfortable, expensive, but life-saving decision to put the airplane down while it's still under control. Sometimes that's on an airport, sometimes not. It's a happy occasion when the pilot can deal with the predicament before his condition becomes terminal.

Such was the case for a 46-year-old private pilot in a Piper Cherokee Six, in an accident that left him and all of his four passengers uninjured.

The 245-hour pilot did not have an instrument rating. He had logged only 13 hours of instrument time, all of it under the hood. He was fairly well experienced in the Cherokee Six, however, having logged some 158 hours in it.

The flight had departed Urbana, Ohio at about 4:45 p.m., bound for Grove City, Ohio. Before departing, the pilot had gotten weather information from the Pilot Automated Telephone Weather Answering Service (PATWAS). According to the pilot, the PATWAS recording had told him of 4,000-foot ceilings with a scattered layer at 2,000 feet. Visibilities were reported as three to four miles in haze and rain. (With the sun going down as departure time approached, he could anticipate this visibility would decrease.)

Less than three minutes after takeoff, the pilot realized the weather was not as advertised. Leveling off at 2,500 feet, the Cherokee began to encounter haze and light rain. The pilot would later write in his accident report, "I called Columbus [Ohio] Approach to receive a [transponder] code and to get an indication as to what the tops were [and] to announce that I was VFR en route to Bolton Airfield and was encountering heavy IFR conditions."

Communications were very poor, however, and the frequency was congested. Undeterred, the pilot pressed on. He soon noticed what appeared to be a clear area above the aircraft. He decided to try climbing to on-top conditions. "Upon arriving at [the higher altitude], we became totally socked in and unable to see even the wings of the aircraft," he later told investigators.

At this point, not even five minutes into the flight, he decided he'd had enough. He made the 180-degree turn to get back to Urbana. Unfortunately, the weather had closed up behind him. "We discovered quickly that the same conditions were now in front of us. In attempting to maintain straight and level flight, I believe vertigo began to set in and the plane began to climb," the pilot wrote in his accident report.

Disoriented, his attempts to regain level flight put the Cherokee into a dive. The airspeed was building—reaching 160 knots, as the pilot later recalled. He pulled the power back and the airplane soon broke out of the clouds at about 1,500 feet. He leveled the wings, but the respite didn't last long. In mere seconds the Cherokee was back in the soup. "Knowing approximately where I was, I elected to put the aircraft down as soon as I was able to break out of the cloud cover," he later recalled.

He spotted a pasture which looked suitable and set up for a landing. The Cherokee touched down and started rolling out as the pilot shut everything down. The airplane rolled through the grass until encountering a steel pipe anchored in concrete in the middle of the field. The Cherokee's right wing hit the pipe, gashing the metal. The concrete base of the pipe snapped off the right main gear. The airplane came to a halt about 110 feet farther on.

Less than 15 minutes had passed since the Cherokee first took off. Columbus issued its regular weather observation at about the same time the Cherokee was rolling through the field. Located 32 miles west of the accident site, Columbus reported a scattered cloud layer at 1,000 feet, with the overcast at 1,600 feet. Visibility had dropped to one mile in haze and rain.

While the pilot surely deserves credit for returning himself and his passengers to earth unharmed, the NTSB felt he could have obviated the need for the precautionary landing by not taking off. In detailing the listing of probable causes, the Board faulted the pilot for inadequate preflight planning and inadequate weather evaluation, among other things.

The Board also cited his VFR flight into IFR conditions as a probable cause. But unlike so many other accidents featuring this probable cause statement, no one was hurt.

In another situation with similar circumstances, the pilot and his passenger escaped injury when their Bonanza struck power lines and a utility pole during a precautionary landing attempt on a road. The 12 p.m. landing was made to escape deteriorating weather.

The 37-year-old pilot had logged a total of 490 hours, of which 270 were in the Beech. He was not instrument-rated.

On the morning of the accident, the pilot called Flight Service and obtained a weather briefing for a flight from Fort Lauderdale to Marianna, Florida, then on to Oklahoma City. He later told investigators that he interpreted the briefing as indicating that the existing weather was to the west of his route and that it would be breaking up at about midday.

The pilot departed Fort Lauderdale just before 8 a.m. and proceeded northwest. As he passed Tallahassee, he tuned in the ATIS, which was reporting a scattered layer at 2,500 feet and an overcast at 8,000 feet. He elected to proceed to Marianna and wait out the weather there before continuing on to Oklahoma City.

He descended to 1,500 feet and got to within nine miles of Marianna when he encountered solid IFR weather conditions, which he described as a "wall of water" that he could neither climb above nor get around. He turned back to Tallahassee and got as far as Quincy, about 20 miles away, when he encountered another "curtain of rain."

He soon realized that he was in a 10-mile-wide hole of VFR weather conditions that was steadily shrinking and moving to the northeast. He continued to descend and flew around inside the hole as it closed in. Finally, the hole was only a mile across, and the Bonanza was less than 500 feet above the ground level.

By this time, the airplane was over the Georgia border, and the pilot decided that it would be better to make a precautionary landing than fly into solid IFR weather conditions. He saw a road below him and made a low pass to confirm that there was no traffic.

During the approach, the airplane hit a set of powerlines and was thrown into a utility pole. The Bonanza then hit a culvert and slid to a stop.

George Can Do It

The advent of the autopilot opens whole new vistas of VFR-into-IFR potential. With "George" on board, the pilot doesn't need to be able to hold the aircraft upright on instruments. The autopilot can keep the airplane under control even if the pilot is totally disoriented. But the autopilot is no substitute for an IFR ticket and a well-planned flight. "George" can have problems all his own. And he'll fly the airplane into a mountainside if the human points him that way.

An autopilot can crash the airplane in much the same way as a human under the same circumstances. An example was provided by the crash of a Cessna P206C, which was found where it had crashed in marshy terrain in a very shallow descent at cruise speed. The 61-year-old commercial pilot, with 16,000 hours logged, did not hold an instrument rating. "The aircraft most probably descended due to a barometric pressure change," said the accident report. The pilot probably never realized that George was carrying him steadily toward the ground.

There are many other accidents which sound very similar, although no mention is made of an autopilot in the accident report. Yet, one can't help but wonder.

For example, there was the crash of a Cessna 177RG near Peterborough, New Hampshire. The 35-year-old private pilot, with some 338 total hours and no instrument rating, departed Albany, New York, bound for Manchester. The Cardinal cruised into a mountainside after encountering IMC weather.

Another example of this might have been the 42-year-old private pilot of a Piper PA-28R Arrow. He escaped injury when the Arrow cruised into trees during an encounter with IFR conditions. Although he had logged most of his 246 hours in the Arrow, he did not hold an instrument rating.

An IFR flight is a well-planned affair. The pilot will familiarize himself with weather, facilities, routing, and a host of other details. He'll do this before the flight, on the ground. He'll have plates and charts at the ready, with no need to fumble for them.

In an unplanned encounter with the weather, even an instrument rating is no protection. Consider the following accident:

> The pilot held an ATP certificate with some 4,946 total hours logged. He was flying a Cessna 401A from Caldwell, New Jersey to Rutland, Vermont, and called the airport when he was about 30 miles out to get weather information. He was

The modern autopilot is as reliable as any of the airplane's equipment, but the pilot has to set it up correctly and then continually monitor its performance carefully.

told that the current weather for Rutland included a 1,500-foot broken ceiling with a 2,700-foot overcast. It was snowing and visibilities were reduced due to fog. The pilot said he'd call again when he got a little closer.

There were no further transmissions from the Cessna. It was found on the side of Dorset Mountain, about 18 miles south of the destination, having missed clearing the ridge by only 215 feet.

Admittedly, a Cessna 401 might be a bit of a handful during an unplanned weather encounter. But even a "simple" airplane can crash from an encounter with the weather.

For example, there was the crash of a Cessna 150M in Narragansett Bay, Rhode Island. The pilot, age 49, held an ATP certificate with some 4,950 hours logged. He had requested a Special VFR clearance out of the Providence, Rhode Island control zone. Weather at the time was 300-foot overcast and one mile visibility in fog.

He was planning to fly from Providence to nearby Boys Town Airport. The controllers on duty at Providence didn't think he could make it on a Special VFR but they couldn't get any additional weather info to back up their skepticism. The SVFR clearance was granted.

One hour later, the Cessna was reported overdue. It was found the next day, in the bay, one mile short of the runway. The pilot and his passenger had been killed.

The Double-Edged Sword of IFR Training

Modern pilot training and certification procedures have forged a two-edged sword with respect to instrument flying. Cutting in one direction, today's private pilot candidate gets more exposure to IFR-level tasks than any predecessor, and, theoretically, he is better equipped than any before him to handle an emergency 180-degree turn in the clouds.

Moreover, his training has been an important first step along the way toward an instrument rating. Instrument flying is becoming-commonplace--fully one-third of today's pilots hold the IFR rating, and the roster continually posts a new batch of names, even during those periods of time when the rolls of new student or private pilots shrink. More and more airplanes come out of the factory equipped at an avionics level that supports safer and less taxing IFR flying.

But when the sword cuts the other way, it's a perilous weapon. That same equipment, and the easy familiarity with IFR procedures gained in private pilot training, can cause a certain group of pilots to override their respect for the hazards of IFR flying. Equipped with an autopilot, a weather radar or Stormscope, an area navigation system or Loran C and a few other items in the panel, a pilot may become a fairly adroit "IFR pilot," but never undergo the serious training and practice it takes, and never actually obtain the rating.

Even pilots who will not go so far as to deliberately engage in illegal IFR flying may nonetheless be insufficiently concerned if the encounter should come inadvertently. Where a prudent VFR pilot's response is a 180-degree turn and a landing in VFR conditions, this kind of pilot might be willing to continue from marginal VFR, into and out of occasional clouds, above a broken to solid deck, and finally into solid IFR conditions. Perchance with autopilot and nav system working well, he has no fear of an upset, nor of getting lost. If he has recently been working on an instrument rating, it may at first seem just like being under the hood. Or he may have a "just a little bit pregnant" notion of IFR flying—he only intends to make one instrument letdown or approach, and he'll be home.

Unfortunately, even skilled and experienced IFR pilots are occasionally unsure of their position, autopilots do occasionally fail, a missed approach is a distinct possibility, and sometime during every flight, an airplane has to be hand-flown according to the time-honored and basic principles of IFR flying. A novice at this skill simply does not have a chance to err and recover; the choice is do it right, or die.

Examples of the syndrome are not difficult to find. We've collected some classics:

SEEING THE LIGHTS

For instance, there is the crash which occurred at Kokomo, Indiana, seriously injuring the 51-year-old pilot in command of a Cessna 150 making its third instrument approach to Kokomo in night IFR conditions. There is perhaps a reasonable chance that he might have "gotten away with it," except that his performance was likely impaired by a medical problem—a burst appendix.

The pilot held a private license and had logged 582 total hours. He was a partner in the Cessna 150, and had more than 300 hours in type. Some quirks show up in his certification records; for instance, although he held a current medical, he had let his biennial flight review currency lapse—it was overdue by three years. Although he had never obtained an IFR rating, he had logged 71 hours of dual instruction in simulated instrument conditions, some of this within the past three months. It is reasonable to conclude that he was working on an IFR rating.

On the day of the accident at about 3:39 p.m., the pilot, who resided in Kokomo, obtained a briefing by phone from the Indianapolis FSS, outlining an intended VFR flight to Lafayette, Indiana and return. In a Cessna 150, each hop on this trip takes about an hour.

The briefer advised him that VFR flight was not recommended due to IFR conditions throughout the route of flight. Unfazed, the pilot immediately told the briefer he wanted to file an IFR flight plan. The briefer asked for and got time to complete the briefing, and then the pilot filed two IFR flight plans, for the outbound and return trips. The plan outbound listed two people on board; the return flight, just the pilot.

The briefer mentioned that Kokomo's ILS system had its glideslope out of service, and that the airport had a new lighting system (pilot-operated by microphone clicks). A cold front was to move through, and airports in the area were reporting 800-foot ceilings. Pilot reports described the tops of that deck at about 2,400 feet, with a higher deck beginning at 7,000 feet. The pilot filed for 4,000 feet.

At about 4:15 p.m., the pilot took off from Kokomo, and at 5:13 p.m., he landed without incident at Lafayette. NTSB records do not give details of this flight, but it was obviously conducted under IFR rules, and weather records around the time of landing showed Lafayette under an 800-foot measured overcast ceiling, visibility four miles in fog.

At 5:25 p.m., the pilot appeared in the Lafayette FSS and requested the latest weather, stating he had just come from Kokomo and only needed an update. He got various pilot reports and the current observations for points along his route. He mentioned that tops in the Lafayette area were about 3,000 feet when he had arrived.

He was ready to depart on the return flight at 5:45 p.m. When he called the tower to obtain his IFR clearance, the controller noted that the pilot gave his preference for a cruise altitude as 3,500 feet (a VFR altitude). When questioned, he amended this to 4,000 feet.

The pilot took off and conducted what apparently was a routine flight under instrument flight rules at 4,000 feet— probably cruising in the clear. Approaches to Kokomo are handled by Grissom Air Force Base, whose controllers gave him vectors and a descent to begin his first localizer approach to runway 23 shortly before 6:20 p.m.

The pilot of another aircraft had shot the approach ahead of him, breaking out at about 600 feet AGL (the minimum for the localizer approach is 500 AGL). He shut down and went over to the FBO's Unicom station, where the FBO attendant was talking to the Cessna 150 pilot, who had requested that the airport lights be turned full up. The attendant told the pilot about operating the lights with the microphone key, and he demonstrated this. Actually, however, the airport lights were on the entire time, having been activated previously.

The Cessna 150 pilot declared a missed approach. The pilot on the ground said he briefly saw the belly of the Cessna through the fog; he said at the time, the airport lights were on full intensity. Nonetheless, during the vectoring the pilot complained that he had not been able to get the airport lights to work. The controller rehashed the light activation procedure. Actually, however, the controller had observed the airplane going slightly to the right of the localizer course, which would explain why the pilot might miss the lights.

The pilot was given vectors for another approach. He started down the final approach course again. In a few minutes, he was back on frequency, declaring another missed approach. This time, the pilot on the ground got no glimpse of the Cessna.

During the climbout, the pilot stated he'd "like to try one more approach, then I'll go to Marion." He was started on vectors for the third attempt. On the way, the controller's supervisor took over the position; he now noticed that the pilot seemed to fly about 20 degrees off an assigned heading. He queried the pilot on this; it was corrected.

The Cessna started down the final approach course again. It dropped off radar, and subsequent efforts to contact the plane failed; it had crashed about 3-1/2 miles short of the runway and about one-third of a mile to the right of the final approach course. The plane had simply descended too low, and struck trees.

When rescued, the pilot had very serious impact injuries, but when these were attended to, the surgeons found there was still another problem: a ruptured appendix. Upon surgery for this, the patient was set on the road to recovery.

When interviewed, the pilot did not have a detailed recollection of events leading up to the crash, although he attributed his problem to not being able to work the airport lighting system. Actually, the lights had been on at full intensity during all his approaches. He could not recall abdominal pain, but NTSB considered it likely that the ruptured appendix played a part, and attributed the accident to physical impairment, as well as the pilot's attempt to fly IFR without a rating.

It is interesting to reflect that, had not an appendix burst, the pilot might not have become a statistic, but could have gone on to fly other IFR trips.

Question of Intent

The Kokomo pilot showed in many ways that the IFR encounter was deliberate. Perhaps less deliberate was an encounter that took place at Autaugaville, Alabama. This one was fatal.

The 66-year-old pilot was the owner of a 1964 Piper Twin Comanche. He had obtained his private license in 1971, and had gone on to get a multi-engine rating. As a businessman-pilot, he had flown frequently, logging a total of more than 5,000 hours, about half of these in the Twin Comanche. But he did not have an instrument rating. He lived in Bessemer, Alabama, and on the fatal flight, was returning home from a trip to Ozark, Alabama. There is no record to show whether he obtained a weather briefing, and no evidence that the flight was in difficulty until about 1:30 p.m., when the pilot radioed Montgomery Approach Control from a position near the Cahaba VOR, roughly 50 miles from his destination. The Twin Comanche's transmissions were scratchy.

Upon initial contact, the pilot radioed, "Ah, I'm on about a 360 radial (unintelligible) VOR, (unintelligible) hundred feet. I'm in the soup and I need a little assistance, squawking 1200." Note that the pilot had not yet made the leap from his VFR-pilot status. He was given another opportunity.

Controller: Twin Comanche Four Three Yankee, squawk 0256, the Montgomery altimeter's 29.92 and ah, say your altitude.

Pilot: Ah, 43 Yankee, I'm at 3,000 feet and, ah, if possible I'd like a Special into Bessemer.

Again, the pilot was avoiding the pretense of IFR capability, although treading closer to it. His request for a Special VFR clearance into Bessemer, an uncontrolled field, could be seen as containing overtones of an urge to be "in the system." If he could get into true VFR conditions, it might be reasoned, he could surely just fly to his destination and land. But in any event, the pilot now crossed the line:

Controller: Twin Comanche 43Y, roger....I'll tell you what, Twin Comanche 43Y, radar contact three miles northeast of Cahaba, there's no other traffic around your position—are you IFR-rated and qualified for IFR flight?

Pilot: Affirm.

Controller: Twin Comanche 43Y, I'm having a little difficulty reading you, are you IFR-qualified and capable of flight?

Pilot: Affirmative. I'm—I can handle it all right. I'd like a Special, if possible.

Controller: Okay, ah, you want to go to Bessemer?

Pilot: Ah, that's affirmative.

Controller: All right now, you can either go to Bessemer VFR or IFR. If you're requesting an IFR flight plan, I'll be more than happy to ah, provide you with that.

Pilot: Ah, do it IFR.

And with the devil's bargain struck, the pilot was now placed on a flight plan that essentially called for him to do only two things: climb from his present 3,000 feet to 4,000 feet, and pick up the Vulcan VOR and fly toward it (north).

It appears he could do neither correctly. It would never be established what altitude he got to, but he never reported reaching 4,000 feet. In addition, his ability to hold a heading was seriously compromised—perhaps due to the fact that he had entered solid clouds now for the first time.

He requested, "I'd like vectors cause my charts, ah, is kinda messed up here and I'm in here by myself." The controller immediately replied: "Fly heading 360." The pilot acknowledged. Nonetheless, only two minutes later, the controller had reason to ask whether the pilot was still on 360 and the pilot answered, "That's affirm." In fact, however, the radar showed the plane wandering erratically, generally northeastward.

The controller now radioed, "You can tune the Vulcan

VOR, frequency 114.4, and advise when you're receiving that. You may proceed on course direct Vulcan, then direct Bessemer, maintain 4,000." The pilot acknowledged, and later reported that he was picking up the Vulcan VOR. But only a couple of minutes later, the controller again asked, "Say your heading?" The pilot replied, "Ah, zero seven five."

The controller confirmed that the nav receiver was tuned to Vulcan, then informed the pilot that his heading should be 350. The pilot questioned this. The controller confirmed it. The pilot replied, "Ah, we've got some radio problems then, or something."

Now the pilot had perhaps his last chance. "Okay, would you like to come into Montgomery and get your equipment checked out?" asked the controller. "Ah, which is the closest, Birmingham or Montgomery?" the pilot responded. "Well, you're only about 18 miles northwest of the Montgomery Airport," said the controller. "Well, I'd rather go on into Bessemer if I could, that's my home base," said the pilot. It was not stated, but the area was under an 1,800-foot overcast at the time.

Again, the controller asked the pilot to fly north, and asked him to check the radial off Vulcan. The pilot did check and agreed that it was 350 degrees to Vulcan. But when asked his heading only half a minute later, the pilot replied, "About 130 degrees." The behavior took on the tone of a person becoming more and more rattled by the minute.

The twin went off the scope with the controller still urging the pilot to fly north and the pilot still acknowledging, but flying in every direction except north. It is clear from impact evidence that the plane went out of control and descended in a tight, high-speed spiral into the woods.

The NTSB conclusion, in light of the evidence, was that the pilot had suffered spatial disorientation. Attempting to hold a heading in the clouds, communicate, tune nav radios and read charts was apparently beyond his abilities.

Amalgamation

If the Indiana case involved a pilot who was unflappable, while the Alabama crash involved one who may have "lost his cool," then the pilot in a Wyoming accident might be considered an amalgamation of the two personalities. While seeming to be well in control of the situation, she nevertheless made errors and misjudgments, right up until her final one.

This accident involved a 47-year-old woman who owned a Piper Arrow III. She was a native of Colorado Springs, Colorado, whose job with a construction company called for her to work at remote locations (in the case at hand, Evanston, Wyoming). In addition to this job, the accident report gives indications that she also was hoping to make money in aviation: after the crash, her construction coworkers gave statements showing that many of them had often flown home to Colorado Springs with her, and she regularly charged them $65 apiece for the round trip. As far as they knew, it was a commercial arrangement.

However, the 1,220-hour pilot had only obtained a commercial license five months earlier, and she had done so without simultaneously getting her instrument rating (she had logged about 19 hours of dual IFR time). As the pilot examiner attested afterward, the resultant limits on her license were clearly explained to her. She would be forbidden to exercise her commercial privileges except in single-engine airplanes, in daylight VFR conditions, on trips within a 50-mile radius.

But the evidence suggests a willful and repeated violation of most of these limits, since more than half a dozen coworkers described paying for trips back and forth to the job site each weekend over the space of many weeks, in nighttime and daytime. The distance between Evanston and Colorado Springs is some 350 miles. Some of the passengers describe trips in conditions that they, as non-pilots, remembered as "bad weather."

At Evanston, the FBO stated that on the Friday before the crash, the pilot left there in a Bonanza she was using while her Arrow was undergoing some maintenance. She took three passengers with her. He said when she showed up at the field, conditions were very poor (indefinite ceiling 800 feet, sky obscured) and he told her this, adding that he was not allowing his own pilots to fly. However, stating that she could "beat the weather," she filed an IFR flight plan for Colorado Springs and took off, presumably completing the flight without a problem, he said. Two days later, it was time to return to the job site at Evanston. The pilot's three passengers assembled at the Colorado Springs airport, and the Arrow took off around 6 p.m., without a flight plan.

VFR—AT FIRST

It can be assumed that the flight went without serious incident for about three hours. At 9:19 p.m., the pilot called Salt Lake City Center and, initially, just requested a local altimeter setting. But after giving that, the controller offered, "Did you want radar advisories?" "That's affirmative, we would really like to have advisories," said the pilot. The controller issued a discrete transponder code and radar identified the Arrow, about 43 miles south of Rock Springs, Wyoming. This meant there remained about 80 to 90 miles more flying, westward to Evanston, some of it over very high terrain. The pilot intended to maintain VFR.

The transcript tells the rest of the story:

Controller: There's a line of embedded thunderstorms, uh, between your position and Evanston, or in the Evanston area. It extends from Fairfield northeast to 67 miles northeast of Rock Springs. Icing and turbulence reported with that system. I can't tell you the bases. The tops (were) reported up to above flight level 300.

Pilot: Salt Lake City Center, I believe we got that, uh, pretty well in sight and we're swinging to the south. Let's see...we're just going to swing towards the south now, on a heading of two-twenty degrees and it looks like we've got a clear path all the way, over.

Controller: You'll get around the biggest portion of the system that we're seeing in about 70 miles. However, there is another system that commences between there and Fairfield, and that system extends southwest to Fairfield. I believe there is a break between those two systems, but I don't know the exact status of that area over there.

Pilot: Roger. We got it pretty well in sight and, uh, we can get through it. If I need any help I'll be glad to holler.

The flight continued on course. The controller, for reasons not made clear in NTSB's report, attempted a handoff of the flight to Denver Center, but this lapse was corrected and the pilot remained with the original controller. Cruise altitude was verified and a new transponder code was assigned. Then:

Controller: The thunderstorm activity is in the Rock Springs area, extends from 40 miles northeast of Rock Springs now to 15 miles north of Vernal, west towards Salt Lake and Ogden. There's numerous buildups in this area. I am unable to vector you clear of them. There's a heavy area of precip just 10 miles southwest of Fort Bridger.

Pilot: Okay, roger. I think we got the thunderstorms pretty well in sight and, uh, I think we got Fort Bridger right in front of us, we—I believe we can make it.

Controller: Roger, Fort Bridger is 12 o'clock and 58 miles, maintain VFR at all times.

Pilot: Roger, thank you, we've got it in sight.

Just a few minutes later:

Pilot: Center, we're going to start our descent, a gentle descent into Evanston, over.

Controller: Roger, you're in an area of high terrain. Are you familiar with the terrain southeast of Fort Bridger?

Pilot: Okay, roger, we'll keep it—we'll be looking out for that mountain, over.

Controller: The Rock Springs altimeter, 29.62.

Pilot: Roger, thank you.

Pilot: Salt Lake City Center, this is Piper Arrow 900.

Controller: Piper 900, Salt Lake, go ahead.

Pilot: What kind of weather do we have at Evanston, over?

Controller: Let me see if there's any weather available at Evanston.

Pilot: Thank you.

Controller: Evanston is missing and Big Piney is missing. Stand by for Rock Springs....Rock Springs is 2,000 scattered, estimated ceiling 5,000 broken, visibility 15, temperature 42, dewpoint 30. Wind 220 at 16, rainshowers of unknown intensity west.

Pilot: Okay, roger, can you give me vectors into Evanston?

Controller: No ma'am. There's too many thunderstorms that I'm not painting on this system, to provide any vectors.

Pilot: Okay, well, I don't know if we should just spin around Evanston until this thing goes away or what.

Controller: Also, are you familiar with the high terrain, the Unita Mountains, just off to your left?

Pilot: Well, we're at 12,800 and I don't think there will be a problem. Do you show that there will be?

Controller: Okay, the terrain just off to your left is up to 12,000 feet, ten miles to your left.

Pilot: I'll stay at 13,000 until we get over Evanston, over.

Controller: Roger, how's your flying conditions now?

Pilot: We're suffering from mild turbulence to severe turbulence, but outside that we're okay.

Controller: Are you in any precip?

Pilot: Yeah, off our right wingtip we're getting a lot of rain, looks like snow in it, but I'm not really quite sure.

Controller: Roger....Fort Bridger is 12 o'clock and 32 miles. If you hold your altitude for another 10 miles you can gradually start down, you'll be clear of the high terrain.

For the next few minutes, the two discussed the lowering terrain and mutually agreed the pilot could safely descend to 11,500 feet. The pilot reported being in heavy precipitation. The controller advised that in about 15 miles, the flight would likely enter an area of less precipitation and that the remaining leg to Evanston looked clear, although there was a big cell about 20 miles northwest of the airport.

Controller: Do you have visual contact with the ground?

Pilot: Very little. Every once in a while I see a light.

EVANSTON "APPROACH"

The pilot discussed descending to 10,500 feet and then did so. She was warned that the lower the altitude, the worse communications would be. Radio transmissions in both directions were already getting weak. Even though the controller had refused to provide vectors, he did in fact now begin to give headings and distances to Evanston, updating frequently. This brought the Arrow to its destination, but not to a landing.

Pilot: We've got a big, uh, glow of lights off our left (wing)tip and it probably is the city, over.

Controller: Okay, where is it from your position?

Pilot: Okay, it's, uh, we seem to be right on top of it. It seems to be on our left and our right, over.

Controller: It should take you, uh, the airport is actually just north of town, so, uh, this heading will put you almost in between the town and airport.

Pilot: Do you think it's safe for me to circle down on that glow and then head north for it, over?

Controller: I can't approve any—or, I wouldn't suggest any descent in IFR conditions.

Pilot: I realize that. I'm only asking for your help because I want to get down, over.

Controller: The highest terrain in that area is 9,000, over.

Pilot: Okay, roger. We're still at 10,500 and the only way I can possibly see the airport or the town is to get down a little lower, over.

Controller: Roger....You can descend at your discretion.

Pilot: (Unintelligible) head for these lights of the city and see if I can't circle and get down a little lower and then head out north and the airport is exactly north of the city, is that correct, over?

Controller: That's correct, and the airport is 12 o'clock and three miles.

Pilot: (Unintelligible) going back to the glare of the city, over.

Pilot: Salt Lake City, this is Piper Arrow 4900....I'm not going to take any chances on going any lower. Can you give us vectors to Grand Junction, over?

Controller: 900, I'm unable to provide vectors to Grand Junction. You'll be below my radar and radio coverage. This is about the best I can do, to Evanston.

Pilot: Okay, we have to get out of here because there is no way we can land. I don't know what the—we have to go somewhere where it's gonna be dry for us to get in. Is there any place that you show on your radar map now that we could get in and land, over?

Controller: Not in VFR conditions in my airspace. Are you IFR-rated and qualified?

Pilot: That is affirmative.

Controller: Okay, I suggest you go over to Rock Springs and land.

NOT OUT OF THE WOODS

This was accepted, and the flight was issued a clearance to Rock Springs at 12,000 feet, via Fort Bridger. This the Arrow pilot began to accomplish, and along the way, even discussed the notion of waiting at Rock Springs long enough for the weather to pass, then continuing to Evanston. But all would not be so rosy. Rock Springs weather was reported as 1,500 scattered, measured 3,000 overcast. There might be heavy rain along the way. And another problem:

Pilot: We're starting to get a buildup of ice on our wings. Is there any way we can go a little lower, over?

Controller: You say you are requesting lower altitude?

Pilot: We're at 12,000, we'd like to go lower, 'cause we're getting—starting to build up ice on our wings, over.

Controller: Piper 900, descend and maintain 10,000.

Pilot: Okay, we're gonna go to 10. Thank you.

Shortly, the pilot reported level at 10,000, and mentioned the plane was in "mild to severe turbulence." At about 10:54, the flight was cleared for the approach into Rock Springs. The pilot therefore switched to the frequency of the controlling facility, which was the FSS on the field.

The pilot came back to Salt Lake Center's frequency, saying that the FSS had reported weather as 1,000 broken. The Center controller called Rock Springs himself to check. The reported weather was 1,000 broken, 3,000 overcast, 10 miles visibility; it would later go to 800 broken and about two miles visibility in snow showers.

The current weather report was relayed to the pilot. The response was:

Pilot: Okay, roger. Can you give me some radar vectors to runway 27, over?

Controller: Uh, 900, what approach did you want to make?

Pilot: Make an ILS approach, over?

Controller: Say again?

Pilot: ILS approach on 109.3, over.

Pilot: Salt Lake City Center, this is 900.

Controller: 900, go ahead.

Pilot: Roger, was that an approval to go to 27?

Controller: 900, say again?

Pilot: Roger. You gonna give me vectors to the runway, over?

Controller: Uh, we're unable to give you vectors to the runway. The only thing I can give you is the ILS, over.

Pilot: Okay, roger. Should we do it now?

Controller: 900, roger. You've been cleared for the approach, over.

Pilot: Roger. We're gonna go right down now, thank you.

Vectorless Vectoring

Although the controller did everything possible to keep from offering vectors in terrain where the radar might not handle the job, he apparently also realized that the pilot needed the extra help of positioning vectors onto the ILS. The controller compromised his position.

Controller: 900, I show you turning south now. You're not to the VOR yet, over.

Pilot: Okay, roger. Should we (unintelligible) on six, then, till we get—till we intercept, over?

Controller: 900, what's your heading now?

Pilot: Okay, we're turning around on a 060 degrees, over.

Controller: 900, roger. Climb and maintain 10,000 and turn left, heading 030.

In this manner, the Arrow was brought to the VOR, put on a heading to intercept the ILS, and cleared for the approach. This did not cure the problem.

Pilot: The VOR—would the airport (unintelligible) the runway be a little bit to the right of the VOR?

Controller: Uh, the airport's to the west of the VOR.

Pilot: Okay, roger, thank you.

Controller: And 900, say your heading now.

Pilot: Okay, we're on a 030, over.

Controller: Roger, you're now 4 miles northeast of the VOR.

Pilot: Okay, northeast, and we'll have to turn. Shall we turn to a 330 degree, over?

Controller: 900, turn right, heading 080.

DOWN FINAL APPROACH

Eventually, the controller led the pilot to the 10-mile fix and positioned her for the ILS final approach course. Along the way, he anticipated other possibilities, and asked the pilot:

Controller: And 900, how much fuel do you have?

Pilot: We got enough for four hours, over.

This, of course, could not have been a true statement, and probably was the pilot's rattled, unthinking reaction to a question that she had answered on the flight plan form many times. In all likelihood, she was nearly out of gas.

By phone, the controller now checked weather in Rawlins, Wyoming, which had a 12,000-foot scattered ceiling. He would hold it ready as an alternate. Meanwhile, the pilot requested to have the Rock Springs runway lights turned up. This had already been done. "Okay, roger. It's probably very foggy," she said.

Although initially the controller was providing left-right steering commands as the plane started down the ILS, the pilot eventually reported, "We have the glideslope right on the money, over." But this good news was short-lived:

Controller: And 900, you're going left of the ILS now.

Pilot: My left landing gear locked up. I can't get it to lock, over.

Controller: 900, roger. Are you going to execute a missed approach?

Pilot: Of course. I'm sorry, but I thought I could shake it loose to lock....My landing—the left landing gear did not lock and I—so I tried to shake it loose, over....It's locked now.

Controller: Roger....And you're three miles from the airport now and about half-mile left of the glideslope [*sic* localizer].

Pilot: Okay, roger, we're coming back on course.

Controller: And 900, the weather now at Rock Springs: indefinite ceiling 800, sky obscured, two miles, light snow.

Pilot: Roger, we're right in it. I can see the snow coming right at us, over.

Controller: You're two miles from the airport and a mile left of the glideslope.

Pilot: Roger, we're gonna turn to the right a little bit.

Controller: And 900, you're two miles south of the airport. You gonna execute a missed approach?

Pilot: No, I'm going to try and make it if we see the light, over.

Controller: Okay, the airport is now 2 miles off to your right.

Pilot: Right. We're moving over to the right.

Controller: And 900, would you like to execute a missed approach and go to Rawlins? Rawlins weather is 12,000 scattered, visibility is 15.

Pilot: Roger, we'll go to Rawlins.

Controller: Say again?

Pilot: That's affirmative. We'll go to Rawlins, over.

SEES THE FIELD

But although the controller and pilot began to coordinate on a climb, a right turn and a cruise altitude of 10,000 feet with the intent of heading for Rawlins, this plan did not last long. Rock Springs came into view.

Pilot: Uh, we got the airport in sight now, over.

Controller: 900, roger. And what's your intentions now?

Pilot: Saw lights, over.

Controller: I say again, what is your intentions?

Pilot: We'd like to land there if we can. We see the lights, over.

Controller: Roger, did you want to cancel your IFR?

Pilot: Uh, yeah, we'd like to land in there at a—if we can, please. And we're gonna swing around into 27 and land at, uh, over here, at this airport, over.

Controller: 900, do you still have the airport in sight?

Pilot: Roger, we sure do.

Controller: Roger. You going to cancel your IFR and go in visually?

Pilot: Roger, we're gonna cancel, we're gonna cancel the IFR.

Controller: 900, roger. Cancel the IFR and you're over the VOR now.

Pilot: Roger, VOR.

Controller: 900, you're a mile east of the airport now, radar service is terminated. Contact Rock Springs Radio.

SAD DENOUEMENT

But the Arrow would not be heard from again. It had crashed. Searchers found it about 1 a.m., just three-quarters of a mile short of the runway.

Although all four occupants were alive when pulled from

the wreckage, the pilot died after about four hours, and the front-seat passenger died the next day. The rear-seat passengers (one of whom had crawled into the aft baggage compartment to sleep sometime during the flight because she was so airsick from the turbulence) survived.

Investigators found that the pilot's license had been defaced so as to obscure the limitations placed on it. They also learned that the passengers had paid for the flight. Furthermore, they also found that the wreckage contained "no evidence of any instrument landing approach charts, navigation charts, or any other type of navigation aid that might have been used by the pilot on this flight." In other words, the pilot had been "fudging it" from start to finish. And she nearly pulled off the charade.

However, the wreckage showed evidence that the black terrain and blowing snow may have confused the pilot about her altitude. The airplane drove into the ground, with gear down and flaps up, as though the pilot simply got too low on final approach.

Self-assurance, a capable airplane, good avionics, and extraordinary help from controllers—none of these could substitute for the IFR skills and ratings the pilot had pretended to possess.

Scud Running

Not everyone simply blunders through the clouds until impacting the terrain. Many try to remain visual by that old tried, but false, method—scud running. The clouds don't go all the way to the ground, and the temptation to sneak along underneath can be almost overwhelming. Especially if the flight is almost at the destination.

Consider the crash of a Mooney M20E near Newark, Indiana. The 50-year-old private pilot had logged some 3,673 total hours, but did not have an instrument rating. He had recently purchased the aircraft in Hickory, North Carolina and was on the second leg of a three-leg flight to get it home.

He had gotten a weather briefing before the flight, but pressed on. He was spotted by two witnesses who saw the Mooney flying at 500 to 600 feet, just below the clouds. It subsequently struck a ridge just a few miles farther on, killing the pilot.

Or the crash of a Partenavia P68C at Goudeau, Louisiana. The pilot, age 54 and the holder of an ATP certificate, had logged some 8,200 hours at the time of the accident. He was attempting to fly from Baton Rouge to Bunkie, Louisiana.

Before he took off, he got a weather briefing which told of fog and low ceilings along his route of flight. He waited until conditions at Baton Rouge lifted to VFR, then departed on a Special VFR clearance.

Navigating by use of Loran, he tried to maintain VFR despite the worsening weather. He made it about 55 miles before colliding with a 500-foot radio antenna. The Partenavia clipped the antenna about 150 feet from its top. Witnesses reported the top of the antenna was in the clouds at the time of the crash, and visibility was only about one mile.

Or the accident involving a Beech C-55 Baron. The 57-year-old, commercially certificated, instrument-rated pilot with some 14,500 hours, was trying to get from Huntington, West Virginia to Pikeville, Kentucky. From the NTSB brief:

"The pilot who was originally scheduled to make the charter flight to pick up the passengers was reluctant to do so due to low ceilings in the mountainous area at the destination."

The owner of the company took the flight and was observed by witnesses near the destination to be flying in and out of clouds between and below the mountain tops. Witnesses estimated the altitude to be between 150 and 300 feet. The destination airport was three miles from the crash site and was completely fogged in with visibility under 100 yards. The aircraft struck the top of a cloud covered mountain.

Mountains, Low Clouds, and Other Factors

Attempting to maintain VFR while flying over relatively flat terrain is one thing, trying to outguess mountain tops is something else entirely. One of the most highly publicized general aviation accidents took place in the Arkansas mountains; in addition to the obvious attempt to maintain VFR, this accident resulted from a rather complicated set of conditions. There are a number of lessons for pilots in this detailed account of a long chain of events which culminated in the accident.

When the S35 Bonanza hit a mountaintop on March 26, 1980 near Board Camp, Arkansas, there was a simple answer for the probable cause report: the pilot had tried to continue VFR flight in adverse weather. He was looking for a way through the hills under a low ceiling, and 2,300 feet wasn't enough altitude to clear a 2,330-foot ridge cloaked in fog.

But the "why" of the fatal accident, and the circumstances which led up to it, were by no means so easy to fathom, nor was the pilot the kind of person who might be expected to make such an error in judgment: he was Donald C. Flower, a name known to thousands in the general aviation community as synonymous with aircraft insurance. He was the founder of Don Flower Associates, the country's largest general aviation insurance broker.

Described as easy-going and amiable by friends and acquaintances, Flower was said to be "utterly unflappable" in the air. He had started flying in 1931 and had more than 6,000 hours, holding a commercial license, multi-engine and instrument ratings. Then in the 1950s, he launched into aviation insurance, concentrating on a market that had not been aggressively pursued by insurers of the time: general aviation. The company grew in step with the burgeoning lightplane industry.

As an insurance broker for more than two decades, he no doubt reviewed thousands of lightplane accidents, and surely must have seen the constant pattern of "get-home-itis" crashes where the urge to be in a particular place at a particular time leads pilots to take unreasonable risks. Yet this was the kind of accident which killed Don Flower.

INTERRUPTED TRIP

The odyssey which ended in Flower's death began on March 25, 1980, when he loaded the Bonanza with belongings he intended to transport from his winter home in Florida to his summer home in Wichita, Kansas. But there was a special stop Flower intended to make.

He liked to keep his V-tail looking new, and the paint job had developed some chips at the leading edges of the wings. It needed a touch-up, and the FBO where Flower always had his aircraft painted was right along the route to Wichita—at

Mena, Arkansas. It was a Friday, and if Flower could get the work done promptly, he would have the Bonanza in top condition for a flight he intended to make the following Monday, when he and some business associates were scheduled to fly from Wichita to Chicago for an important meeting.

Unfortunately, the weather did not cooperate. A strong front was crossing the southeast United States, and Flower found his way blocked by thunderstorms. Though he was no stranger to rough weather, according to long-time acquaintances, a taste of this front was enough to convince him to put in at Meridian, Mississippi for the night.

The following morning, there were still clouds covering much of the Mississippi Valley, although Flower was able to wend his way from Meridian to Hot Springs, Arkansas, arriving there about 11 a.m. Though no one can now say what Flower's motive was in landing at Hot Springs, circumstances suggest that the low ceilings and the knowledge of terrain at the destination may have played a part. Crossing the flatland underneath the weather doubtless was easy enough, but the western half of Arkansas rises sharply in 2,500- and 3,000-foot mountains, and Mena is tucked up in a valley there. Hot Springs was a likely place to stop and get an idea whether Mena was reachable.

It is known that Flower called the Little Rock FSS for a report on Mena. Since there is no observation station there, the briefer gave him an area forecast, as well as current Hot Springs and Little Rock weather. Hot Springs was reporting 1,100 feet overcast, visibility 7 miles, with light spots in the overcast which the briefer interpreted as patches of blue sky.

There were some signs that the weather was improving, according to the briefing. But it is noteworthy that Hot Springs is at an elevation of 535 feet in flatland, while Mena is 1,069 feet, in the mountains 65 to 70 miles to the northwest.

Flower also called the paint shop at Mena, and was told that if he brought the aircraft in, he could have the paint touched up immediately and be on his way.

ILLEGAL IFR APPROACH

Flower took off and headed for Mena. He was later to tell authorities that he followed a major road up through the hills, got within about four miles of the field, couldn't remain VFR and climbed in the clouds. However, this does not jibe with the story told by the Mena Unicom operator. He told investigators that Flower shot the VOR approach to Mena, then executed a missed approach.

According to the Unicom operator, the ceiling was 400 to 500 feet overcast at Mena (which not only made the airport IFR, but below minimums), and he told Flower that when he started the approach. The Unicom operator later added, "I told him, 'It'll be real close if you do make it in here.'"

The VOR-DME approach to Mena calls for an initial approach fix at Rich Mountain VOR, which lies to the northwest of the field. To get to the VOR from Hot Springs, Flower would have had to go past the airport and turn around. The Unicom operator recalls him reporting the VOR inbound. The approach starts at 4,000 feet and the MDA is 2,240 feet. The missed approach calls for a climb to 4,000 feet to the hold point.

At 11:45 a.m., Flower called Hot Springs Approach Control and told them he was at 4,000 feet in the clouds in the vicinity of Mena and needed assistance. This was the first known contact with ATC since he had departed Hot Springs; authorities believe he conducted an instrument approach without permission from controllers.

The controllers at Hot Springs were concerned because the Bonanza was actually just outside the periphery of their jurisdiction, in Fort Worth Center airspace, and being without radar, they could not tell whether he might be in conflict with other IFR aircraft. But the tower supervisor on duty quickly arranged for coordination to allow the flight to be handled, and instructed the pilot to squawk the emergency code (7700) on his transponder. Flower was brought back to Hot Springs on an ILS approach, which he executed without incident and landed.

The supervisor asked Flower to telephone the control tower. In the phone conversation, the supervisor took down the information necessary to file an official report of the incident—one which could well have led to enforcement action against Flower.

About an hour later, Flower himself showed up in the tower cab. He and the supervisor had a calm conversation, not only about the incident, but a lot more: "I showed Mr. Flower the sectional chart and I pointed out to him the mountainous terrain in the vicinity of Mena," the supervisor later told investigators. "I asked Mr. Flower if he was familiar with the instrument approach procedures at Mena. He said he knew about the instrument approach procedures at Mena, but that the minimums were too high for the weather at the time.

"I pointed out to Mr. Flower that the field elevation at Mena was 1,069 feet. I told him that if the cloud layer over Hot Springs at the time extended to the Mena area, then the ceiling at Mena would be very low," the supervisor said. "Mr. Flower and I discussed the fact that there had been quite a few aircraft accidents in the Mena area because of the steeply rising terrain, especially when associated with low ceilings and visibilities. I pointed out to Mr. Flower the warning notes in the vicinity of Mena that were on the sectional chart. I told Mr. Flower that some aviation charts were even marked in red in that area because of the danger. He acknowledged that fact." The supervisor said Flower even pointed out that the name of the VOR in the area had been changed from Page to Rich Mountain to call attention to the mountainous terrain.

"Mr. Flower and I talked about the problems involved in trying to make low-altitude turns in mountainous terrain in low-ceiling, low-visibility situations. I mentioned to Mr. Flower the problem of flying into a box canyon situation," the supervisor also recalled.

The conversation was conducted in matter-of-fact tones, the supervisor later said, and when Flower left the cab, the supervisor was satisfied that he understood the seriousness of the previous incident. Flower had his Bonanza serviced with fuel and oil, and he made another call to the paint shop at Mena. He was again told that the weather was "very lousy," although it might get better later in the day.

SECOND ATTEMPT

Flower then did something which in retrospect may seem unbelievable. He started up the Bonanza, taxied out and left to make another try at Mena.

The tower supervisor had a hard time believing it. When he heard Flower getting takeoff clearance, he got on the radio: "You're going VFR, is that correct?" he asked the pilot. "That's affirmative, VFR," replied Flower. The Bonanza took

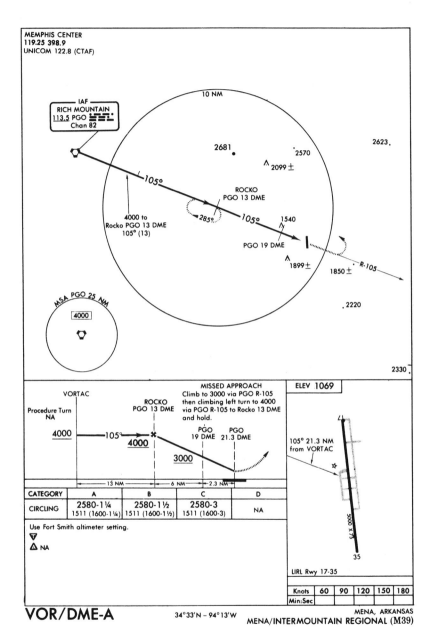

VOR/DME-A

34°33'N – 94°13'W

MENA, ARKANSAS
MENA/INTERMOUNTAIN REGIONAL (M39)

The weather at Mena, Arkansas was between 400 and 500-foot overcast, well below the MDA for the circling-minimums only approach into the airport.

off and requested a right turn out of the pattern—towards Mena—under a 1,300-foot ceiling.

Not long thereafter, the Unicom operator at Mena again heard from Flower, this time apparently some distance away. "He wanted to know if I thought he could get into the airport," the operator said. "I told him it didn't look any better than the first time he had tried."

A hunter was in the valley about 20 miles southeast of Mena when Flower's plane came into sight flying westbound, just beneath the low clouds. The hunter told authorities it went west a short distance, turned and flew north to the other side of the valley. Then it turned and headed south over the hunter's position. "The base of the clouds apparently sloped downward right at the mountain...the upper half of the mountain was in the clouds," the hunter told the NTSB. The hunter watched as the Bonanza flew into the clouds and struck the mountain; he heard the sound of impact. Prior to the crash, he had observed the plane in level flight, with the engine running normally.

In all likelihood, Flower had been looking for a way through the valleys under the clouds, and made the final error by accepting flight into a cloud that contained a mountain. He was 30 feet below the top of the mountain, and it was the highest mountain in that vicinity.

OTHER FACTORS

Nothing in the wreckage indicated any pre-impact malfunction of the airplane. But it was notable that the altimeter was set to 29.94 inches, even though the setting given to the pilot as he left Hot Springs the last time was 29.85 inches. This difference would cause a pilot to be approximately 90 feet lower than his altimeter indicates. However, the instrument face was destroyed, so it could not be determined what the altimeter might have read at impact, and it was not deemed to have a direct bearing on the cause of the accident, since the plane was in visual conditions under the clouds until just before the crash.

The investigation turned to the possibility of incapacitation, but the evidence would not support such a conclusion. While the pilot was just short of his 76th birthday, he was in good health; only a couple of days beforehand, he had been pronounced in good physical condition by a doctor, according to the NTSB investigator.

On the one hand, during the second stop at Hot Springs, a lineman observed Flower having trouble working a vending machine. The lineman said Flower was not able to exert enough force on the knob, so he pulled it for him. However, it was learned that Flower had chronic arthritis, which may explain the incident. On the other hand, Hot Springs tower has no elevator, and the supervisor recalls Flower having no difficulty climbing the stairs to get to the tower cab.

If physical factors aren't the answer, then perhaps psychological questions are appropriate to ask, although NTSB investigators are largely prohibited from delving into such matters. What kind of motivation would allow a competent pilot to attempt a scud running flight to Mena when his first attempt had not only failed, but got the attention of the FAA? Part of the answer may be Flower's total self-confidence in the air. "He loved to fly, and was perfectly at home in the airplane," his wife later told *Aviation Safety* magazine. "There were lots of times when I thought it was too rough, he didn't consider it rough at all," she said.

Mrs. Flower said she could recall missed approaches, bad weather and turbulence, none of which fazed her husband. "He was always very calm and collected," she said. And one long-time friend of Flower's recalls an incident that underlines the point: "We were both on the same frequency down near Atlanta one day, and I think Don must have been in or near a thunderstorm. He called the controllers and said he was in heavy rain, severe turbulence and thought perhaps there was even some hail. He said he was going to slow down because of it, and just thought they ought to know."

But perhaps the most telling insight may be information added by Mrs. Flower which was not in NTSB's report. Flower had been extremely ill several times in the past few years. He had had a severe attack of phlebitis a year previously, which had been successfully treated. Two to three years previously, he had undergone an operation for prostate cancer. Such a disease is common in older men, and usually is successfully dealt with by removal of the prostate gland.

But the doctors found more, according to Mrs. Flower. She said a very large tumor was found blocking one of Flower's kidneys to the point where the kidney had to be removed. There followed a long series of treatments with chemotherapy and radiology to destroy the rest of the cancer.

On the day prior to leaving Florida (two days before the fatal crash), Flower called his wife with wonderful news. "He was overjoyed," she said. "The doctor had just told him that as far as all the testing could show, he was now totally free of cancer, and was physically in very good shape." After the long period of illness, Flower told his wife he was "about 95 percent back to where he used to be."

Whether Flower's relief at the reprieve from cancer was enough to influence his judgment two days later—whether it gave him the conscious or subconscious feeling that he could take other risks now that the sword no longer hung over him—cannot be determined. But it is probably fair to say that it was an influence, along with the paint shop appointment and the commitments in Wichita, which contributed to his last and fatal misjudgment.

And at the risk of belaboring the point, if such an error can be made by a pilot of this stature, it can be made by any pilot who is not willing to let the weather win today, so he can fly tomorrow.

A Forecast is Not a Promise

Sometimes pilots get "suckered" into scud running by unforecast conditions. But this is no excuse for not turning around. Especially when the conditions are all stacked against the pilot, the 180-degree turn may be the only option.

There was, for example, the 179-hour private pilot of a Beech C35 Bonanza. He was attempting a night cross-country flight from Seymour, Texas, to Woodward, Oklahoma. He later told investigators that the forecast for his route of flight was VFR. But while en route, he started to encounter clouds.

Trying to stay VFR, the pilot let down to 3,200 feet from his cruise altitude. The clouds got lower, forcing him down to 3,000 feet and finally down to 2,500 feet. He decided he probably couldn't make it to Woodward and changed his destination to Gage, Oklahoma.

"He thought he was cruising below the clouds at 200 to 300 feet AGL," said the NTSB in the accident report. "Subsequently, the aircraft collided with the terrain in a wings-level, flat attitude at a reported elevation of 2,473 feet." Miraculously, the pilot and his passenger escaped with minor injuries.

IFR: "I Follow Roads"

Another "time-honored" variation of scud running is the pilot who tries to fly by reference to roads. When the weather is good, following the road is no problem. But when the weather gets bad, the road can be a highway to hell.

Typical of this type of accident was the crash of a Beech M35 Bonanza near Valley View, Texas. The 24-year-old private pilot, with no instrument rating, had been briefed on IFR conditions all along his route of flight. Despite the warning he launched anyway. From the NTSB brief:

"Several witnesses observed the aircraft flying in and out of the fog and low ceilings. At one point the aircraft was observed flying down an interstate highway. The aircraft impacted the ground in a 42-degree nose-down, 46-degree right-bank attitude. A witness who observed the impact estimated the weather as a 200-foot ceiling and 1/2-mile visibility with fog."

Another private pilot was more fortunate. He and his passenger survived an accident while scud running down a highway. The 235-hour pilot was flying a Cessna 170 from Helena, Montana to Mullan, Idaho.

From the NTSB brief: "The aircraft collided with a telephone line during maneuvering to stay VFR and clear of ground obstructions. The pilot said he was approaching Lookout Pass at about 500-600 feet AGL and was following Interstate 90 westbound. He inadvertently entered IFR conditions as he tried to turn left to follow the highway. The left turn angle of bank increased and the aircraft lost altitude. The pilot tried to climb eastbound to avoid rising terrain. As the pilot approached the summit eastbound, he was nearing a stall with an overpass straight ahead. A dive and pull-up to clear the overpass resulted in a collision with the wire. A full stall followed and the aircraft collided with the ground."

Some flight instructors will challenge an advanced student's stick-and-rudder skills by asking him to fly circles around a moving point...and one of the very best targets for this maneuver is a truck, because most of them drive at constant speeds. In the next example of scud running, the CFI picked out a truck to follow, but the episode turned into more than a training exercise.

The 23-year-old flight instructor and her 21-year-old student died when their Cessna crashed while apparently attempting to follow a truck on a highway under IFR conditions. The CFI, a Swedish national, had only recently gained her instructor rating. She began her flight training on March 2, 1988, and in only six months obtained her instrument, commercial, multi-engine, instructor, and instrument instructor ratings, gaining the commercial and multi-engine tickets on August 29. By the time of the accident, she had logged a total of 368 hours. She was working as an instructor for three months at the time of the accident.

The student, a Greek national, was one of her first students, and had progressed rapidly through his training. He had accumulated some 40 hours of flight time and was reportedly getting ready to take his private pilot checkride.

The pair had departed Meacham Field at Fort Worth at about 5:30 for a local flight. They did not get a weather briefing, but investigators found the student's kneeboard on which he had copied the ATIS information at the time of departure. The weather was marginal, with visibilities reported as four miles in fog. The forecast for the area was for conditions to deteriorate. By the time of the accident, conditions had dropped to a 300-foot indefinite ceiling with two-mile visibility in fog.

At the time the Cessna departed, the CFI's boyfriend happened to be flying as well. He told investigators he heard her call on the radio and thought they would be coming right back, since the weather was so poor. He reported that he had taken off just after them and encountered what he called IFR conditions on the downwind leg of the traffic pattern.

There were no further communications from the Cessna. It was next spotted by a trucker driving on Highway 27, heading southeast. The trucker said it appeared the Cessna was trying to follow him, as it stayed behind him and weaved from side to side. Eventually, it collided with a static wire on a powerline set some 80 feet above the ground. The wire flipped the Cessna inverted and it crashed onto the road.

INTO THE MURK

A final example shows just how far things can go. This accident involved a 37-year-old commercial pilot on a Part 135 flight in a Piper PA-32R-300 Lance. He was to transport prisoners from Winston-Salem, North Carolina to Knoxville, Tennessee. The pilot had logged some 600 total hours and held an instrument rating. The pilot was told that VFR flight was not recommended. But Winston-Salem was VFR, and at 1:38 that afternoon he departed.

The direct route of flight from Winston-Salem to Knoxville lies slightly south of due west. Yet, the pilot proceeded north, following Interstate 77 up into Virginia. He may have been trying to fly I-77 north to Wytheville, Virginia. There, he could pick up Interstate 81 and follow it to Knoxville.

The Lance was next seen near Lambsburgh, Virginia, by witnesses who observed it flying north near I-77 at about 200 feet. One witness stated the airplane was well below the mountains that were ahead of it, mountains that were obscured by fog. A minute or so after seeing the Lance fly by, the witnesses heard it hit the mountain. All aboard the aircraft were killed.

The Rotorhead Advantage

Another part of the popular mythology about flying in the weather concerns helicopters. Some feel that helicopter pilots don't need to worry so much about IFR conditions. They can always stop and descend slowly to a safe landing. Or at least, they can travel slowly enough to avoid any obstructions that might loom out of the fog. But like most myths, this one reads better than it plays in real life.

A tragic example involved a 20-year-old, 117-hour pilot in a Robinson R-22. He was trying to get back to Grand Forks, North Dakota from Sisseton, South Dakota.

He called for a weather briefing before the flight and was informed of fog in the area. During the briefing, the FSS specialist had the pilot look out the window to determine the local sky conditions. The pilot noted he could not see any stars (it was very early in the morning). "You should run out from under that fairly shortly going north," said the briefer. "Well, I think I can get out from underneath it with a helicopter, no problem," said the pilot.

Almost two hours later, the pilot took off into the fog. He only made it a mile and a half before crashing in a farm field, out of control. He had become spatially disoriented.

Another accident shows the fallacy of believing that a helicopter can always descend slowly to a safe landing, avoiding obstructions by virtue of low speed and good maneuverability.

The 866-hour private pilot at the controls of this Robinson R-22 was lucky enough to escape with only minor injuries.

He had taken off from Ruston, Louisiana, bound for Shreveport on a night VFR flight. While cruising at about 500 feet, he encountered IFR conditions. He decided to descend and get underneath, and let down until the chopper hit a tree about 75 feet above the ground and crashed to earth.

Even in a well-equipped helicopter with a highly qualified pilot, VFR into IFR can be fatal. Consider the crash of a Bell 222UT helicopter near Galax, Virginia. The helicopter was working for an emergency medical service. The pilot, holding a helicopter ATP with a helicopter instrument rating, had logged some 8,085 hours, most of which was in helicopters.

The chopper had been dispatched to pick up a patient with a head injury and return to Winston-Salem, North Carolina. Before departing, the pilot got a weather briefing, during which he was advised that IFR conditions prevailed over most of the area and VFR flight was not recommended.

The flight launched anyway. The chopper pilot climbed to 4,500 feet and cruised towards the destination. In his last radio transmission, with the hospital, he said he was only twelve miles from Galax, where the patient was waiting. At about the same time, a witness in the area heard the chopper. The witness told investigators that the sounds stopped suddenly when he heard a "thud," but he couldn't see anything because of the fog.

The wreckage was found the next day. The chopper had made it to within ten miles of Galax when it hit a ridge. All three persons aboard were killed.

"Inoperative" Can Sometimes Be Worse Than "Not Installed"

When you need the basic flight instruments, you really need them...and in a situation where spatial orientation is absolutely necessary to save the day, a pilot who suddenly discovers that there's something wrong with the instruments is in a world of hurt, as this helicopter pilot found out.

A quick scan of the instrument panel should be a part of any pre-takeoff check. Even if he doesn't intend to do anything but fly by visual references, a pilot would be expected to look at the panel some time during a flight. To wait until instrument information is vitally needed can be a mistake.

Such was the case for the 37-year-old commercial pilot at the controls of a Bell 206B helicopter. The pilot, flying a medical evacuation flight in the mountains of Idaho, escaped with serious injuries and the other three occupants of the chopper were unhurt in the accident.

The pilot was well qualified for the flight, having logged 8,810 total hours, 4,700 of which were logged in the Bell 206. He later told investigators he was also very well experienced in the geographic area of the air ambulance operation he worked for.

According to the pilot, he had received a call to pick up an injured skier just before noon. He drove to the helipad to inspect the chopper for the flight and to assess the weather conditions. He found both to be adequate for the flight. He did note, however, that there was a layer of high thin clouds at about 10,000 feet, with another scattered layer around the mountains at about 7,200 feet. This was about the altitude of the pickup location.

He was about to lift off when he received a radio call from "Mountain Control." The weather in the pickup area looked good and seemed to be clearing, they said. He told Mountain Control that he would personally assess the weather at the pickup point.

On arrival, the pilot noted visibilities of between 1/2 and 1/4 mile, but he was able to land without difficulty. There was a five-minute delay waiting for the injured skier to arrive and be belted in. While waiting, the pilot noted he could see the top of Mount Baldy, elevation 9,200 feet.

Because of the cloud layer blowing by at the pickup point, the pilot called Mountain Control for a weather update. Mountain Control replied that the clouds the pilot was seeing appeared to be isolated. They too could see Mount Baldy, as well as the intended destination—the Moritz Hospital.

The pilot decided to go, since the hospital was only three miles from his present location and Mountain Control said weather was otherwise good all around.

The pilot took one last look around at the weather. Visibility had dropped to an eighth of a mile, which he later characterized as "marginal VFR, but with visual reference still possible."

With the injured skier aboard, as well as a nurse and a ski patrolman, the pilot lifted the chopper off. He climbed vertically to about 400-500 feet AGL to ensure clearing any trees, as well as to get a better look at the surrounding terrain. Unfortunately, things did not improve at this altitude. He started the helicopter forward, using "immediate visual references [including] 'linear streak patches' of blue sky."

They had only traveled about a quarter-mile when "it became apparent that...IFR transition was necessary to continue the flight," the pilot later reported. Returning to the pickup point was out of the question due to the weather conditions, the pilot added.

He transitioned to IFR flying, using the instruments. It was now that he discovered he had less than a partial panel. He looked at the artificial horizon, only to see the warning flag hanging across the instrument face. He noted it showed a slight left bank. As he processed this information, the chopper entered the clouds.

The pilot's next choice was to use the turn and bank indicator. There was another unpleasant surprise for him here. "I re-discovered the needle portion of the gauge was 'blackened out' due to [it] being inoperative prior to commencement of this contract (VFR day only and inadvertent IFR not anticipated)."

Things were not going well at all. He knew he had to use the only remaining instrument which could keep him heading straight—the magnetic compass. "Knowing its location (right bottom side of the right front window), I did not want to turn my head in fear of inducing acute vertigo and possible

Under the best of circumstances, medical evacuation flights are hazardous. They're made riskier by poor weather, even in a helicopter with as good a safety record as Bell's popular 206 JetRanger.

inverted flight configuration," he wrote in his accident report. "I slowly glanced at the mag compass and at that time verified the left turn configuration," he continued. He moved the cyclic to the right, but it didn't feel like the chopper was responding, so he put in some more.

The chopper had accelerated to about 100 mph by this time. He glanced through the windshield to see a tree looming out of the fog. They missed it, but not by much. Before he could do anything about their proximity to the ground, another tree came out of the fog, heading straight for the Plexiglass. The pilot pulled back on the cyclic and swung it to the left while bottoming the collective. He knew he couldn't avoid the tree, but he hoped he could at least lessen the impact. The helicopter plowed into the tree and then hit the ground.

In his accident report, in the space where pilots are asked for ways in which the accident could have been avoided, the pilot blamed the lack of functioning instruments. "I feel my accident could have been avoided had the aircraft had an operable turn-needle," he wrote. His responsibility for checking the condition of the aircraft and instruments prior to flight was not mentioned.

The NTSB took exception to some of the pilots assertions. The Board apparently did not believe the inoperative instruments came as a surprise to the pilot. In pronouncing probable cause, the Board named the pilot for "operation with known deficiencies in equipment," as well as "flight into known adverse weather conditions" with the inoperative instruments.

"It's Only a Thin Layer of Fog, Clear on Top"

One of the most tantalizing and dangerous weather phenomena in aviation—especially for the VFR pilot—may be a mere thin layer of fog. Fine VFR conditions beckon above the fog layer, and the pilot can think of lots of ways to convince himself that getting on with the flight is worth the risk of a few moments of instrument flying. But the possible consequences—high-speed impact with obstacles, or an out-of-control dive into the ground—should awe any airman.

One pilot who counts himself very lucky survived the crash of his Cessna 150 after an attempted takeoff in fog ended in the trees. The accident demolished the Cessna, however.

> The pilot, age 38, had logged some 278 hours since achieving his private certificate, 249 of those hours in the Cessna 150. He had only logged three and a half hours of simulated instrument time, however. The pilot's accident report tells the whole story:
>
> "On the way into Happy Camp from my home three miles up the Klamath River, I found the usual morning fog covering the airport. The same fog had prevented me from making even minimal use of my airplane as a commuter to my job in Treka.
>
> "[The fog] appeared to be a couple of hundred feet thick as I could see above it. On top, the ceiling looked to be 25,000 feet and scattered with unlimited visibility. [Witnesses later said the weather was a 100-foot obscured ceiling with about one-eighth of a mile visibility—Ed.]
>
> "I went on to the airport and preflighted my airplane while I waited for the fog to burn off. I had been faced with the same

situation a hundred times over the past several years, but I had never even considered taking off in it.

"After about 45 minutes, while waiting at the end of the runway, for reasons I still don't understand, I decided I could keep the airplane in a normal climb attitude long enough to get through the fog. I could list many reasons contributing to my inexcusable decision to 'go for it,' but the main ones were my wife's failing ability to cope with our separation during the weeks since my accepting the Treka job, and my boss' explicit instructions the evening before that he didn't want anyone late or off the next day. I also felt a need to prove...that an airplane could be dependable transportation.

"In what now seems like a daze, and not even checking what heading I would have to maintain, or what precautions I should take to help insure a successful takeoff in very unfavorable conditions, I proceeded to take off.

"Once in the air and in IFR conditions, I suddenly realized what I had attempted. While keeping the plane in a level climb, I let it drift to the left towards the hillside to the west of the runway. About the time I was starting to get things sorted out, the trees appeared out of the fog. I pulled back hard on the yoke. I struck a fir tree about 50 feet above the ground and then dropped straight down to the ground, nose first. The plane then fell over upside down. I don't remember getting out of the airplane and walking down the runway."

Prep and Plan

Flying IFR is not inherently dangerous. But a safe IFR flight requires thought and planning. Unplanned encounters with the weather deny the pilot the chance to gather information and plan the flight.

Faced with a surprise weather encounter, the temptation to press on can be very strong. But flogging around in the weather with no definite plan invites disaster. Pilots who are instrument rated should air-file an IFR flight plan and follow it. Those pilots who are not would be best advised to turn around and get out of the weather as quickly as possible.

For those who elect to continue, the decision may well be the last one they make. Statistics clearly show that more than 80 percent of all VFR-into-IFR accidents result in deaths. Those are odds most gamblers would refuse.

Cold Weather Operations

T he mobility range of today's general aviation
airplanes—even the smallest of them—presents the opportunity for pilots to travel far
outside the local area, sometimes into unfamiliar climates and
environments. Even though many pilots are quite content to remain
in parts of the country that never see the onset of winter, there's
always the chance that the "northland" will beckon...a trip to a colder
clime, perhaps just for a day or two, but maybe enough exposure so
that some knowledge of the peculiarities of cold-weather operations
will prove helpful.

Of course, for those who fly throughout the winter just because it's
there, cold-weather operations are second nature...or are they? The
discussion which follows, using several accidents and incidents to
illustrate the points, shows that flight in a low-temperature environment can present problems to beginners and veterans alike.

Everything Slows Down

Absolute zero is the point at which all molecular activity stops;
fortunately, that super-cold state is achieved only in laboratories.
But as the temperature drops from what we consider a "normal"
range, people and machines begin to slow down. If protective or
remedial measures aren't taken, cold can cost us the ability to make
rational decisions, and can set up situations which lead to accidents.

Special precautions are in order for cold-weather pilots, not the
least of which are those required for getting a reciprocating airplane
engine started. Low temperatures reduce the cranking power of

storage batteries, and this, coupled with cold, high-viscosity oil can bring even the strongest battery to its knees in a hurry.

In such a dead-battery situation, pilots are tempted on occasion to employ the old faithful "Armstrong" starter—pulling the prop through by hand. Now there was a time when hand-propping was the only way, and the GA fleet still counts among its venerable members a number of airplanes with no electrical system at all. But the pilots of these airplanes are well versed in hand-propping procedures and safety measures, and the engines involved are mostly very low horsepower, easy to pull through and not likely to move the airplane much if it's not properly secured.

Here's a pilot who attempted an "Armstrong" start on a larger, more powerful aircraft, and when the engine caught, the airplane demonstrated a mind of its own.

> The 42-year-old private pilot suffered minor injuries while attempting to hold back the Piper Archer after hand-propping. The plane ran off unoccupied when the engine started.
>
> The 575-hour pilot told investigators there had been a "record cold" the previous night and the plane's battery was exhausted when he tried to start the engine. He set the parking brake to "full pressure" and started the engine by hand-propping, then attempted to board the aircraft. He said he had just reached the tip of the wing on his way to the cabin door when the airplane began to move. Despite his efforts, the plane got away, traveled across a field, through a fence and over a barrier onto an airport perimeter road. Pieces of the Archer struck a passing van, but the occupants were uninjured. After the plane came to rest, a fire broke out and destroyed it.
>
> In the space on the accident report form where the pilot is asked to suggest how the accident could have been avoided, the Archer pilot wrote, "We should institute FARs regarding hand-propping and we should insure that all ground schools and pilot training include a course on hand-propping."

We agree that more care should be taken by those who need to start their airplanes by hand. Indeed, it's impossible to be too careful, but general regulation and training might well induce more people to use this procedure, and defeat the intent. Rather, take note that a whirling propeller—even one that whirls only once, or a part of a turn—must be considered nothing less than a rotary guillotine. When people and propellers tangle, the prop always wins.

Cold Engines Need Lots of TLC

In his book, *Stick and Rudder,* Wolfgang Langeweische pointedly differentiated airplanes from cars: "It may sound like one and smell like one, and it may have been interior-decorated to look like one; the difference is—it goes on wings." Langeweische's point also applies to an airplane engine—it's not like a car's either.

The reason an aircraft engine needs different treatment from a car's lies in the basic construction of the engine. In an auto, the block is usually cast iron and the crankshaft is steel; these metals expand at about the same rate when heated. In contrast, the horizontally opposed aircraft engine has an aluminum crankcase supporting steel components such as the crankshaft and camshaft. The cylinder barrels are steel with aluminum cylinder heads tightly attached.

The rate of expansion for aluminum, as it is heated, is twice that of steel. This also applies as it cools—aluminum shrinks in size twice as much as steel.

Because the engine was designed and assembled at room temperature, its clearances between parts can shrink dramatically when the severe cold of winter sets in. At temperatures as "high" as -11 degrees Fahrenheit, one popular engine can completely lose crankshaft bearing clearance. No wonder they turn over hard when they're cold! Even warm oil can't help when there isn't any bearing clearance. Many pilots have ideas on how to operate their engines in cold weather that come from their experience with their automobiles. As a result, there are some popular misconceptions.

Misconception: If You Can Start It...

Myth: "The main purpose of preheating is to start the engine: therefore, if you can start it, you don't need preheating."

Fact: An automobile engine survives quite well when cold-started, but an airplane engine can be severely damaged.

Because of poor fuel vaporization, an engine with cold cylinders is hard to start. But if it is started while they are cold, the cylinders are easily damaged. The top end of the cylinder bore is smaller than the base end—this is called "choke." It's designed to allow a nearly straight cylinder wall once the engine is at operating temperature. The choke has little effect at start-up in moderate ambient temper-

When the temperature plummets into the teens and below, engine preheat should be standard procedure.

atures. But the colder the temperature, the more the cylinder is choked. When the cold engine is turned over, the piston is forced into the smaller-than-normal top end of the cylinder.

Another thing happens when the cylinder is cold. It concerns the wristpin, which in normal operation floats freely, axially within its bore in the piston. But the differences between metals in cold weather may change that. The piston, being aluminum, grips the steel wristpin. When a piston which last stopped at the bottom of its travel cools down, the wristpin end may be locked against the cylinder wall. When this engine is started, the wristpin end may wear against the cylinder wall.

The piston-to-connecting rod juncture also becomes stiff in a cold engine, causing the piston to tip at an angle as the engine is started. The first few times the piston travels in the cylinder, it may do so with its piston rings cocked at an angle and the piston skirt contacting the cylinder wall.

As if this weren't enough damage to the cold cylinder, one more thing occurs—once the engine starts, the aluminum piston grows at a faster rate than the cylinder diameter. The result is scuffing of the cylinder wall by the piston until the temperatures equalize.

This all might be enough to make the owner of a $12,000 aircraft engine grimace to think of the pain his engine already may have undergone. But there are worse effects from cold-starting. Starting the engine with cold cylinders may result in excessive wear—starting with a cold crankcase could cause main bearing failure.

Misconception: Warm Oil, Warm Engine

Myth: "When preheating, the most important thing is warm oil." This idea is similar to some early preheating methods in automobiles, which even in autos were not too successful. The "dipstick heater" heated automobile oil but didn't help greatly in producing the start.

Fact: Warm oil may not even help if the rest of the engine is cold. Looking again at the automobile engine, the most successful means of preheating is the "in-block" type of heater, which heats the coolant. This automobile preheater heats only the cylinders and the block areas—the oil isn't heated at all. It relies on multi-viscosity oil to flow once the engine start occurs. If oil heat were the only significant thing in an aircraft engine, then the new multi-viscosity and synthetic oils would be the only kind needed. But actually, the aircraft engine, with a cold crankcase, may have reduced bearing clearance which won't accept any oil at all—hot, cold, or synthetic. The bearings and journals may be in metal-to-metal contact at the first instant of motion.

Oil Quality: It Pays to Observe the Specs

Engine manufacturers know what their products need in the way of lubrication, and somewhere in the paperwork for each powerplant you'll find a table or chart which indicates the special engine-oil requirements for cold weather. The problem stems from that "molecular slowdown" we mentioned at the outset—as the temperature drops, the viscosity of engine oil goes right along with it. And when the oil is so thick that it can't flow into and through the tiny passages in the engine, some parts are going to go without; that's disaster for pieces of metal rubbing against each other at high speed.

One way to make sure there will be lubrication in a cold-weather environment is to preheat the entire engine before a start is attempted; of course even the most thorough preheat can be defeated by using the wrong grade (viscosity) of engine oil. Some new respect for having

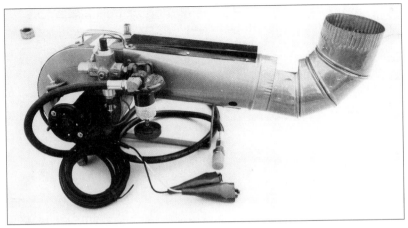

One popular preheater is Flame Engineering's Red Dragon. The unit is propane-fired and has a battery-operated blower.

the right grade of oil as well as preheating an aircraft properly may have been instilled in a pilot who crashed one cold February day at Crested Butte, Colorado.

The pilot made an emergency landing in five feet of snow after the engine of his Piper Comanche 260 quit within two minutes after takeoff. None of the four persons aboard reported injuries.

The temperature at the time of the accident was 2 degrees Fahrenheit. The pilot told investigators that the engine was preheated for about 25 minutes, and after startup, was run 10 to 15 minutes to "warm it up" before takeoff. The pilot, who held a private license with approximately 800 total hours of flight time, said all the engine instruments were normal as he commenced the takeoff.

About two minutes later, the engine made a loud noise followed by what sounded like a "mild" explosion, the pilot related. He said an oil inspection door was blown off and black smoke began coming from the engine. He made a prompt emergency landing.

Investigators found that the engine's connecting rod bearings and their journals on the crankshaft showed evidence of failure from oil starvation. Two of the connecting rods had broken, and in flailing around the crankcase, had punched holes in the case, probably accounting for the black smoke that was observed.

The investigator noted that the engine was some 300 hours past its TBO, and the logbook had an unusual entry. There was an indication that the engine had been disassembled, given a major overhaul and re-installed but the entry concerning the overhaul was then scratched out. It also was not apparent whether the engine was in compliance with an Airworthiness Directive concerning oil pump gears in Lycoming engines. As it turned out, these items were discounted, since further investigation seemed to indicate other reasons for oil-related failure.

The NTSB investigator said the personnel who preheated the plane had been unable to put the hot air duct into the bottom of the Comanche's cowl, as should have been done, so they inserted the duct through the top front opening. Such a position does wonders for the top of the engine, but provides little heating of the engine crankcase and its cold oil.

It was also learned that the oil in the engine was a straight 50-weight oil, the investigator said. Engine manufacturer's instructions call for a much lower-viscosity oil when operating in cold temperatures, due to the possibility of thick oil cavitating in the oil pump and failing to flow properly through the oil galleries of the engine.

Cozy Cylinders

Myth: "If the cylinders are warm, you're preheated." Some methods of preheating heat only the cylinders. These engines start easily and it appears that the plane is "home free."

Fact: while a car lives quite well this way, an airplane may be in trouble because it has reduced bearing clearances due to that cold crankcase.

Many failures have occurred in aircraft engines over the years that have been the result of improper preheating. It's my belief that most of these may have been blamed on other things because the nature of the problem was not understood. Some types of failures that are caused or aggravated by improper preheating are as follows:

Cold crankcases may "burn" or excessively wear main bearings even though the engine has warm oil or cylinders. This is usually incorrectly blamed on "stiff oil" or a congealed oil cooler.

In extreme cases the bearing insert may rotate, blocking oil flow

Cold-starting an engine with no preheat is likely to cause serious piston and cylinder scuffing.

to the entire crankshaft and thereby causing a massive failure of the engine. In less severe cases, the engine may exhibit poor propeller control due to oil pressure losses in the worn main bearings. Twins might demonstrate this by propellers that won't stay "in synch" and won't respond to cures such as overhauling the props and governors. Other clearance-related problems may occur within an engine with a cold crankcase, such as improper fit of the camshaft and the valve lifter bodies.

If an engine has a warm "top end" and cold oil, this may create its own problem. When using a straight grade of heavy "summer" oil, the oil system may not be able to draw oil to lubricate the engine once start-up occurs. The newer multi-viscosity oils do a much better job in this respect.

Drier Consequences

Myth: "Since the engine is a closed system, moisture is not a problem in preheating."

Fact: The engine is not a closed system. Moisture is produced whenever the engine is run, and any preheater vaporizes this moisture. Regular flying of the aircraft is necessary to clear out moisture whether it is summer or winter.

This is an area not commonly understood. If only the engine's lower end (oil sump) is heated, the moisture vapor rises and condenses on the cold parts such as the crankshaft and cam. (One can see the same thing occur on basement water pipes in the summer.) This moisture will produce rust and acids. But also, under the right conditions, it may freeze in the oil breather tube, blocking the breather. If this occurs, the crankshaft nose seal can in many cases be blown out of the engine, followed by the entire supply of oil.

The only way to avoid such problems is to assure that the preheater system preheats the entire engine and that the pilot has taken the proper precautions to winterize the engine.

A list of winterizing items should include winter grade oil, an oil cooler cover, an insulated breather tube with an alternate hole, and a check to see that the engine's baffle strips are in place. A winter front should also be used if approved for the airplane. (This is also a good time to check the cabin heater for exhaust leaks!)

Certification

Myth: "Since the airplane is FAA approved, it should operate well under any temperature condition." How could such an expensive device as an airplane engine exhibit such poor characteristics? Didn't FAA approval require it to operate in these conditions?

Fact: The FARs under which the engine was certified didn't require it to meet standards for low-temp operation. This isn't all bad, but the engine's operator should be aware and take some precautions.

In below-zero weather, the engine develops more horsepower than it was certified to develop—possibly as much as 15 percent more! To counteract this, it's the practice of many cold weather pilots to add carb heat once the throttle is opened full (and to remove it when they reduce power). Also, they don't sit on the runup pad with the carb heat on for long periods, since it may raise the temperature just enough to cause frost in the induction system. This could cause the engine to die when the throttle is opened.

"One Heater's Like Another"

Myth: "Any preheater that is FAA-approved or that has 'No Hazard Approval' will preheat my engine properly." When a preheater is advertised as FAA-approved, doesn't that mean that it will do a proper job of heating?

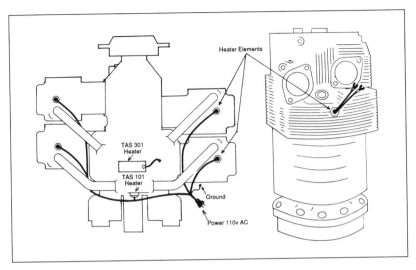

In cold northern climes, Tanis engine heaters are popular. They feature both heated cylinder plugs and a crankcase heating pad.

Fact: Since the FAA has no regulatory standards for cold weather operations, to gain approval a preheater may not have to meet any standards—it may not even work. Many preheaters don't have any kind of "approval," nor are they required to, because they are not installed on the aircraft.

The crankcase, the part of the engine most critically in need of preheating, is also the most difficult part to preheat. This is because of a kind of "wind chill factor," analogous to what people experience in cold, windy weather, which is transmitted through a not-so-obvious mechanism—the propeller.

Typically, the propeller accounts for the largest heat loss on an engine being preheated. It sits outside the cowling in the wind, drawing heat from the crankshaft and case. While this "wind chill" can't cool an engine to lower than the outside air temperature, it will demand more heat output from the preheater to warm the engine to a given temperature. Because of this, an insulated cover for the cowl and propeller is desirable when trying to preheat.

Every preheater has limits as to how much wind chill it can handle. At a given sub-zero temperature, some don't have enough output to heat properly on a calm day—when wind chill is added, even the best at some point will no longer do the job. When an aircraft owner is shopping for a preheater, he should find that the reputable manufacturer of the unit is able to discuss what temperatures his unit will produce—as measured at the crankcase of the particular engine—and the effect wind chill will have on this performance.

Manufacturers of preheaters make many claims in their advertising—some claim BTUs of heat, others watts of power, and still others that you can "start in only 10 minutes" (or 15, or 20). But considering that the information really needed is whether the preheater will produce safe starting temperatures, it's enlightening to compare preheaters by the same standard. One can try converting manufacturers' claims to the same measurements. Conversion factors are available in any high school physics book for such things as watts to BTUs. (One BTU equals about 0.293 watt-hours.) One thing to remember is that there are losses every time energy changes form or is transferred to some other object.

Obviously, the best standard to use would be temperature within the core of the engine. In the absence of the ability to measure this precisely, spending more time preheating, assuming adequate preheater output, can be like buying extra engine insurance.

Once the threshold of output has been met, there are some other differences among types of preheaters.

Most preheaters sold today are of the "air blower" type. Through one means or another, air is heated and then blown around the engine compartment. Since heat rises and it's often hard to position the blower to be sure that hot air travels by all the cylinders as well as the crankcase, there are often parts of an engine that are extremely cold after what seemed to be a hearty preheating session. Sometimes, the blown air is simply mis-applied, and never gets to the critical engine parts. If it's applied without proper engine covers in windy conditions, the blown hot air just blows uselessly away. But the most common mistake is to believe that all that hot air applied for 15 minutes equals a warm engine, when it could take *hours* to do the job, with some heaters.

Provided these pitfalls are avoided, there are some hot air preheaters which can do a reasonable job, when properly employed.

Another type of heater being sold today heats the oil pan electrically. However, it does nothing for the "upper" engine, particularly the cylinder heads. There are also dipstick-style heaters, which we can dismiss for reasons mentioned above.

And there is the Tanis pre-heater, in which electric heating elements are installed at strategic places around the engine—not only a 120-watt element on the oil sump, but other elements on each cylinder—and the airplane is simply "plugged in" to a 110-volt outlet for about 5-6 hours prior to being started. (It can be left plugged in continuously, keeping the engine constantly ready for starting.)

It has been my experience that any "air blower" with less than 50,000 BTU is just too anemic to work well. Yet an insulated system such as the Tanis TAS100 will do an acceptable job on as little as 250 watts. Why is this? This particular system operates for a longer period of time, makes fewer exchanges of energy and transfers heat by conduction, which is very efficient.

Whatever type of preheater is employed, its effectiveness can be vastly enhanced by using thermal blankets around the cowl to keep the heat from being blown out of the engine compartment. Again, there are conditions of wind and temperature which can make it impossible to preheat the engine to the extent needed for a safe start.

The Ultimate Question

At this point, one may consider another question: When the temperature or wind chill drops into the negative teens, should we really be flying? If a pilot had a forced landing, could he survive long enough to reach shelter? When the wind chill reaches -30 degrees and lower, a pilot who is normally systematic and safety-conscious can be turned into a madman whose only concern is to get the door closed, the engine started, and the cabin heater turned on. Some cold-country pilots don't fly much below -20 degrees unless it's an emergency. At these temperatures a pilot may have trouble keeping cylinder temperatures up, and as a result produce more cylinder wear.

To summarize, when the temperature is below 20 degrees, be sure to thoroughly preheat the engine. If you want to determine the "quality" of your preheat, the cylinders, nose case, and the oil should all be warm to the touch. If they aren't, don't start.

Too Much of a Good Thing

Cold weather sometimes makes engine starting an artful procedure. Three ingredients are still required for combustion—air, fuel, and ignition—but getting them together in the proper proportions can create a problem. What's normal doesn't usually work, because internal combustion depends on vaporized fuel, and cold gasoline gives up its vapor grudgingly. The only answer is to increase the amount of liquid fuel going into the engine to the point where there is sufficient vapor. Of course when the engine fires, things heat up in a hurry, and with all that extra gasoline in the induction system, a fire is a distinct possibility.

Picture yourself in a small airplane at a small airport on a cold morning. You pulled the prop through, primed the engine and cranked, but the engine ran only 30 seconds and died. So you primed a little more and cranked a little more, and it ran 10 seconds and died. So now you prime one more time and crank with the last ounce of juice in the battery and...the engine's on fire! What do you do now? For one Skyhawk owner, the answer was, you watch your aircraft burn.

The owner had gone through the aforementioned sequence of events, and found himself with an engine fire. He remembered the age-old advice about carburetor fires: keep cranking the engine, to suck the flames into the carburetor and extinguish them. He tried this for several seconds, but the smoke kept rising from the cowl. He had no urge to keep trying after that. "I'm sure that advice is correct, but you try sitting in an aircraft with flames up front and 40 gallons of fuel above your head!" he later told *Aviation Safety*.

His next step (and a wise one) was to evacuate his passenger, a dog and himself, grabbing the airplane's fire extinguisher as he did so. By this time, a definite conflagration was in progress in the engine compartment. He said he discharged the small extinguisher's contents into the cowl, but "it had absolutely no effect." He told us it was his impression that he couldn't direct the dry chemical extinguisher far enough back and underneath the engine, to the source of the flames.

As he stood with the empty bottle in his hand, he now faced a predicament that would be the same for thousands of pilots at airports throughout the country: no help in sight. It was a holiday morning, and the airport was nearly deserted. Moreover, as investigators pointed out, the nearest fire extinguisher (had the pilot been aware of it) was a whopping big 15-pound job situated at the fuel pit of the airport—1,000 feet from the airplane. Not even O.J. Simpson, with his demonstrated ability to race across airports, could have sprinted to get that extinguisher and returned in time to do any good.

Plan B was the fire department, of course. The passenger ran for the phone. Unfortunately, the phone was 1,200 feet from the airplane, and the fire department was in the center of town—three miles away.

Consequently, the answer was to watch from a safe distance as the Skyhawk burned, and wait for the firemen to arrive. The pilot told us there now arose another fearsome factor: the plane's prop began turning. The fire apparently melted insulation in the wires and caused a short, which energized the starter. The pilot had the horrifying thought that the engine might actually start, and the flaming airplane take off. But luckily it didn't. The prop turned several revolutions, stopped, turned several revolutions again, then stopped for good. The fire department arrived in due course and hosed down the front of the airplane (the fuel tanks never did ignite). But in their zeal, the firemen also took axes to the cabin windows, and pumped gallon after gallon of water and foam into the Skyhawk's innards. According to the pilot, had they not attacked the cabin, the plane might have been repairable. As it was, the Skyhawk had to be "totaled out" by the insurance company.

The pilot said he learned a lesson, to wit; with a carbureted-engine airplane, it's a good idea to station an accomplice with a fire extinguisher—and a big one, bigger than the aircraft cabin size—near the cowl during a cold-weather start.

He also said he has solved the problem another way—he bought a fuel-injected Mooney to replace the Cessna. Fuel-injected engines start better in cold weather, and have no carburetors to catch fire.

However, there are some other points about engine fires worthy of note: First, the common carbureted-engine fire usually results from overpriming, which drips raw fuel out of the intake manifold, down through the carburetor and into the carburetor air box. So far, this is not a severe fire hazard, and this situation is the one where continuing to crank may put the fire out; but likely as not, the pilot has the throttle just-cracked. This means the carburetor butterfly is closed, or nearly so, and that means very little suction can be developed through the carburetor. Therefore, contrary to a pilot's normal inclination, experts advise opening the throttle to about the 1,000-1,500 rpm range while continuing to crank.

Our favorite mechanic also advises that overpriming is only part of the reason for the fire. The source of ignition, often a misfiring spark plug, is the other half of the equation. Faulty ignition generally doesn't happen when a battery is fully charged, but rather, after it has been nearly exhausted. This also happens to be about the time the pilot has primed for the third or fourth time, creating the conditions for the fire. The mechanic also points out that the fire begins with an unforgettable "bloop" sound and the prop stopping abruptly. That's the signal to keep cranking, at least with the textbook- case carburetor fire.

It is well to remember the reason for doing this is to deal with the fire, not to get the engine running and continue the trip. The engine may actually start at this point, and the fire may be out, but problems are not over. The carburetor fire may have frizzled the air filter, fried some engine wires or hoses, and we know one engine overhauler who believes he's seen evidence of carburetor fires severely warping the carb's primary venturi. No pilot can guarantee that the airplane is undamaged. The solution is to shut down and have a mechanic inspect the engine before further flight.

But the fire may not be the textbook kind. Sometimes, the fuel doesn't stop at the carburetor air box. It drips down onto the lower cowl, and more often than might be imagined, makes a puddle on the ground underneath the airplane. If all this ignites—and it can—no amount of cranking on the engine will do any good. It is time to evacuate and extinguish.

If the pilot anticipates this problem, he may do a lot of good by quickly shoving the airplane back out of the burning puddle, or having a lineman or competent passenger do it. This can be done with greatest safety by pushing on the tail of the aircraft.

It may be obvious, but the pilot should shut off the fuel selector, pull the mixture and throttle back, turn off the mags and master switch and grab the fire extinguisher as he leaves the airplane.

Pilots operating fuel-injected engines should change their thinking about engine fires. If a fire does arise, it is not in the carburetor (there is none) and cranking will do no good. Thus, the answer is to secure the airplane, evacuate and extinguish.

And of course, the bottom line in safety on cold-weather starts is to have a lineman with a king-sized extinguisher standing by. In military aviation, the ubiquitous "fireguard" position is filled, summer and winter, for every engine start. Scouting up somebody to do the job may be inconvenient and often unnecessary, but it sure beats having to stand by helplessly and watch an airplane go up in smoke.

Learning from Alaskans

Word association test: "Alaska." If you countered that with "cold," you are probably not alone; almost everyone thinks that winter and Alaska go together. For the most part, that's true—after all, our 49th state is way up north, but the Alaskan climate is not all frigid. For a pilot, cold weather operations are certainly the feature, but not the entire menu of Alaskan flying.

Each year several hundred pilots from the continental U.S. heed that alluring "call of the wild" and make the long cross-country flight up through western Canada to Alaska. During the booming heydays of the oil pipeline construction, the prospect of well-paying jobs stimulated this aerial migration, but lately, business growth has slowed, so now most flying visitors are simply tourists determined to experience the grandeur of America's last great frontier.

Before a person flies in Alaska, there are quite a few things he should know. Alaska's air-safety record is about twice as bad as the rest of the U.S.'s. Let's examine some of the major causes and probe for some of the cures.

Terrain

First-time visitors to the state are stunned by its enormous size and geographical diversity. Its 586,400 square miles make it more than twice the size of Texas. Its total population, however, is only about 400,000, of whom nearly 80,000 are native Indians and Eskimos. Due to its scant population and challenging terrain, Alaska has virtually no roads outside its few largest towns. Indeed, Juneau, the capital city, is accessible only by plane or boat, and all the towns and villages in the western half of the state are equally isolated.

This makes Alaska dependent on air transportation to an extent that most Americans from the "Lower 48" would find difficult to comprehend. Traveling by air is as ordinary and routine to Alaskans as traveling by car is to Californians. Food, medicine and all other necessities of life are brought by air to virtually all the smaller communities. In fact, even the kids on high school athletic teams are taken from game to game by bush pilots flying lightplanes. Since aviation is so necessary to Alaska, it's no surprise to find that pilots are a much larger relative share of the population than in the rest of the U.S. There are about 10,000 pilots and 7,000 airplanes in Alaska. This is about eight times as many pilots, and 16 times as many planes, per unit population, as elsewhere in the States. Likewise, the average number of hours flown per pilot is about 16 times that of other American pilots.

Not surprisingly, considering the law of averages alone, this vast amount of flying generates a higher level of accidents. But even after accounting for exposure, Alaskan pilots have an accident rate that is about double that of the rest of the country. Alaska has about 23 accidents per 100,000 flight hours, versus about 10 accidents for the rest of the U.S. Likewise, Alaskans have close to three fatal accidents per 100,000 hours, versus roughly two for other Americans.

Safety is further complicated by a variety of unique terrain and weather factors. The topography varies enormously; vistas of flat, water-logged tundra give way to awesome mountain ranges and areas of active volcanos. At 20,320 feet, Mt. McKinley in the Alaskan Range is the highest peak, but 18 other mountains reach above 14,000 feet, and flight routes through the passes are frequently treacherous due to high winds and low ceilings.

The arctic area of Alaska north of the Brooks Range gets very little moisture (although it suffers snow "whiteouts" and 24-hour darkness during winter months). But down south in the coastal region around Ketchikan, more than 200 inches of precipitation fall each year, virtually guaranteeing severe icing problems in all but the warmest summer months.

Temperatures vary widely within the state, especially in the interior around Fairbanks, where summertime highs can reach almost 100 degrees Fahrenheit and winter lows occasionally plunge to a mind-numbing 70 degrees below zero. While most pilots are familiar with density altitude problems in high temperatures, another variation occurs in extreme cold: at minus 40, an aircraft engine will put out some 30 percent too much power at full throttle, and Vmc for twins will go up accordingly if a pilot unwittingly overboosts his engines on takeoff. Also, engine pre-heat is an absolute necessity in winter, and most Alaskan planes are rigged with Tanis plug-in heaters plus padded engine blankets.

Seasonality

Some of Alaska's rather dismal safety record can be correlated with the time of year. FAA data shows sharper peaks and valleys on graphs of Alaska's monthly accidents, in comparison to graphs of other U.S. accidents. Alaska's accidents stay relatively level during the early winter months. An initial upward trend in March and April could be due to increased crashes of ski-equipped planes on lakes that are just beginning to thaw. A major upward spike in June and July comes in a season of very active fish-spotting and fish-haul flying (often at over-gross weights).

But the highest jump occurs in the August and September, which is the time of greatest lightplane activity and the prime hunting season. Alaskan pilots have nicknamed a type of accident occurring in this period as the "moose hunter's stall."

Air Taxi Record

Aviation officials often find it easier to analyze the safety record of the air taxi/commuter segment because the Part 135 scene is under greater scrutiny and accountability than most Part 91 operations. This has a special validity in Alaska, since it's estimated that air taxi pilots fly about 45 percent of the total hours flown in the state (versus only about 10 percent elsewhere in the country). A preponderance of the flying is done in smaller single-engine airplanes, such as Super Cubs, Cessna 185s or 206s, or DeHavilland Beavers. (Significantly, the major Part 121 airlines operating in Alaska do not have a radically greater accident rate than other U.S. airlines, presumably because they operate on IFR flight plans and land at only the best of Alaska's many airstrips.) In any event, a look at Part 135 operations may disclose some whys and wherefores of air crashes in our northernmost state.

NTSB Special Study

In 1980 the NTSB published a special study, "Air Taxi Safety in Alaska," based on extensive interviews with both operators and officials around the state and a careful scrutiny of accident statistics for the five years 1974-78. During this period, NTSB found the rate of non-fatal air taxi accidents per 100,000 hours was five times higher in Alaska than in the rest of the United States, and the fatal accident rate was double.

As mentioned before, Alaskan figures show a higher rate in the summer months and lower in winter, compared with the rest of the country, due to the relative activity levels, especially of float-plane operations. Also, while Alaska shows a lower relative rate of in-flight and mechanical failure accidents, and an identical percentage of landing phase accidents, the state has a much higher rate of accidents in the takeoff phase (32 percent versus 18 for the Lower 48). No doubt this is due to the deplorable condition of many of the short, ill-maintained bush strips and to the well-known cavalier attitude of Alaskan pilots about legal gross weight limitations ("If I can fit it in or tie it on, I can yank it off the ground").

For instance, there was the (mighty shaky) takeoff of a two-seat Super Cub near Fairbanks with six people aboard (wives and kids atop the laps of their derring-do husbands). Also, the crash of a Cessna 185 near Shungnak in a VFR landing short of the runway killed seven occupants and injured two more—in a plane that seats four comfortably and six in a real pinch.

The NTSB study concluded that there are three main causes for the high rate of air taxi accidents in Alaska: (1) The "bush syndrome," (2) inadequate airfield facilities and communications of airfield conditions, (3) inadequate weather observations or communications and insufficient navigational aids. It's obvious that these factors would affect most Alaskan flying, not just air taxi pilots. We feel the lack of navaids is so significant that it probably should have been itemized separately. Let's take the factors individually.

Bush Syndrome

The average Alaskan air taxi pilot appears to be highly qualified, especially since most operators (goaded by their insurance companies) require pilots to have at least 2,000 total hours and 500 hours of Alaskan time or equivalent special experience. Statistics support these figures, since 80 percent of the Alaskan air taxi pilots involved in accidents had more than 2,000 total hours and 100 in type. Also, 80 percent had instrument ratings (although maybe not legally current) and 20 percent had ATP licenses. Why, then, is the pilot listed as a prime cause or factor in 86 percent of Alaskan crashes?

Descriptions of the "bush syndrome," according to the NTSB, "range from a pilot's casual acceptance of the unique hazards of flying in Alaska to a pilot's willingness to take unwarranted risks to complete a flight." Unfortunately, it is common for Alaskan bush pilots to attempt VFR flights in extremely poor weather, or to land in places that are, at best, only marginally suitable for the task.

Legends abound of "old, bold" pilots who have dared greatly, tempted fate often, and survived numerous accidents to tell their tales...and many of today's pilots subconsciously feel compelled to test themselves against this aura of intrepid invincibility. As the NTSB reported, "The bush syndrome goes beyond the realm of poor judgment compounded by pressures and into the area of unreasonable risk-taking." Taking chances is often considered a standard part of flying in Alaska, by the pilots and even by the passengers, who frequently demand to be flown to their destinations regardless of darkness and weather.

Indeed, passengers turned down by one operator will usually amble right over to the next operator on the field, and economic necessity being a powerful force, will often find some pilot bold enough to risk the worst odds. (And there's no telling how much "midnight air taxi" flying is being done, by pilots not associated with a licensed operator.)

Examples abound. For instance, the NTSB cited a case where two passengers at McGrath sought to be flown to Tatalina. The first operator they approached refused, since the Tatalina strip was unlighted and it was a very dark night. However, a pilot for another operator agreed to take them (supposedly without the permission of his boss). Immediately after takeoff the Piper PA-32 entered a steep right bank and descended into the trees about a mile from the McGrath strip. Investigation revealed that the pilot had previously been involved in three other accidents and—most germane to the fatal flight—didn't even have the instrument rating required for a night Part 135 flight. This was a clear case of "bush pilot" disregard for the rules plus the "bush passenger" attitude of wanting to fly under any conditions.

Similarly, a Cessna 206 based in Anchorage tried to depart from an Indian village strip west of Anchorage across the bay. It was about 4:30 p.m.—some two hours after total darkness had arrived—and the overcast ceiling was estimated at a scant 400 feet. Undaunted, the pilot and his three passengers managed to get airborne and then promptly made a descending left cartwheel into the inky waters of the Knik Arm. Since a 20-knot tide was flowing out to sea, no trace of the plane or passengers was found. Spatial disorientation and failure to transition properly to the gauges in the total absence of outside visual clues, plus VFR flight foolishly conducted into IFR conditions beyond the pilot's capabilities, are all too common in Alaskan flying.

A final, somewhat humorous example of the "bush syndrome" and its pervasiveness: An Anchorage operator confidently hired a new pilot with an ATP certificate and more than 10,000 hours of experience with a major commercial airline, only to hear several passengers complain that the ex-captain was "obviously a lousy pilot." Finally, concern prompted the operator to quiz one of the complaining passengers, who elaborated: "This guy can't be a good pilot—he flies everywhere with a map on his lap, so he obviously doesn't know where he's going!"

Facilities

The NTSB found "inadequate airfield facilities and communication of field conditions" a major problem area in Alaska. For instance, 13 percent of air taxi accidents are attributed to the pilot's selecting terrain unsuitable for landing, and 19 percent of non-fatal accidents involve collisions with obstacles on takeoff or landing.

FAA figures for 1978 showed Alaska had 756 airport facilities, including 520 for landplanes, 194 for seaplanes and 42 for helicopters. Most of these are infrequently used and ill-maintained even though 537 are publicly owned. The state Department of Transportation and Public Facilities (DOT/PF) claims that it actively attempts to maintain 211 landplane airstrips (of which only 38 are paved), but maintenance and snow-plowing are contracted out to local residents who have not proved to be entirely reliable at the job. Of these 211 airports, 154 have no lighting, and the majority are too short, too narrow and too poorly surfaced to be considered reasonably safe, especially for multi-engine operations.

While gravel is a preferred runway material in rural Alaska, it is expensive and difficult to transport by air, so at least half of all bush strips are dirt-surfaced. They become treacherous during rains or at the spring break-up when the tundra thaws and the snow melts. At these times landing aircraft get coated with a layer of tenacious mud, and takeoff runs can easily exceed the available field length.

As if all these problems aren't challenge enough, Alaskan bush pilots—professionals and eager-beavers alike—frequently attempt fixed-wing landings at off-airport sites that would terrify a Vietnam veteran helicopter pilot. High on the list of these super-STOL spots are a variety of log-strewn beaches and rock-studded sandbars dotting favorite bear-hunting coastal areas or virgin fishing streams.

Needless to say, the mortality rate on landing gear is crunchingly high. (One well-known Anchorage pilot claims a solution of sorts: each summer he bolts a brand-new pair of metal wheel-skis to his Super Cub, then blithely spends the next three months landing on river bars so rocky that, without the skis, the landing gear would instantly be torn off.)

Further, information on present runway conditions is often non-existent, based on hearsay, or even baldly fallacious in occasional cases where back-country villagers let their desire for a prompt air delivery overcome their responsibility to report accurate local airport conditions. It takes a dice-roller to operate into these areas where scant, if any, runway or weather reports can be obtained.

Weather/Navaids

Which brings us to the third NTSB causal area, "inadequate weather observations or communications and insufficient navaids." In addition to the sporadic reliability of native weather observers hired by the NWS, many of the weather observers in the bush areas are hired by specific air taxi operators who, for competitive reasons, don't share weather information with either the FAA or other operators.

Another aspect of the problem is that whenever the FAA tries to crack down on air taxi operators going VFR into IFR conditions, the pilots are quick to start turning in phony PIREPs to protect themselves from a violation. Under a waiver, the legal VFR minimums between Nome and Kotsebue are 500 feet and two miles. In recent years "600 and two" became something of a joke as a PIREP in that area when an FAA inspector began issuing $1,000 fines to pilots foolish enough to report the real weather they were braving.

Several types of automated weather reporting stations have been installed in various parts of Alaska, but reliability is doubtful, and pilots almost universally distrust them. Also, scanning TV cameras were installed by FAA on the airport at Unalakleet and in the waterway narrows at Valdez, with the pictures transmitted to the Nome and Cordova FSSs; these also have occasional reliability problems.

Navigation

It's amazing to discover that the entire state of Alaska, huge as it is, contains only 54 NDBs, seven VORs (four are VOR-DMEs) and 26 VORTACs in the FAA-operated system.

Numerous low-power NDBs have been privately installed at various strips by airline operators and others, but these are often not charted and operate sporadically. Alaskan bush pilots love their NDBs because they provide a useful signal at low altitudes. VOR reception is seriously degraded below 10,000 feet in many areas due to terrain.

Considering this paucity of navaids and instrument approaches in out-back Alaska, it's not surprising that most bush pilots shun IFR flying like the plague—relying instead on all manner of death-defying (and frequently illegal) VFR tricks. No pilot, even the hairiest-chested of the Alaskan species, likes to continually push his VFR luck in IFR weather, but often the economic pressures force some operators to tacitly condone it, and the pleadings of ignorant passengers sometimes sway a pilot's judgment. (Along coastal areas of southeast Alaska, FAA recognized this situation and granted local seaplane operators a waiver to fly VFR in "300 feet and two miles" over the water.)

In a survey of some 87 air taxi operators, the Alaskan Aviation Safety Foundation discovered that 62 percent did not participate in any kind of recurrency training or FAA safety seminars in the past year. This "you can't teach me anything" attitude is yet another aspect of the deadly "bush syndrome."

With neither a regular program of instrument proficiency training or the routine opportunity to practice honest IFR flying, Alaska's bush pilots cannot be expected to make significant reductions in their alarmingly high accident rates. In the 1974-78 period, Alaskan air taxi pilots had 75 accidents attributed directly to "initiated/continued VFR into adverse weather" and/or "spatial disorientation," while the entire rest of the U.S. recorded only 74 such accidents.

Obviously, no one simple answer exists to solve Alaska's air safety problem. However, if any Lower 48 state, like California or Texas, managed to remotely approach Alaska's five-year total of 1,251 accidents at a rate of more than 23 per 100,000 flight hours, you can bet the FAA would react with the same kind of alacrity it showed after the Cerritos mid-air collision.

Pilot Programs

What is being done to deal with the pilot—the 86 percent factor in the accident equation? FAA and some private groups do have programs to directly reduce accidents by changing the habits of the pilots through training and education.

One item we gleaned from an FAA seminar could easily save the lives of perhaps half a dozen people in Alaska during the summer season. An FAA test pilot related that while flying a Super Cub in calm air with full flaps and circling in a 60-degree bank, he had repeatedly flown into a vertical component area of his own wake turbulence which each time caused an uncontrollable stall with an immediate loss of at least 500 feet. This may well be the technical reason behind the "moose-hunter's stall."

Researchers looking at pilot attitudes were surprised to discover that no matter which part of Alaska they were in, local pilots invariably rated their own turf the least dangerous in the state. North Slope pilots could comfortably brave whiteouts, but were terrified of the "high traffic" areas around Anchorage. Pilots in the Bethel area dreaded the fog and low ceilings of Juneau, while those from the Southeast were apprehensive about flying windy mountain passes at high altitudes.

Such a discovery leads to a final conclusion: Pilots from the Lower 48 who are reasonably proficient in their flying skills and—more important—who are professional in their attitude toward aviation, need have no great fears about flying around Alaska in their own planes. It would be helpful but not essential to have an instrument rating. However, seaplane pilots from Florida, Louisiana or Michigan will feel at ease over the bays and beaches of southeastern Alaska. Pilots from the Rocky Mountain states won't feel out of place nosing around the Alaskan Range near magnificent Mt. McKinley. And fliers from the Pacific Northwest will feel right at home in Alaska's wet summertime weather.

There are enough wide and well-groomed runways so that, with planning, one doesn't have to risk a new A36 Bonanza or Cessna Crusader on any dubious beach or gravel bar. One should be sure his Continental U.S. insurance policy will cover him in Alaska, and above all, not let the "bush syndrome" start to cloud his better judgment. Experiencing Alaska by air is one of the greatest thrills any pilot can ever have.

Keep the "Alaska experience" in mind as we consider the effects of cold weather on airplane operations in general.

Narrow Runways, High Edges

Cold weather almost always comes equipped with frozen precipitation, and conscientious airport operators do their best to keep runways clear of snow and ice. In the very act of cleaning a surface so that pilots can do their thing, it's not unusual for something less than the full width of the runway to get plowed, and the snow is frequently heaped up alongside, creating yet another hazard to cold weather operations.

The experiences of one low-time private pilot illustrate just the sort of trouble Old Man Winter can cause; this pilot had the misfortune of running his Cessna 172N Skyhawk into a snowbank—twice.

The 34-year-old pilot had logged a total of 124 hours before the accident, of which 69 were in the Skyhawk. One February day, he set out on a cross-country flight from Glens Falls, New York to Rochester, with an stop at Duanesburg. He obtained a weather briefing indicating that the weather at Rochester was deteriorating, so he elected to simply make a round trip to Duanesburg.

He took off at 4:30 p.m., and was soon over Duanesburg. A call on unicom for advisories elicited no response, so he flew over the runway to check its condition and to take a look at the wind sock. Runway 28 at the snow-covered airport was favored, and the pilot could clearly see the runway asphalt, indicating that it had been plowed. A normal landing was made, and the airplane had decelerated to about 15 knots when the left main wheel ran into the snow at the edge of the runway. The Cessna turned into the snow, tipped over to the right and hit the frozen snowbank with its right wing tip.

The pilot secured the airplane's systems, and he and his passenger got out. Though the left main wheel and nose wheel were in the snowbank, they were able to pull the Skyhawk out and push it to the ramp, where they inspected it for damage. The plastic wing tip was broken; there was a scratch on the underside of the right wing near the tip; and there was a dent in the cowling.

The pilot called the FBO that rented him the airplane, and personnel there suggested he perform an extensive walk-around check, a run-up to 2,000 rpm and a taxi around the airport to see if there was any other damage. He did all that and found all systems normal. After another discussion with the FBO, he decided it would be safe to take off.

The pilot did a second thorough preflight check and run-up but still found nothing wrong. He taxied out, lined up on the runway centerline and began to roll. At rotation speed, he quickly checked the engine instruments and noted that all was still well.

He increased back pressure to lift off, and just as the airplane was leaving the ground, the left main wheel again struck the snow on the edge of the runway. The left wing hit the snow, and the airplane turned to the left. The right wing came down and hit the runway, and the airplane's nose went into the snowbank. The Cessna came to rest upright, and the pilot and passenger were able to shovel the snow from the wheels and push the airplane to the ramp once again.

A portion of the pilot's written statement provides insight into his inability to keep the Skyhawk out of the snow. "The runway is 50 feet wide. I had landed there previously and knew the surface to be good," he wrote. "On my flyby, it appeared clear and dry. My assumption was that the runway was plowed to its lateral margins. Not until landing did I find it was only plowed to a width of 24 feet. My level of experience did not allow for a safe landing in that width.

"I believed that my control on takeoff would be adequate to maintain the runway center and take off safely. I do not know why I contacted the snow; either a gust of wind or inadequate rudder compensation.

"In this case again my level of experience did not allow for a safe takeoff. I relied upon information from another source which I felt had more experience than I, but they were not at the airport, and I may not have made the conditions clear enough for them to make a fair judgment.

"This accident occurred because of a poor judgment made by the pilot to land and take off at an airport with an inadequately plowed runway. The level of experience of the pilot did not allow for recognition of the unsafe width of the runway from the air.

"I would recommend that airports that do not properly clear the runway of snow be so listed in the Airport/Facility Directory, just as those with trees and powerlines are listed. Secondly, I would stress to pilots in training the dangers of close snowbanks and how to recognize them. In winter flying, minimums should be set for the size and condition of the airports to be used, and these guidelines should be adhered to."

Don't Believe Everything You Hear

Advisories on unicom from small airports are not always the most reliable; and if no one answers the call for information, a pilot has no recourse but to make a visual inspection and decide for himself. Even that is sometimes not enough, especially in winter, when things are not always what they seem.

As a case in point, a 35-year-old, 763-hour pilot and his passenger escaped without injury when he landed his damaged airplane, following an encounter with an icy runway.

The VFR flight had departed Republic Airport at Farmingdale, New York, that morning and was bound for Rutland, Vermont. While en route, the pilot chose to land at Mount Snow Airport in West Dover, Vermont instead. He was receiving VFR advisories from Boston Center, and he requested airport information from them. He was told that the airport was open, with no hazards reported.

The pilot canceled advisory service and attempted to contact Mount Snow on the unicom frequency, but got no response. On arrival at the airport, he made some low passes to check the runway for snow and obstructions, but saw none, so he elected to land. A normal approach and touchdown were made, but the Piper encountered a coating of clear ice, which the pilot said covered the entire runway. The airplane began to skid, and the pilot tried to abort the landing and get airborne again. Unfortunately, the airplane was no longer aligned with the runway, and went off the left side, where the left main gear struck some rocks. It sheared off, damaging both the left flap and left aileron. The Piper had attained flying speed, and the pilot continued the takeoff.

Once airborne, he climbed to 3,500 feet and radioed Bradley Approach. He was able to reach them, but their replies had to be relayed through a passing aircraft. Bradley told the pilot to contact Albany approach, but he was unsuccessful. Ultimately, he was able to contact Boston Center. The pilot declared an emergency and requested radar vectors to the nearest airport, which was Turners Falls. Upon landing, the airplane continued off the end of the runway, sustaining severe damage.

In some parts of the country, that's called "black ice"—a condition in which clear ice forms on an otherwise clear roadway or runway, and especially when you're looking straight down at it, there appears to be nothing but clear asphalt. But wait until touchdown! You may be in for the surprise of your life.

An icy runway is bad enough at any time, but it's particularly hazardous when a pilot isn't aware of the condition; the sudden realization that you're in command of a vehicle that isn't moving fast enough to fly, and too fast to get stopped is one of the most helpless feelings in the world. Airport advisories can be a great service at uncontrolled fields to help make a decision to land or go somewhere else. But pilots should always be at least a little leery about what the unicom operator tells them. They should, so to speak, take what's said with a grain of salt.

The pilot of a Cessna 340 likely wishes he had taken that grain of salt and spread it on the runway at Frankfort, Illinois before he attempted to land there one wintry day. The pilot received minor injuries in the accident, but his passengers escaped unharmed when the twin slid off the icy runway during landing.

The pilot held an ATP certificate, and had logged some 356 of his 3,858 total hours in the Cessna 340 he was flying. The flight from Lexington to Frankfort was uneventful. Weather along the route offered some hints of the future, though;

witness a SIGMET for freezing rain in the Frankfort area. Mindful of the icing potential, the pilot requested vectors to the final approach.

The approach went well, with the airplane breaking out more then 200 feet above the MDA. The Cessna had picked up some ice, though, and the windshield was now coated with it. However, the passenger in the right seat spotted the runway to the right, and the pilot swung around, circling to land. As he circled back towards the runway, the pilot called Unicom for runway information. A voice came back over the radio telling him the runway was "slippery" and that he should be careful.

The Cessna crossed the fence at 90 knots, touched down, and the pilot started braking immediately. He later recalled that, while the braking action wasn't great, it was good enough along that portion of the pavement that he felt he could get the airplane stopped on the runway...until he encountered the ice which covered most of the runway. Braking action dropped to nothing and the Cessna simply slid along. It was too late now to go around. The pilot started thinking fast. He decided to try something a little desperate. As he later wrote in his accident report, "I tried to slow the aircraft by putting one wheel in the snow" along the side of the runway. That approach didn't seem too promising as directional control was too difficult. He pulled out of the snow, back onto the icy pavement.

Time and runway were running out fast. He could see the end of the runway, and a ditch just past it. Hoping to avoid wiping out the nosegear, he pulled the yoke all the way back. The aircraft bounded over a small ditch, across a road, and across another, larger ditch. It finally came to a halt about 100 feet later in the middle of a field off the end of the runway.

The pilot shut everything down and evacuated the passengers. The Cessna was considered a total loss.

The pilot felt he had been short-changed on his runway advisory. In the space on the accident report where pilots are requested to offer advice on avoiding such an accident he wrote, "This accident could have been avoided had I been told there was nothing but solid ice on the runway, in which case I would not even have attempted a landing." The NTSB didn't see it that way. In its own peculiar language, the Board stated the probable cause of the accident was, "Weather

evaluation—not understood—Pilot in Command." The lack
of an accurate evaluation of the runway condition by the
Unicom operator was considered a factor in the accident, but
not a cause.

There's an old hangar-flying story about icy runways which we offer
mostly for amusement, since there's probably no way to prove its
authenticity, and we certainly don't recommend this procedure
except as the very last resort. It has to do with a four-engine bomber
that touched down on a long runway completely covered with ice.

When the pilot realized there was absolutely no braking action,
and that he hadn't nearly enough runway left to get back into the air,
he reversed the two left engines, waited until the airplane had swung
a full 180 degrees, then applied full power to all four, effectively
generating a huge amount of "reverse thrust," and bringing the
bomber to a safe stop before sliding to the end of the pavement.

Quick thinking, logical, and rational...and it worked! But the
potential hazards of a trick like this are monumental. In most cases
of uncontrolled sliding, it's probably best to shut down systems to
reduce the possibility of a fire, and take your chances with a
controlled crash straight ahead. Better yet, make *certain* you know
the condition of the surface on which you're about to plant your
airplane's wheels. When in doubt, go somewhere else.

Velocity, Mass, and Ice...Bad Combination

The wintertime no-way-to-get-stopped problem is not unique to
small airplanes; if anything, the heavy iron is more susceptible
because of the increased momentum. More weight, more speed, and
no braking adds up to monumental increases in stopping distances.

For example, a Falcon captain and his copilot were both
seriously injured when their jet ran off the end of a slippery
runway while landing. The flight was a Part 135 cargo trip
from Memphis, Tennessee to Binghamton, New York, and
resulted in the complete destruction of the airplane.

The captain reported that he received a weather briefing
from the Jackson, Mississippi, Flight Service Station before
departing, and at that time, he was told the weather at
Binghamton was good, but there was patchy ice on the
runway. He did not think this would present any problems.

The Falcon departed Memphis at 4:35 a.m. The en route

portion of the flight was uneventful, and the flight arrived in the Binghampton area at about 7:15. The captain stated that approach control reported braking action on the runway was poor. Also, ATIS information indicated that a vehicle had reported the braking action as poor. However, the captain still felt this would present no problems.

The Falcon touched down on runway 16 at 125 knots—a normal touchdown speed. The copilot applied the brakes, but the captain soon noticed that the Falcon was not slowing down. In seconds it became apparent that the aircraft could not go around and it would have to be stopped on the runway.

The captain took over. The Falcon did not have thrust reversers, but was equipped with a drag chute, which the captain deployed, but it streamered and did not open. With the end of the runway coming up, he tried to steer the Falcon off to the right to avoid the approach light stanchions at the end of the pavement. However, the slick runway provided no traction and the airplane merely drifted to the right.

The Falcon ran off the end of the runway, and traveled 115 feet before encountering a 62-foot dropoff. At this point it became airborne and flew down the slope, striking some small trees before crashing at the bottom. In his statement to investigators, the captain complained of not getting a braking action update before landing. "Had I been advised of nil braking action, I never would have landed," he wrote.

From One Extreme to the Other

A Falcon Jet is possessed of a great amount of power, which doesn't exempt it and its ilk from the perils of winter; even on the other end of the power scale, a sailplane—completely powerless—can get its pilot into wintertime trouble as well. In this case, you'll see the involvement of a number of factors, not the least of which are those precipitated by cold weather. The chapter of the *Airman's Information Manual* titled "Medical Facts for Pilots" is a cool, dry piece of reading. It is up to pilots to use their imaginations (or the experiences of others) to breathe life into the story.

One pilot whose practical experience covered several sections of this chapter on cold-weather operations in one flight was in command of a Schweizer 1-34 glider which crashed at the Air Force Academy Field in Colorado Springs, Colorado.

The 31-year-old airman had been a Marine in Vietnam and sustained extensive shrapnel injuries when struck by artillery fire. Because of chronic pain from these injuries, he routinely took several common drugs. During the 24 hours prior to his flight, he took doses of Phenergan, Darvon and Talwin. (A pharmacist we consulted said these are an antihistamine and two pain-killers, respectively.) The airman was under the impression these medications were in the same order of effectiveness as aspirin, and contained no sedatives. (The pharmacist agreed that they are not intended to have a sedative effect, but also pointed out that this may be a side effect, as specified in the medical explanatory notes supplied with the drugs.)

The pilot set out on a cold day from the Black Forest Glider Port with the intention of setting a personal altitude record in the 1-34. This is a natural step in a soaring pilot's career; he had some 401 powered-aircraft hours, as well as 75 hours in gliders. He was towed to a release altitude of 15,500 feet and dropped to 14,500 before getting set up to climb in the mountain wave just east of Pike's Peak. He said it took him the next 3-1/2 hours to climb to 27,000 feet, most of that time being spent in the last 3,000 feet of ascent.

Despite his heavy clothing and gloves, it was very cold in the glider's cockpit, and the canopy built up a layer of heavy frost on the inside from his breathing. He was able to keep a section of the canopy clear on both the left and right forward positions (approximately 18 by 12 inches) with his gloves, he later related to authorities.

An Air Force investigator who interviewed the pilot related this part of the flight as follows: "After approximately three hours of flight while at 26,700 feet MSL, he noticed that his airspeed was fluctuating more than normal, and he suspected he might be hypoxic. (The pilot) said that the oxygen mask didn't fit well, and in order to get a good seal, he had to lower his jaw. He suspected that with the extreme cold he might have tightened his jaw and allowed a leak.

Upon noticing his apparent hypoxia, he leaned forward to adjust the oxygen regulator. When he leaned forward, he felt he was getting vertigo and decided to start a descent. The vertigo probably also was aggravated by the cloud conditions. He had started his ascent with scattered cloud cover and bases at 18,000 feet. After being aloft and above the clouds for so long, now he noticed the cover was more broken than scattered, and he found himself circling down through an opening about two miles wide and five miles long. "Plus, the ground directly below, that was still clearly visible, was entirely covered with snow," he told investigators.

He got to cloud base at about 12,500 feet and as he headed for the glider port, the bases descended to 10,500 (terrain in the area is about 6,000 to 7,500 MSL). He flew north and concedes that he went through the "very bottom wisps" of the clouds. In short order, the outside of his canopy was nearly covered with ice. He came in sight of the Air Force Academy field and headed for Black Forest, which lies about eight miles to the east. But, he said, he went about 12 miles east and still was unable to visually identify the field. So he turned west and headed for the Academy field.

Impediments to safe flight were piling up. At some point, the radio "malfunctioned." He later said he was unaware that the transmit portion was working or he would have used it. This point became moot, since, he explained, "I had intended to inform the Academy tower of my approach; however, my hands were so cold that when I attempted to unfold the paper on which I had the tower frequency, I dropped it in a position from which I was unable to recover it."

He said that when he arrived at the field he still had sufficient altitude for a normal left pattern to runway 34L (he noticed operations on 34R). But as he turned downwind, he saw an aircraft do a touch-and-go on 34L. "It was at this point, with restricted visibility, no radio contact, and no light signals from the tower, that I decided not to risk being involved in or causing a mid-air collision." He continued, "I had noticed as I crossed the boundary of the airfield from the east that there was a service road. It was not until I had completed my turn and was almost on the service road that I saw the fence ahead of me. At that point, I attempted to force the aircraft down onto the road and groundloop it in order to try to avoid the fence."

The force of initial impact so stunned him that there was little he could do to control the aircraft. It bounced 50 feet into the air and traveled forward about 300 feet, striking the fence. The pilot had back injuries, but survived.

The pilot conceded that he "certainly was dazed and a little confused immediately after the accident," but apparently felt he was well in command of his faculties before it. NTSB apparently disagreed, and cited "physical impairment" among factors in the probable cause.

Perhaps it would be helpful to review the pertinent sections of the *Airman's Information Manual,* keeping in mind that it was cold weather that started this whole operation downhill:

Medication

Pilot performance can be seriously degraded by both prescribed and over-the-counter medications, as well as by the medical conditions for which they are taken. Many medications, such as tranquilizers, sedatives, strong pain relievers, and cough-suppressant preparations, have primary effects that may impair judgment, memory, alertness, coordination, vision, and the ability to make calculations. Others, such as antihistamines, blood pressure drugs, muscle relaxants, and agents to control diarrhea and motion sickness, have side effects that may impair the same critical functions. Any medication that depresses the nervous system, such as a sedative, tranquilizer or antihistamine, can make a pilot much more susceptible to hypoxia.

Hypoxia

The altitude at which significant effects of hypoxia occur can be lowered by a number of factors. Carbon monoxide inhaled in smoking or from exhaust fumes, lowered hemoglobin (anemia) and certain medications can reduce the oxygen- carrying capacity of the blood to the degree that the amount of oxygen provided to the body tissues will already be equivalent to a cabin pressure altitude of several thousand feet. Small amounts of alcohol and low doses of certain drugs, such as antihistamines, tranquilizers, sedatives and analgesics can, through their depressant actions, render the brain much more susceptible to hypoxia. Extreme heat and cold, fever, and anxiety increase the body's demand for oxygen, and hence its susceptibility to hypoxia.

Illusions in Flight

Coriolis illusion—an abrupt head movement in a constant-rate turn that has ceased stimulating the balance organs—can create the illusion of rotation or movement in an entirely different plane. The disoriented pilot will maneuver the aircraft into a dangerous attitude in an attempt to stop rotation. This most overwhelming of all illusions in flight may be prevented by not making sudden, extreme head movements, particularly while making prolonged, constant-rate turns under IFR conditions.

Cold Weather Affects Flight Instruments, Too

When the mercury plummets, all things mechanical are affected. Pilots need to be aware that some instrument indications tell terrible lies in a cold environment, as this pilot discovered.

The 56-year-old pilot was on his way from Duluth to Fergus Falls, Minnesota. His home was only a block from Battle Creek Airport, which he probably would have preferred, but that field was closed for the winter. So on this January evening, he intended to go the extra 18 miles and land at Fergus Falls.

But first, he told investigators, he wanted to make a pass over his house to let his wife know he had arrived. This was accomplished, and he and his passenger headed on toward their destination. "My mind was on my family and two grandsons who were visiting that I was to have dinner with and my thoughts were on them instead of flying," he later told investigators. After the low pass over his house, he said, "I climbed to what I thought was a safe altitude over Silver Lake and proceeded over open rolling farmland."

There are two ways of viewing the ensuing accident— from the ground and from the air. We'll do both: A man and wife who happened to be student pilots were in a car just leaving their driveway onto the county road. "We observed an aircraft approaching from the east with its landing lights on at an altitude of approximately 100 feet. Thinking it was in trouble, we slowed down," they told NTSB. "It continued to descend and came directly towards us. At this point we realized we were in danger of getting hit and attempted to accelerate. Our vehicle was on ice and would not respond. The plane hit the power lines slightly to our rear at an altitude of approximately 30 feet. There was a bright flash as the wires parted. The plane gained enough altitude to clear the tree-covered hill to the west. We then lost sight of its lights." According to the pilot, "An automobile was coming out of a driveway with lights on about one-quarter mile away and it was then I realized I was too low, at which time I pulled up, striking the powerline at the same time. I was able to keep the plane in the air and proceeded to climb slowly out over north Turtle Lake and on to Fergus Falls Airport even though the windshield was knocked out and the temperature was -15 degrees."

The pilot made it to a safe landing at Fergus Falls. The Piper Cherokee 180 had parted two high-voltage powerlines and nicked a third. The collision had broken off the spinner, notched both propeller blades, broke out both windshield sections, tore away the comm antennas, cut off the upper half of the vertical stabilizer and tore off the rudder. But it flew!

In their report on the accident, investigators noted that the pilot had set his altimeter upon leaving Duluth and had not changed it. The airplane had gone from an area of low pressure to an area of high pressure, which would cause the altimeter to read lower than the actual altitude. However, because the plane also was in an extremely cold area, the altimeter would have another error that would cause it to read higher than the actual altitude. The two errors were not quite offsetting; investigators believe it likely that the plane was 20 feet lower than the altimeter said.

The pilot later suggested why he might have been so low without recognizing it. "I recently purchased a new pair of 'photo gray' trifocal lens glasses," he told NTSB." These glasses change color with the brightness of the day and should return to clear lenses when indoors or out of the bright light. I have noted particularly at dusk that these glasses bother me a lot and I have to take them off. I have no problem with distance, so I can get along fine without them with the exception of having to read anything close up. These glasses do give me a false perception at dusk and into the night, at which time I do try to get along without them unless I am driving a car or flying a plane and of course, need the glasses for reading the instrument panel. I was wearing these glasses at the time of the accident."

Icing—But Not on the Outside

A flight instructor sustained minor injuries and his student escaped injury during a forced landing after the engine in their Warrior lost power while flying in snow showers. An FAA inspector reported finding a buildup of ice in the aircraft's induction system.

The Warrior was on a VFR training flight from Park Rapids, Minnesota to Grand Forks. When heavy snow was encountered, the instructor obtained an IFR clearance. The aircraft was being vectored to Runway 35L at Grand Forks Airport and was descending when the engine lost power. Weather was IMC with a 900-foot broken ceiling and four miles visibility in snow.

The instructor said he applied carburetor heat and attempted unsuccessfully to restart the engine. The private pilot continued the descent, and when he made visual contact with the ground, the instructor took the controls and landed the aircraft in a plowed field. The Warrior was substantially damaged in the forced landing.

The matter of carburetor icing has been extensively dealt with in aviation education (although it continues to cause accidents!), but precious little is said about *induction* icing. To be sure, carburetor icing is a form of induction icing, but in the sense of the accident described above, we're talking about particles of ice or snow that accumulate in the system—not ice that is created as the result of refrigerative cooling in a carburetor.

The result is the same, of course. If enough ice—from whatever source—manages to build up in the engine's "throat," the flow of air will be choked and the engine will quit. The methods of prevention and correction are considerably different, however. In the case of classic carburetor ice, the introduction of heated air ("carb heat") should physically melt the ice that has formed, and prevent the formation of additional ice. But when the situation is conducive to classic induction system icing, the problem occurs upstream from the heated air's entry point, making it virtually impossible to get rid of the nasty stuff by melting it. In fact, once accumulated, induction ice won't go away until you fly back into above-freezing temperatures.

Airplane manufacturers have provided for this; in the case of carbureted engines (which are especially susceptible to refrigerative icing), the carburetor heat system usually does the job. If the pilot is quick to recognize that he's losing power without a change in throttle setting, or if an otherwise smooth engine begins to run rough, application—full application—of carburetor heat will normally solve the problem. Power is reduced, the mixture setting must be readjusted to accommodate the less-dense air going to the engine, but reduced power is much preferred to no power at all.

True induction system icing is encountered only when you're flying through crystalline precipitation; i.e. particles of snow or ice. Now, the particles may collect on the air filter, or at bends in the induction system piping; and if enough of it accumulates, the engine will be choked...literally. The only solution at this point is provide an alternate source of air to the engine, a source which draws from an area free of the troublesome particles; a frequently used location is inside the engine nacelle, which also provides a modicum of heated air—not a bad deal when you're trying to get rid of ice.

Engines fed by carburetors are of course also susceptible to induction system icing, and you should be aware that a carbureted engine *also* comes equipped with an alternate air source which can be used very effectively to combat ice and snow crystals. When the carburetor heat system is activated, the air filter is bypassed, supplying the engine with warmer air, but more importantly right now, with air that can flow unimpeded by a blocked filter.

The early symptoms are the same in both cases—relatively slow reduction in power output, and usually a rough-running engine. Whereas carburetor ice can occur in clear air at temperatures way above freezing, induction system icing depends on visible snow or ice particles for its formation.

Either way, when induction system icing is suspected, take the appropriate action; and begin to think seriously about Plan B, in case the icing becomes more vigorous than the engine can handle.

More "Inside" Icing

One of the reasons for the demise of the big flying boats on trans-Atlantic runs was the inescapable problem of water freezing on the hulls during takeoff and landing in the winter. The seaplane pilot faces a special set of circumstances when the weather turns cold, circumstances which lead many with "water wings" in northern climes to tie down their airplanes for the winter, and wait for the lakes and rivers to thaw.

One extra fact of preflight life for float pilots is the importance of keeping floats (and hulls, if applicable) free of water. This is also important when storing the airplane, particularly in cold weather. One pilot removed his amphibian from cold storage for an early spring flight and discovered the true meaning of frozen controls. He was seriously injured and his airplane destroyed in the mishap.

The private pilot set about preflighting his Lake LA-4-200 Buccaneer for a flight from his strip in Le Roy, New York, to Swanton, Vermont. The 58-year-old pilot had 1,078 hours, with well more than half of that time logged in the LA-4-200. As is recommended for new Buccaneer owners, he had attended a Lake Aircraft owner training course at Tomball, Texas. Here he obtained his single-engine seaplane certificate and became familiar with the airplane.

Outside air temperature at the 8 a.m. preflight was about 30 degrees Fahrenheit. During the procedure, the pilot noted that fore and aft elevator control movement was restricted and that the fuel sump drain was clogged. The Buccaneer had been drained of water the previous summer, according to the pilot, and had not been in the water since. The plane spent the ensuing months tied on open ground.

The Buccaneer's elevator control system is actuated by pushrods situated in its hull, and Lake stresses the importance of proper hull drainage and ice prevention in its owner training course. By means of a kerosene-fueled, forced-air heater, the pilot was able to apply heat to the hull and free up his pitch control and drain the fuel sump. His preflight was then complete. He had obtained a weather briefing via broadcast media earlier in the day and he departed for Vermont in VFR conditions without a flight plan.

After cruising for about an hour at 5,500 feet, the pilot noted that his elevator control was beginning to freeze up again. Investigators concluded the temperature at this altitude would have been 10 degrees. The pilot was able to solve pitch problems by using the hydraulically-activated trim tab, and continued his flight, at one point climbing to 7,500 feet to avoid turbulence over the Adirondack Mountains en route to Vermont.

At about noon, and still controlling pitch with the trim tab, he was ready to begin his approach to Franklin County Airport. However, the prevailing winds were distinctly uncooperative, estimated at nearby Burlington as 330 degrees at 20 knots, gusting to 30. Lined up for Runway 1, the pilot was having an increasingly difficult time substituting trim tab for elevator.

At about 40 feet above ground the plane was hit by a gust

which pushed the nose down and, according to the pilot, recovery without the elevator control was impossible. The airplane nosed over right wing low and hit the ground at a 30-degree angle about 1,000 feet short of the runway.

On impact, the Buccaneer sheared its nosegear and slid about 40 feet, coming to rest with the nose crumpled back to the cockpit seats. The pilot sustained severe chest, abdomen and back injuries and multiple cuts, but survived.

During its post-accident investigation, the NTSB discovered among the airplane's documentation a Lake Aircraft Service Letter counseling owners on proper hull drainage. The Letter urged periodic inspection of the bulkhead weep holes which allow water to drain effectively to the hull drains and finished by stating, "Freezing of water in the hull has been reported, in one recent instance, to have resulted in jamming the elevator controls. Particular care should be taken to thoroughly check the hull for water before flying the airplane into an area of below freezing temperatures."

Closing Thoughts

Not all cold days are bad. On some cold days we may climb into warm air and have a beautiful flight. Cold weather flying can be some of the most enjoyable of all flying. The air is smooth and the airplane will perform well. Cold moonlit winter nights can be great flying.

The beautiful thing about winter flying is that once we understand it, we can properly prepare for it. A pilot can dress properly for winter and be comfortable. Try that for hot weather—impossible!—I much prefer winter.

Pilots, Passengers, And Survival

6

Oil gets thick, engines die from lack of lubrication, altimeters tell lies, controls freeze...the list of mechanical problems that result from cold weather goes on and on. But the most cold-sensitive component of any aviation operation is *people*. When people get cold, they begin making bad decisions, which often translate to accidents.

Regardless of how pilots and their passengers get into cold-weather accident situations, the matter of survival takes on prime importance. The amount of abuse the human body can tolerate while surviving after an accident is considerable, but survival doesn't "just happen." Survival success requires planning and education; here are some thoughts and examples of how cold-weather accidents with catastrophic potential can be survived.

One person died but four survived a Christmas Eve crash on the slopes of Mount Yale, near Buena Vista, Colorado; the crash prompted the largest search and rescue operation ever mounted in the state.

It took five and a half days to find and retrieve the survivors in the crash of a Cherokee Six at the 11,600-foot level of the snow-covered 14,200-foot mountain within sight of the Continental Divide. Heroic efforts by mountain rescue teams and military personnel using snowshoes, snowmobiles and helicopters eventually resulted in the rescue of two adults and two teenagers who had survived by staying in the intact fuselage and eating snow served up in an empty briefcase, which was said to be the sum total of the survival gear available.

The airplane departed the Dallas, Texas area without a flight plan on December 24, headed for Aspen, Colorado, with the pilot's family and a friend aboard. It crashed around 2 p.m. after encountering what survivors described as a "downdraft" encountered on approaching the mountain which left the plane unable to top it, despite full power. It was crash-landed in eight feet of snow.

About 15 minutes after the crash, the pilot told the others he was going for help, and waded off into the snow. When rescue teams arrived later, they found his tracks disappeared under an avalanche, and he was presumed dead. (It is a fundamental rule of survival that one should stay with the wreckage.)

The family, bound for a skiing vacation in Aspen, had sent their heavy clothing ahead and were forced to share clothing during their ordeal.

The airplane's emergency locator transmitter activated, but apparently the pilot did not inform his passengers of its existence before he left the wreckage. The ELT continued to operate well beyond its rated cold-weather minimum of 48 hours, and though weak, the signal eventually led rescuers to the airplane. The Cherokee Six, which was mostly white in color, by that time had been buried under two feet of snow left by storms that hampered the search effort.

The ELT signal was reported to Denver Center by two pilots within about an hour of the crash, and Center officials maintained that word was passed to the Air Force Rescue Coordination Center at Scott Air Force Base, Illinois. But officials there said they had no record of such information being received December 24. Denver Center did notify a Civil Air Patrol official, who made a check of area airports and found no one reporting reception of the signals, nor any planes overdue.

The search was not begun in earnest until a new round of reports about the ELT were received on December 26. Combined Army, Air Force, CAP and civilian personnel participated in the effort. The plane was found the afternoon of December 29 and three of the survivors were lifted out by Chinook helicopter before a snowstorm and nightfall stopped the operation. Seven members of the rescue team stayed with the remaining survivor, who was brought out by sled, snowmobile and four-wheel drive vehicles the next day.

Survival after the crash can be as difficult and questionable as during the crash itself. In some cases, only clear thinking will save the day. By retrieving and using the emergency locator transmitter after a crash, the 85-hour private pilot of a Cherokee 140 probably saved both his own and his passenger's lives after being forced down in the mountains in the middle of winter. The 22-year-old pilot was seriously injured in the crash, while his passenger received minor injuries. The aircraft was demolished.

The pilot had received his certificate only two months before the accident, which happened on a pleasure flight from Great Falls to Bozeman, Montana. Weather for the flight could only be described as marginal at best, with ceilings of 9,000 feet (in mountains rising nearly that high) and scattered heavy snow showers throughout the area.

All had gone well until the airplane was approaching Bozeman. The pilot noted that the visibility was deteriorating around the mountain peaks, which reached up to 8,000 feet. The visibility continued to drop until it was about three miles in scattered heavy snowshowers.

Attempting to remain on course, the pilot started a correction to the left to regain the centerline of the radial. At this point, the passenger told the pilot they were flying directly into a hill.

Simultaneously with the sighting of the hill ahead, the aircraft encountered downdrafts, probably due to mountain wave effects. The pilot attempted to climb out and over the ridge, but found that the aircraft could not outclimb the downdraft. Airspeed and altitude decayed as the ground came closer. The pilot, sensing an impending stall, lowered the nose. The airspeed would not increase enough to permit a climb, so he raised it again and stalled. As the nose pitched down, the left wing struck a tree and broke off. The rest of the aircraft crashed into the mountainside and came to rest inverted in about five feet of snow.

The crash had left the two survivors about three miles from the nearest road in harsh, snow-covered terrain. Al-

Careful planning—including filing a flight plan and carrying survival gear—improves the odds of surviving a crash in a remote area.

though he had received serious facial injuries from hitting the glareshield during impact (the aircraft was not equipped with shoulder harnesses), the pilot was still able to walk. The mountain slope was so steep that the passenger tumbled 100 yards when he released his seatbelt and exited the airplane.

A cardinal rule of survival is to stay with the airplane until help arrives. The step of leaving the craft should never be taken without some rational plan of action. Thus, the pilot and passenger hung on for one night, making use of the airplane for shelter. They tore up the seats and furnishings to stuff into the cracks in the cabin and provide warmth. The temperature was about 25 degrees F at the time.

The pilot went to the tail section and removed the ELT. The switch was in the "Arm" position—possibly activated, but possibly not. He turned it to "On." It should also be noted that the ELT's battery was fresh, having been replaced by a conscientious mechanic at the plane's last annual (even though this isn't exactly specified in the airplane maintenance rules).

According to an account in a local newspaper, the pair decided to walk out after spending their first night in the wreckage. Taking the ELT with them, they made their way down a ravine through waist-deep snow. Lady Luck smiled broadly on them. Although there could have been a bleak night facing them, after hiking for a few hours, they found a small cabin. Inside was a stove, some wood for fuel, Tang breakfast drink, and coffee. They were thus able to warm themselves and dry their clothes.

After spending that night in the cabin, they decided to move on. They wrapped their feet in plastic to keep them dry (the pilot was wearing only tennis shoes; his companion had hiking boots). The ELT was still working as they set out. Sometime later in the day, a helicopter which had followed the ELT signal appeared, circling above them, and picked them up in short order. The probable cause, as determined by the NTSB, was the pilot's improper planning and decision making. The pilot evidently agreed. In the space on the accident form where the pilot can suggest ways the accident may have been prevented, he wrote, "Not flying close to the lee side of mountains."

Moreover, the pilot told investigators he would always carry a survival kit, as well as a "shock-proof, voice-capable radio," and would henceforth fly in aircraft equipped with shoulder harnesses.

It Pays to be Prepared

Survival depends in large part on preparations that begin long before the airplane leaves its home base; most pilots are not ready for post-crash survival. Nowhere is this more apparent than in the amount and kind of survival equipment aboard most of the nation's aircraft.

A casual trip around any airport, peering into aircraft cabins, will demonstrate that pilots simply do not expect to crash, and therefore feel they need take no particular precautions: most lightplanes have no survival equipment of any kind aboard. Even when there is some, it is likely inadequate to the task, inaccessible in a critical situation, or unfamiliar and even unfathomable to pilots and passengers.

Some scenarios: Pilot A. Smith has crashed in a Cessna 150 he uses for weekend flying. He thought he had quarter-full tanks when he left his home field, but the engine quit about half an hour after takeoff. He did his best to land in a clearing, but missed and hit trees. He has a broken ankle and is in pain, but is in no immediate danger of dying. He is only about five miles from civilization, but unfortunately, no one saw him crash and since he was just going "out flying," no one knows exactly where to look for him. Because the Cessna was just a fun plane for local flying, Smith has had the plane's ELT "out for repairs" for the past two years. He has no survival gear, nor has he ever contemplated what he would do if he crashed. It was warm when he got into the plane, but now, with darkness approaching, he wishes he had a jacket.

Pilot B. Jones comes to with blood running down his forehead, blood that he thinks at first is rain (he was trying to stay VFR and got into clouds just before his memory went blank). The bump on his head from hitting the instrument panel has made him groggy, but his mind clears instantly as he realizes there is a fire growing from the engine compartment.

Adrenaline pumping, he shoves his unconscious wife out the broken cabin window, drags her to a safe distance, and watches the plane burn. Because of his diversion around the clouds, the high-mountain crash site is miles away from the direct line between the departure and destination airports. Pilot Jones has kept the ELT in good repair, but it's in the tail of the plane and soon will be burning. He even had a rudimentary survival kit in the back of the plane—just about where the flames are reaching now.

Pilot C. Brown is unconscious and dying. His wife and daughter have dragged him away from the flaming wreckage of their airplane. As they left the plane, Brown's daughter remembered instructions he had given long before: "If we crash, we take that orange survival pack with us." Brown is bleeding from cuts all over his body. They open the pack and find a manual which instructs, "Clean the wounds with soap and water, or apply antiseptic, and a bandage." They look for such items, but the kit actually contains only a couple of two-inch gauze pads and five adhesive-strip bandages of the kind suitable for cut fingers. Though they attempt to bandage him with pieces of clothing, Brown succumbs.

His death paralyzes the two survivors, but after a long period of inaction, his wife and daughter realize they must fend for themselves. They also realize they are hungry and thirsty. They look in the kit again and find it contains several packets of powdered soup and powdered cocoa. Where is the water to make these? "Water is not

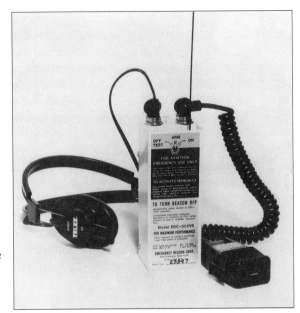

Besides being a legal requirement, a properly maintained ELT makes it easier for search crews to find a missing aircraft.

included," says the kit's instructions. "However, materials to make a solar still are provided." Brown's wife and daughter have never heard of a solar still and have no idea how to make one. Besides, darkness is making it difficult to read the instructions.

Perhaps some other, even grimmer scenarios can be imagined. The point is, the real survival situation will probably be nothing like a Boy Scout campout, and yet that is about all most pilots, passengers—and even their commercially prepared survival kits, if aboard—are prepared to handle.

The Better Way

Anyone can vastly increase his chances of post-crash survival by merely acknowledging that a crash could occur and preparing for that possibility. It is only necessary to dispense with a myth nurtured by many pilots: "I won't crash." The reality is, "I probably will never crash, but it could happen."

Getting beyond this first step, the second becomes obvious: the pilot will want to learn modern techniques of survival. It would be fair to say that survival thinking has undergone a revolution in the past 20 years, while many laymen (and most manuals) have not caught up with the changes. The kits and manuals tend to foster an idyllic myth which portrays the survivor as so competent, well-equipped and energetic that by the time help arrives (perhaps a week after the crash), he is nearly at home in his wilderness camp.

It's a silly picture. For many reasons, in modern times it is fair to expect that rescue will come within 24 to 72 hours after a crash (although hedging one's bets by having the means to survive longer is okay). But more important, a survivor's aim is not to live in the woods indefinitely, but to get out of the woods as soon as possible— something many kits and manuals do not emphasize.

The third step is to assemble equipment to help achieve the aim of surviving long enough to leave the woods. At this stage, the pilot may have already discovered that "survival kits" offered for his use are sometimes grossly unsuited to the task, being inferior in quality and with items that have no relationship to the needs of a downed pilot. And even relatively well-reasoned kits of good quality cannot possibly address the special needs of each individual, nor account for peculiarities of the local area.

Finally, some envision the survivor as a modern-day "Robinson Crusoe," expected to fend for himself away from civilization for years; in the continental United States, this is an unlikely requirement.

By customizing his survival kit, a pilot can cure all these problems. Furthermore, since he becomes intimately involved in preparing the kit, he is much more likely to make good use of it—as opposed to the pilot who buys an off-the-shelf kit and gets his first look inside it after the crash.

Rules for Survival

In pursuit of the elusive "perfect survival kit," I consulted with experts in the field, and distilled the contents of some of the more popular survival manuals.

All the credible experts make some preliminary points before they even discuss post-crash survival gear:

1) Filing a flight plan is extremely good insurance, and IFR or flight-following interaction with controllers is even better. Planes downed on IFR flight plans trigger almost instant search and rescue (SAR) attempts, and because there was an identified target on the scope, the search area is considerably narrowed. Even a VFR flight plan gets a rescue effort going much sooner than none at all, and it indicates the course line to be searched, again vastly reducing the number of square miles that must be searched. The pilot who wanders off on a

Even a rudimentary survival kit, with flares, strobe, signaling mirror and short rations, can make the difference between surviving a crash or succumbing to the elements before rescue.

vague sight-seeing flight without telling anyone can practically assume that he's on his own if he crashes.

2) Crashing with the airplane under control (as opposed to upside down or cartwheeling) will dramatically increase the odds of survival, along with the use of seatbelts and shoulder harnesses.

3) The pilot's mind is his most important piece of survival gear. First, survival in the true sense (not the camp-out meaning) is a fundamental driving life-force. Having a positive mental attitude and willing oneself to continue to survive no matter what, is the essential ingredient. Second, a pilot who has stored away knowledge about survival methods is capable of improvising his way to safety, even if he has not a shred of equipment identifiable as survival gear. The pilot who hasn't done this is going to have to catch up on his reading mighty quick—he has a whole survival manual to finish, and it's getting dark.

4) The most efficient means of getting to safety is to communicate. If there is a choice between carrying gear that makes living in the woods more pleasant, and gear that helps communicate (or signal) to rescuers, pick the latter.

5) One such piece of equipment is the plane's emergency locator transmitter. Ironically, it appears from analysis of accident reports that carriage of ELTs may have decreased in recent years, just when the ability of the ELT to save lives is being dramatically enhanced. For many reasons (a high false alarm rate, corrosion problems with lithium batteries, lack of faith in their efficacy), ELTs have had a bad reputation. However, the advent of Soviet and American satellites that can promptly pinpoint an ELT signal should finally give the ELT program the capability that was originally intended.

Thus, a flight plan, a seatbelt and shoulder harness, an ELT, some signalling equipment, and the mind of a survival-trained pilot, all could be considered basic survival gear.

In addition, considering the utter efficiency of direct communication as a survival technique, our choice of the top priority in survival hardware would not be found in most kits: a modern, 720-channel portable transceiver.

Hardware

This stated, we can turn to the "stuff in the orange bag." What should one carry in a survival kit? Is it smart to buy a prepared kit, or make one from scratch? Is there any standard of quality or completeness to apply to survival kits? One answer is, of course, that except in northern Canada, survival kits can consist of anything the pilot wants to carry, at any level of quality.

Consequently, products marketed as "aircraft survival kits" may range from a "sick joke" all the way to a deluxe weekend camping outfit, at prices from about $20 to $600. Components of the kits may be well made and useful, or almost totally useless.

Customize

There are a number of these survival kits available, but in view of the cost, we believe anyone who has the time and inclination is far better off creating his own kit, by merely making a list of needed items and going to any large camping/sporting store to shop for them. He can nearly match the kit price, even though he is paying retail, and he will gain the ability to select the type and quality of equipment he wants.

To help that effort, we have combined features culled from more than a dozen custom and commercial survival kits, and suggestions from various survival manuals. This is not intended to be a "perfect" kit or a complete course in survival, but we believe it will help pilots to begin building a survival kit which will serve the needs of an aircraft crash survivor. Our top priority remains a portable radio costing anywhere from $200 to $800, and some "kit builders" may be inclined to stop right there. This would be foolish, since the added protection of other survival gear can be included at very little additional expense.

We've grouped our suggestions according to logical categories of survival gear. Some explanation for the items on our list:

Make a Fuss

Heavy emphasis on signalling, particularly the portable transceiver, most efficiently addresses the primary goal of the survivor: to get out of the hostile environment by summoning help. Other kits place emphasis on living in the environment, even indefinitely. This is Robinson Crusoe thinking.

We'll assume that the survivor knows the location of the airplane's ELT (as opposed to the kit's) and has checked to see whether its switch is on and its antenna is deployed (if that's broken off, any piece of wire may be substituted).

Some hints not covered in many manuals: If the radio unit is an ELT, broadcasting on emergency frequency 121.5 MHz (plus 243.0 MHz, the military channel) is the only choice, and makes sense.

New Soviet and American satellites may be able to fix the position of the downed aircraft within about four hours, with an accuracy of about two miles. If the unit is a transceiver, we'd advise tuning to other frequencies, such as 122.0 (Flight Watch) or 122.8 (Unicom) as a more efficient means of getting attention from other aircraft (not all FAA facilities monitor 121.5 and even those that do may be shielded by mountains).

Furthermore, nothing beats looking up the area ATC frequency on an IFR chart, if available. This is a great way to contact an airliner passing overhead, in the best position to receive one's signal.

An IFR or VFR flight plan, or direct communication of this kind, are the more likely ways authorities would be alerted in time to launch an SAR attempt on the same day as the crash. If these are not in a survivor's favor, then there's a strong chance of an overnight stay, since it will take time before late arrival at destination is detected, authorities are called in and checking around airports along the route is accomplished. By then, it may be nightfall, and prudent SAR teams will probably wait until dawn to begin the search.

Therefore, it is well to save flares and other pyrotechnics until a plane or other vehicle is close at hand. Shooting them off promptly after the crash, as one might be tempted to do, is merely a waste.

A campfire, though useful for other reasons, also is not an obvious distress signal; three campfires in a row might be recognized as such. The advantage of the strobe light at night is that it does attract attention, even from casual passersby, who may come to investigate.

The modern heliographic signal mirror is the only one to have. Plain mirrors are extremely hard to aim at a passing plane.

Get Under Cover

Because survival kits imitate camping equipment, too much emphasis is placed on shelter equipment, in our opinion. Getting to shelter is very important, but defining "shelter" is the problem. The ubiquitous "tube tent," found in many kits, is an example. It's a plastic tube that does indeed rig quickly, and can be a useful shelter. (Hint: given the choice, run the line through the tent to serve as a ridgepole, instead of cutting the line in half and tying it to either end). However, the tent also traps body moisture and becomes a clammy, uncomfortable place. Further, one might be tempted to close one end off, then get cozier and close the other. What manuals do not always warn about is the resulting serious danger of suffocation.

For a few dollars more, one can purchase a tent of good quality that will take up the same space in a pack, weigh the same or less, and have none of these drawbacks.

But it is not necessary to equate "shelter" with "structure." Since the aim of survival shelter is to protect the body, space blankets, plastic ponchos or even large garbage bags made into tunics will suffice. Moreover, a structure can be a large pile of dry leaves or evergreen limbs, a hollow log, or the like. The airplane can be used, although crawling into the tailcone is of dubious value, since the aluminum skin conducts body heat away in short order.

Warming Up

Fire is an essential for many reasons, and kit makers may seem to go overboard insuring ways to get a blaze started. However, the plethora of wooden strike-anywhere matches, waterproofed individually and then encased in special containers, plus tinders and associated paraphernalia, cannot disguise an appalling lack of common sense in these kits.

Sure, it doesn't hurt to pack a container of these matches. But wouldn't it be easier to use a disposable butane lighter? Why not pack several in the survival kit? (Hint: guard the triggers with adhesive tape and pack the lighters where impact forces will be cushioned.) Tinder, in the form of steel wool, cotton balls and the like, is useful enough, but there is ample, fine tinder in the foam of aircraft seats.

In any event, people unfamiliar with building campfires can have lots of tinder and yet be unable to get a fire started. Reason: they've been equipped with a saw and pre-disposed to believe they must use it to get wood. Thus, the novice's first act will be to attack the nearest sapling—a waste of energy, since its green wood will not burn.

Life-saving fact: Wherever one goes in the world, wood that is dead but still attached to a tree will be burnable, even after a rain. It also snaps off the tree readily. Literally tons of wood can be gathered in this way, and broken into fire-sized pieces merely by whacking it over the sharp edge of a rock. No tools necessary.

Even supposing the saw is useful for cutting wood to use as a shelter, we'd wager few non-Bunyans would have the steely hands to work with a wire-type saw for more than a couple of logs. Some directions do give away the secret that the first cuts should be to make a bow-like handle for the saw. Even so, only an expert woodsman would succeed with this, we'd expect. Wire-type saws get into survival kits because they are cheap and compact, not because they are necessarily useful.

Likewise, the magnifying glass packed in many kits as a fire-starter has little purpose; most cannot focus enough sunlight to start a fire. Kits and manuals which discuss fire bows and other exotic fire-starting techniques are doing no one any favors. Amateurs would have almost no hope of succeeding; experienced woodsmen would think of better ways.

Water Above All

There is no dispute that a healthy person can go without food many days longer than he can without water. Yet because it takes some extra volume, weight and cost, kit makers tend not to put in water. Also, sealed water tins last indefinitely, but water in canteens must be changed periodically. Some survival kit makers appear to assume the kit will not be checked until it's really needed—hence, no water.

We think it reprehensible that the same kit makers can include manuals which blithely inform the survivor that a human being comfortably at rest needs about two quarts of water a day, and that a small change in water balance can seriously affect one's performance, mental and physical. It's a sick joke for them to include "foods" such as dried soups, which require the unsupplied water.

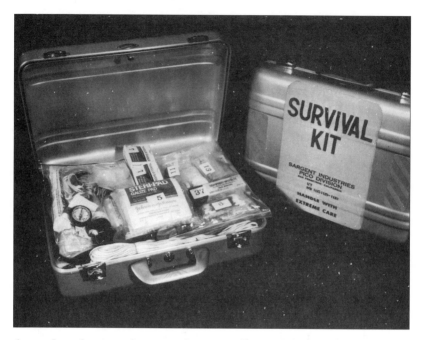

A number of companies manufacture well-equipped survival kits intended for aircraft use.

We believe a survival kit ought to contain a quart of water per person, in a steel or plastic canteen (steel is preferred, because it doubles as a cooking utensil). Extra water might be desirable, although there's a limit to the weight and bulk one can manage to remove from an airplane quickly. Self-locking plastic bags can be good water containers in a pinch, and in snow country, they can be used to bring snow inside an outer layer of clothing to melt it without need of a fire.

Contrary to the beliefs of some, the first thing to do with available water after a crash is not to ration it, but to drink it and go look for more. Water is helpful against shock and injury, helps to maintain mental and physical performance, and without it, dehydration may make a survivor unable to eat or drink when he *does* find water.

There are lots of ways to find water in the wild, and manuals cover these adequately. Nearly all discuss the solar still, which is made by digging a large hole, centering a container in the bottom and putting leafy materials around it. Then a "wettable" (surface slightly roughened) plastic sheet is draped on top in such a way that droplets of condensation from the leaves collect on the plastic and fall into the container. Although this idea is workable, it takes a lot of time and energy to dig the hole, and more time to wait for the water. Therefore, it probably won't yield anything useful on the day of the crash.

Alternative: If the survivor has a large black garbage bag, he has a much simpler solar still. Partially fill the bag with leafy material, prop a stick up to form a roof, and position the mouth of the bag to collect the dripping condensation. Getting water in this way still takes time, but little energy.

Treating Injuries

First aid is a subject which is adequately covered in most manuals, but there is no substitute for prior knowledge and training; some emergencies, such as arterial bleeding or cardiopulmonary failure, leave no time at all for looking up the procedure in the manual. Further, Red Cross, Scout, or other first aid training can be used to overcome a lack of supplies (e.g., by using articles of clothing for bandages), but aircraft crashes are often a lot more severe in their demands than other mishaps envisioned by the kit makers. Therefore, we would assemble a supplementary stock of first-aid items, as well as a prepared kit. The supplementary materials cover big-wound, big-area burn injuries, and the like.

One thing a lot of first aid kits have not caught up with is an almost complete change of thinking on snakebites. Nearly everyone has been steeped in the notion that a rattlesnake bite requires an instant skin-cutting, blood-sucking operation. This has been largely discredited. Unless the "surgeon" is expert and nearly as fast as the snake, the procedure will just add a cut-up leg to the victim's list of injuries. Doing nothing but keeping the wound cool and the victim calm may be the best treatment. Modern manuals will specify the proper techniques.

Sustenance

Noticeably well down on the list of survival requirements is food. For a survival period of one to three days, food is not at all critical. However, if food is to be carried in a kit, it should have the highest caloric value possible. Soups and broths are psychological boosts, but have minimal caloric content. Candies (rock candy especially), various rich and concentrated food products, and just about anything that would make a dieter feel guilty, is the kind of food for survival. Ideally, it should require no preparation.

Tools

For a survival tool kit around airplanes, we'd want at least a hacksaw blade (the whole saw if we could carry it) and vise-grip pliers. A good-quality knife, especially a "Swiss Army Knife," would complete the basic kit.

Additional items would be some fishing gear, snare wire and rope. Some deluxe kits have axes and folding shovels. These are fine, but heavy. As mentioned above, lots of woodsmanship isn't necessary for a short stay, since most of what is needed can be broken off the trees without tools.

Somewhere in every airplane should be a good flashlight, and it could be considered part of the tool section of the survival kit— assuming that's where it's kept.

Kits which supply fishing lures like streamers or trout flies are only furthering the Robinson Crusoe image. These are hard to use without extra tools like a rod and reel, not to mention some fishing luck. In survival, the aim is not to give the fish any sporting edge. Consequently, the really good kits include a gill net (which is outlawed in most places because it works so well). A worm on a hook works almost anywhere; even without bait, ganging hooks on a line and using them to snag fish is effective, if unsporting.

An item considered a tool in some kits is a firearm, particularly a collapsible rifle. Such a weapon is required in wilderness Canada. A person with this equipment should know ahead of time how to care for it, how to use it to kill game, and what to do with the dead animal to make it edible. Lots of manuals don't cover this area (the Air Force manual does), and besides, these are not skills which come easily from reading. Snares, deadfalls and other passive traps for game are safer, if not as effective. A manual which helps to identify edible plants, nuts and berries will in most terrain obviate any need for fish or fowl.

The Kitchen Sink

It's important to stress again that no survival kit is perfect, and individuals may have their own knowledge of what to add to the basic kit to account for special personal needs or local conditions.

However, there has to be an upper limit, and it should all fit into one container or knapsack, preferably one that is bright orange. To test whether the kit is still manageable, try it in the airplane. If the weakest likely passenger can pick it up with one hand and leave the airplane, it passes. If not, it might be just another part of the airplane that burns after a crash.

And So We End

While any discussion of post-crash survival may seem like a macabre conclusion to our first book in *The Command Decisions Series,* view it as an affirmation of continued living rather than as a glorification of gloom. Pilots who go down and survive will suffer a great deal of mental anguish and self second-guessing. Their abilities will be scrutinized and questioned—most severely perhaps by themselves. But they will be alive to share the tale with friends and family—and perhaps to fly again!

And on that optimistic note, I'll conclude *Aviation Weather.* We've reviewed the key weather problems that both VFR and IFR pilots will face on both local and cross-country flights, and perhaps I've helped you develop the decision-making skills you'll need to confront tough weather situations.

The next book in *The Command Decisions Series* looks closely at pilot proficiency in a variety of flight environments for both fair-weather and instrument pilots. *Pilot Proficiency* is intended to take you beyond the textbooks, beyond what your CFI ever told you, by conveying correct pilot technique. As with this volume on aviation weather, *Pilot Proficiency* will continue the method of demonstrating proper piloting by exploring accident case histories.

I think you'll find it useful.

Index